# SIR THOMAS BROWNE'S
## RELIGIO MEDICI

UNIVERSITY OF MISSOURI STUDIES LIX

# SIR THOMAS BROWNE'S
# RELIGIO MEDICI

## AND TWO SEVENTEENTH-
## CENTURY CRITICS

### BY JAMES N. WISE

UNIVERSITY OF MISSOURI PRESS

ISBN 0–8262–0130–X; Library of Congress Catalog Number 72–84204; University of Missouri Press, Columbia 65201; Manufactured in the United States of America; Copyright © 1973 by The Curators of the University of Missouri; All rights reserved.

FOR HESTER AND GARNETT

# ACKNOWLEDGMENTS

My debts have grown over the years as this study has undergone several transformations in its development from a doctoral dissertation to its present form. At least five individuals played important roles in its original version as a dissertation at the University of Florida. Professors Alton C. Morris, C. A. Robertson, and my chairman, Robert Bowers, all of the Department of English of the University of Florida, and Professor Francis C. Haber, now of the Department of History of the University of Maryland, helped and encouraged me during their service as my doctoral committee. The fifth individual to whom I am grateful for having introduced me to seventeenth-century English literature and to Sir Thomas Browne is Professor Ruel E. Foster of West Virginia University, who remains my best teacher and guide. It is impossible to acknowledge the exact contribution of each of these men to this study, but as scholarly presences in and out of the classroom they have my deep appreciation.

Through the years many students have studied sixteenth- and seventeenth-century English literature with me, and I appreciate their contributions as they helped me to discover the lines of argument that continue to be significant to modern man.

But most of all I wish to thank the many librarians who have provided me with the materials and assistance that I needed to complete this study. I express my gratitude to the staffs of the libraries of the following universities: Vanderbilt, Western Kentucky, Kentucky, Louisville, and Missouri, and more particularly to those of the University of Florida Library. I am grateful to the Newberry Library for providing me with Alexander Ross's *Medicus Medicatus*, and to the Henry E. Huntington Library and Art Gallery for much help, in particular for permission to use material from their collection as illustration for the jacket of this book. The frontispiece has been reproduced from *Posthumous Works of the Learned Sir Thomas Browne*, London, 1912, in the Rare Books Collection of the Library at the University of Missouri-Columbia. The final research on this book was largely completed during a leave in 1969 to the Huntington, made possible by a special Faculty Improvement Grant from the University of Missouri.

Finally, I proffer my thanks to my typist Mrs. Mary Ann McCelvey, who reproduced this study in all of its various stages with great care and enthusiasm.

Above all I thank my wife and my son, who contribute the love that sustains.

J.N.W.
University of Missouri—Rolla
July 11, 1972

# CONTENTS

# SIR THOMAS BROWNE'S
## RELIGIO MEDICI

# I.

## BROWNE AND HIS CRITICS

Why should we look once again at the writings of three controversialists of seventeenth-century England—Sir Thomas Browne, Sir Kenelm Digby, and Alexander Ross? Browne has become so traditionally a part of the history and texture of classic English prose style that we sometimes unconsciously undervalue his ideas and their power to arouse dispute in his time. The primary purpose of this study is to assert his significant, albeit ambivalent, position in the history of ideas in seventeenth-century Europe. Only minimal attention will be paid to Browne's stylistic excellence as such—a matter forcefully and definitively analyzed by other critics, including Coleridge, whose superb comments were collected as recently as 1955.

In Chapter II I provide a condensed reading of *Religio Medici*, which emphasizes areas of controversy in the work that were not closely examined by either Digby or Ross. In doing so I have explicitly avoided a survey of the existing scholarship, yet it should be clear to the reader that my discussion of *Religio* derives a great many of its assumptions and implications from the work of other scholars. Browne has been especially fortunate in the high quality of scholarship his writings have attracted; any new work on *Religio Medici* is clearly indebted to and buttressed by the work of such scholars as Joan Bennett, Jean-Jacques Denonain, W. P. Dunn, Frank L. Huntley, E. S. Merton, Leonard Nathanson, while, in the case of Sir Kenelm Digby, I am most grateful for the biography by R. T. Petersson.

The only major feature of the art of *Religio Medici* that this study emphasizes time and again is Browne's masterful control of tone. *Religio* is implicitly—rather than explicitly—a piece of contemporary argumentation. The tolerance, skepticism, and charitableness of the persona—that self-image which permeates and unifies the work—conflicts with the climate of his times without Browne's needing to call attention to the fact. His carefully structured ambivalences in matters of reason, faith, and intuition follow naturally the course of his thought processes. The juxtapositions of self-effacement, hyperbole, and candor resemble the artistry of Montaigne's persuasive methods.

Browne recognized that his character was controversial, since his profession was scandalous, his education skeptical, and his manner objective. Even with this stance in mind, the reader quickly realizes that *Religio* is only implicitly a personal characterization, if personal allusions are a measure. It is, to be sure, self-centered and self-aware, but it is not autobiographical or private. Allusion replaces illusion in the Olympian perspective of Browne's personality. On the other hand, a warning or at least a reminder may be necessary at this point that emphasis on eccentricity—the so-called "quaintness" so favored by the romantics when discussing Browne and his contemporaries—is missing from this study because I believe distance in time and thought should not endue disbelief in the seriousness of earlier thinkers and artists. *Religio* is a witty, a paradoxical, even at times a facetious work of art, but it is always serious, never *quaint*. So too were the controversies real in the climate of the seventeenth century. For the reader who enters that climate, it will be unnecessary to personalize the intensity of the arguments that lay between Browne and his critics, Digby and Ross.

It is necessary to examine once again the remarkable degree of sedate tolerance Browne held toward both Christian and non-Christian—sedate because Browne did not bother to protest his magnanimity. His conscious sophistication and relativism distinguish him clearly from the zealots and absolutists he challenged with such charm and wit. The cyclical nature of experience and truth verified for Browne the judiciousness of his understanding. The catholic breadth of his mind and feelings enabled him to represent through pointedly contemporary references the modernity of his religious and philosophical principles. Conflicts, contradictions, fluctuations, and uncertainties excited him, so he substantiated his faith and enriched his skepticism by viewing the flux around him with a philosophical detachment.

To treat Browne simply as an exponent of certain crosscurrents of seventeenth-century thought is to restrict him unjustly, but to detach him totally from his intellectual environment is to overstate his universality. Thus, unlike Hobbes and Milton—whose contemporary disputativeness was simply an adjunct to their already major reputations—Browne emerges as more rounded, more significant, and more argumentative than he was in his time—nearly on a plane with Sir Francis Bacon. Bacon's ideas and style are clearly significant beyond their contemporary relevance, but his work also represents distinctly the climate of ideas within the seventeenth-century boundaries of his influence.

Browne's own admission of youthful heresy and his perception that heresies recur in a man's mental history are reminders of half-realized truths. The circumference of knowledge, truth, and faith is ever expanding because reason endlessly speculates about knowable truth. In Browne's vision there was no closed universe of the mind.

The compulsive God-centeredness of his faith swept aside the need for literal scriptural evidence, miraculous revelations, or dogmatic theological proofs. Instead, intellectual awareness —a perception of the imaginative powers of his own *oh altitudo*—provoked in Browne a coherent love of mystery and metaphor powerful enough to tempt out of reason's way a myriad of religious paradoxes and ironies. Thus the light of reason becomes revelatory and exploratory; reason becomes transmuted into faith.

His apprehension of the mysteries of God's wisdom, eternity, and providence led Browne into contemplation of the mysteries of number, division and unity, dualism and totality. Such abstractions compel a humbling acknowledgment of the difficulty of attaining complete knowledge even through the mingling of man's will and God's. Thought on the absoluteness of causation, the immanence of the divine force in natural law, the omnipotence of God's artistry made the outer reaches of Browne's reasoning powers so pliant that even atheists and materialists could not disturb his geniality. Contradictions, ambiguities, and doubts were absorbed by his charitable appreciation of the fact that dogmatism must not intervene in one's worship of God.

How severely Alexander Ross and at times Sir Kenelm Digby attacked the placidity of Browne's perspective on divine truth will emerge in the discussion of their reactions to his work. The responses of both Ross and Digby provide the simplest rationale for their attack—their utter confidence in being right in their thinking. Their rebuttals—not the inner workings of Browne's metaphorical argument—are the major concern of this study.

The final section of this discussion of *Religio* explores Browne's random speculations about man's soul and the world of spiritual beings. The conjectures about the reality of witches, the middle state of man's existence, the nature of the soul's birth, and—in their turn—the death of the body and the death of the world form the broad divisions of Browne's metaphysical extensions. Just as his views on witches brought him later notoriety, so too his general doubts about the process of traduction as an explanation of the soul's passing into the body at conception made him relatively controversial at that time. Browne's probing imagination placed him beyond—not within—the orthodoxies of the period.

He doubted the reality of ghosts as well as the ascension of religious martyrs into heaven—matters perhaps too esoteric for modern tastes but closely related to his unwillingness to fear death, a concern not so easily ignored by men today or then. Even if Browne moderated somewhat his earlier audacity about death, an over-all tone of reasoned assurance produced his famous affirmation of resurrection and regeneration. The immortality of the Form and the indestructibility of the Idea or seed signify the patterns of reconciliation that Browne constructed around his thoughts on immutability versus corruption. Out of these convolutions came a celebration of harmonious order within the universe, within man, and within the soul's relationship with God. Such a superstructure could be best explained, Browne believed, by a realization of the progressiveness of man's capacity to love. That the expressions of these forms of love may prove paradoxical did not disturb Browne, because these paradoxes are real and ordered.

The real order of things? Perhaps not. For, in addition to the attacks by Digby and Ross, others have found *Religio* inflammatory, irreligious, unprintable, atheistic, pretentious, and misguided. Certainly *Religio* was not ignored in the seventeenth century, nor is it today, but the rebuttals by Sir Kenelm

Digby and Alexander Ross have been largely neglected, although several books—most particularly R. T. Petersson's excellent biography published in 1956—have been written about Digby. If the intellectual blending process that takes place in *Religio* continues to be provocative today, what about the critiques by Digby and Ross that grew out of it?

The flamboyant personality of Sir Kenelm Digby nearly eclipses his contributions to the movement of thought in the mid-seventeenth century. Praised for his energies, dubbed the "compleat gentleman," admired for his sympathetic curing powers, he also was ridiculed for his bragging and his lying. The extravagant modesty that characterizes Digby's letters to Browne set the tone for the debate that followed in his *Observations*. Since Digby made little reference to the style of *Religio*, I follow his emphasis in my discussion of his criticism of the work. Coleridge noted long ago the inherent fault in Digby's approach. "He ought to have considered the *Religio Medici* in a dramatic & not in a metaphysical view—as a sweet Exhibition of character & passion, & not as an Expression or Investigation of positive Truth." Nevertheless, there is much that is worth exploring within Digby's rationalistic framework.

The immortality of the soul is not central in present-day thought, but Digby, as well as his contemporaries, was deeply involved in philosophical considerations of the soul—a fact that is clear in his *Observations*. So engrossed was he, in fact, that it is necessary to consider his work, *Two Treatises concerning the Body and Soul of Man* (1644), in order to give his rebuttals to *Religio* a full sounding. Digby attacked, in this work, those who would explain corporeal processes in spiritual terms by means of qualities and powers and then try to explain the incorporeal soul according to "a corporeall occult quality." Subsequently, Digby attempted to separate quantitative "notions" from qualitative according to causation and function. Thus, in Digby's opinion Browne the physician was professionally unqualified from the outset to judge such matters.

On the other hand, Digby qualified himself as a deductive reasoner working from first principles—perhaps the earliest English exponent of the theories of Descartes. By this reasoning the body–soul question represented for Digby a study of the operations of the mind; he pondered its thinking and ap-

prehending powers at the same moment that he explored the
biological origins of the soul through traduction. For Digby,
the soul's birth could not be separated from the soul's purpose
—the acquisition of the knowledge needed to prepare one for
afterlife. This approach to reality immediately became less
esoteric when it led Digby to contemplate along Cartesian
lines the response of the nervous system to external stimuli.
Digby's small but significant role in the history of the study of
human perception has been clearly documented for some
time now, and no new interpretation about his role is intended
in this study. What will be emphasized is the total context of
Digby's viewpoints, which include the nonphysical, spiritual
responses of the soul—not just the interactions of bodies in the
modern sense. In the same sense Digby's reinforcement of
spirituality influenced his recognized contributions to the
science of plant and animal generation. His attempts to explain the theories of epigenesis and pangenesis relate to the
religious assumptions that he and Browne made about the
creative process in nature.

To argue the truth or falsity of their theories in the light of
modern developments in these sciences would be to judge
Digby as pedantically as Digby—or Ross, for that matter—
judged Browne. Without overstating or overspeculating on
how much direct impact Digby's criticisms had on Browne, I
will throughout this study single out some of the changes
Browne made in the 1642 edition that appeared in the 1643
version of *Religio*. After considering Digby's comments, this
study will present Ross's reactions not only to *Religio*, but also
to the *Observations*. Naturalistic, materialistic, and mechanistic explanations of natural phenomena have supplanted the
Neoplatonic and quasi-Aristotelian theories of these writers,
but this shift in the basis for theory does not invalidate the
lasting impression of these three minds at work and what they
express about their age.

In his reaction to Browne's work, Digby developed further
the intricacies of the body–soul question by dealing with such
matters as eternity, Providence, and salvation, which Digby
also viewed in terms of the spirit–matter problem. Here, too,
Digby answered Browne by pursuing a methodology of rational
verification based on a system of absolute causation. An

"open" rather than "hidden" system allowed Digby to reject the workings of fortune, astrology, chiromancy, and other related explanations of causation, giving him a more rational perspective than some of the facts of his own life would seem to indicate. Once again, his mechanistic tendencies rested in unequal balance with his spiritualism; God's providence is open to those who see, closed to others.

A great many of Digby's individual points of attack can only be loosely gathered under the broad concept of causation. Such matters for contention as the principles of contrariety, the annihilation of the world, the secrets of numerology, the concept of notions, the existence of ghosts, the process of sympathy, the aptness of allegory, and the natures of time, light, death, angels, perception and understanding, damnation and salvation, and happiness rest on Digby's pedantry, quasi rationalism, and single-mindedness for substantiation.

What view of God finally emerges from Digby's commitment to the foregoing ideas? Digby's God can best be seen in the light of his conception of virtue and grace. Defining *virtue* in terms of Christ and *grace* in terms of effect (the beatific state), Digby presented the Deity in much the same language that he used to describe the noncorporeal soul earlier in his arguments. He thereby contrasted a correspondence between divine and human excellence with what Browne defined as a more temporal and worldly morality in *Religio*. Strangely enough, Browne thus became the spokesman for the human conscience and Digby a repudiator of this world for the next. By trying to justify his morality rationally Digby made the greater compromises in his positions. By stating his case so emotionally, he endorsed a series of moral abstractions that confirm the incompatibility of his absolutism on morality with Browne's humanism.

Digby concluded his analysis of *Religio* by pointing the way to happiness in heaven, rather than on earth, since the final object of man's life and love is God alone. His long night's labor was over, except for a sudden afterthought that he had omitted his discussion of grace—a most ironic omission in the light of his over-all perspective.

So Sir Thomas was both too intuitive and too worldly for Sir Kenelm, who instead looked for a rationalized system of causation open to intelligent perception while being at the same time linked inextricably to a parallel system of grace and reward. The tests of faith and of reason must coincide, but without an admission of the paradoxes inherent in Browne's view. Unwilling to allow for Browne's love for unindoctrinated truth, Digby did not disclose how near to Browne he was on such key questions as the primacy of the Divine Will and the supremacy of the human soul. A rigid complex of mechanism, materialism, and rationalism obscured forever Digby's capability of seeing *Religio* for what it is.

If there is at times a frustrating imprecision in Digby's *Observations* that reveals a misunderstanding of Browne's mind, there is in Alexander Ross's *Medicus Medicatus* an antagonism and a dogmatism that obstructs, not merely obscures, any possible tendency toward agreement. Ross wrote to warn young minds against the dangers in *Religio*, and he rejected out of hand Browne's wish to be understood rhetorically and metaphorically in his arguments. No, Ross answered; he would apply "the rigid test of reason." Renowned for the inclusiveness of his controversies with several of the advanced thinkers of his day, Ross was epitomized by his most significant adversary, Thomas Hobbes, as "one who may be said to have had so much Learning as to have been perpetually barking at the works of the most learned."

Ross voided his claim of objectivity by distorting what Browne said. Ross's argumentation is a clear reminder of the general tendency to reject frank expressions of self-analysis when preconceptions are so narrowly partisan that opponents are dismissed as gullible fools. Browne's relativism, his tactful avoidance of sectarian controversies, his general breadth of mind were ignored in the single-mindedness of Ross's attacks.

Ross declared that Browne was inaccurate in significant matters of faith, particularly the immortality of the soul, but the battle this time did not center on Cartesianism. Instead, it was Aristotelianism versus Platonism, although Ross, when necessary, claimed Plato as his ally. Ross's Christianized rationalism soon became his personal explanation rather than the authoritative analysis he desired it to be. Reward and punishment, angelology, antimaterialism, anti-Platonism, antitraduction mark the major divisions of Ross's arguments about the nature of the soul. Many times his views take a deliberately negative perspective, for he was a determined opponent, rarely an advocate. Ross was far more concerned than even Digby that the soul might be somehow besmirched by any association with the body. Scriptural proof and outright assertion typify Ross's documentation. Browne's notion on the regeneration of plants provoked a long series of rebuttals— again strongly Aristotelian—except that in this context Ross invoked materialistic persuasions to support his argument. Browne's speculations about the spiritual correspondences between form and matter drew orthodoxies wrapped in tones of ridicule and facetiousness.

Ross's reservations about Browne's notion on the regeneration of plants led to his statements on nature. Once again his antipathy was thoroughly Aristotelian in basis as well as rigidly literal. Here, too, Ross attacked Browne's analogies with analogies of his own while soberly and with great particularity dissecting Browne's exploratory manner. Probably Ross was unaware that he was a spokesman of the waning reverence for Aristotle as a Renaissance authority. Yet his traditionalism serves even today as a model, albeit of misdirected enthusiasm. His speculations were so narrowly framed that even when he made a telling point against Browne's own brand of rationalism, it is apparent that Ross was only generally aware of the true significance of their quarrel. Casting himself as the defender of orthodoxy, Ross clearly did not attempt to grasp the striking imaginativeness of *Religio Medici*.

Ross concluded that Browne read the Bible "mystically," a practice he deplored. For Ross, the "literal sense" was substantiated by both the Church's "consent" and right reason; Browne's candid attempts to investigate the accurate meaning of the literal interpretations were therefore denounced as "impious and ridiculous."

Ross's certainty about Scripture is still more pronounced in his convictions about the nature of the Deity and his relationship to it. He supported a merging of the thinking of Aquinas and Scotus on being and non-being and *ens* and *ens rationis* in order to verify the absoluteness of God's knowledge and power. Speculations based on fortune, astrology, chiromancy, palmistry, and other providential influences he dismissed quickly as merely dangerous superstitions. He dealt with atheism and doubt angrily, while he regarded the spiritual realm—except for witches—as largely irrelevant to a clear understanding of God's providence. Any concept that allows for self-doubt concerning salvation was "infidelity," not "humility," in his opinion. So Ross offered little magnanimity to "bad Christians" and "bad men," among whom he included the author of *Religio*.

Browne's personal allusions and his views on charity, friendship, marriage, and death provoked strong responses from this critic. Ross castigated Browne's whimsicality about his sins, his pride, his "modest ignorance," his aversion to cohabitation. Browne's mannered equanimity and introspection were wholly wasted on the dogmatic Ross, who concluded his attacks with —curiously—a prayer for Browne.

As a type-figure Alexander Ross is well worth remembering; intolerant in religion and reactionary in philosophy, biased, elliptical, unimaginative, dull, and graceless, Ross chose to react to *Religio* by offering points of view that incorporated the very philosophical and teleological arguments his opponent endorsed.

The final chapter of this study turns attention to a brief examination of Ross's rebuttals to Digby's *Observations* and summarizes generally the works of all three authors. In his rebuttals to the *Observations* Ross dismissed curtly Digby's elaborate concerns about the nature of light, the inexactitude of traditional philosophical diction, and the quality–quantity debate; all these matters were clear to a true Aristotelian. His brief rejection of Digby's concerns epitomized precisely the insularity against which Digby was complaining. As would be expected, Ross diagnosed the glimmers of ecumenical spirit in both Browne and Digby as signs of dangerous gullibility. An apocalyptic cadence punctuates Ross's dislike of such relativism.

Ross devoted nearly a third of his animadversions upon Digby's work to the question of the resurrection of the body. He found Digby guilty of nine errors ranging from the semantical to the nearly heretical. The key to the argument, which also touches on the question of traduction, is Digby's admission of the dependence of the soul upon the body. In rebuttal

Ross reaffirmed the superiority of the soul, dodged the theory of epigenesis, and finally described the body as simply an instrument of the soul.

The final state of the soul's identity in the afterlife fascinated Digby, but Ross was much more concerned about the moral proprieties of the soul. As to the immutability of the soul, the first matter, and the heavens, Ross perhaps went beyond Digby in his endorsement of the orthodox positions on these subjects. Ross wrote that God is, after all, the absolute cause of all things, even to the point of self-contradiction and annihilation, although such actions are "repugnant" to Him. Ross's subsequent disagreements with Digby on the debated properties of angels, light, ghosts, and grace may be characterized as lessons in literalism where Ross's thinking is concerned. Ross was quantitative when it suited him and qualitative at other times.

The underlying propositions of Plato, Aristotle, Descartes, and other great speculative minds range throughout these discussions, except that here it is possible to see how eclectically such thinkers influence the undercurrents of any age's ideas. Protestant and Catholic, literalist and metaphysician, ironist and extremist are all exposed in quarrels such as these. More than any other factor, Sir Thomas Browne's personal genius as expressed in *Religio Medici* reveals itself clearly when the bias of pedantic superiority, the lack of willing imagination and the posture of surface objectivity are set against it.

# II.

## SIR THOMAS BROWNE

### An Apology for Privacy

Although Sir Thomas Browne intimated that he did not intend *Religio Medici* to be matter for dispute, private and public controversy have from the first surrounded the work. Browne's view of himself, implied throughout his writing, is that of a fearlessly unconventional thinker. His self-characterization, his concerns for tolerance and charity, and his views on God, the soul, and the supernatural make up the broad divisions of what became, in the minds of his contemporaries, a sharply controversial book. That it should be so is understandable, for the general continuity of a sturdy faith in Christian teachings bridges subtle shifts in tone from tolerance and skepticism to simultaneous declarations that both reason and intuition are valid guides in science and religion. He was, in the thought of his time, a latitudinarian, and therefore a fit target for the shafts of sectarians.

Browne's short explanation "To the Reader," with which he prefaced the 1643 authorized edition of *Religio*, might well be titled "Apology to the Reader." It opens with a paraphrase of a moving passage from Seneca's tragedy, *Thyestes:* After Atreus slaughters Thyestes' three sons an unnatural darkness blankets the earth, provoking the chorus to cry out poignantly against the immensity of the crime. Their concluding wail, "Greedy indeed for life is he who would not die when the world is perishing in his company,"[1] was adapted by Browne for hyperbolic juxtaposition with his complaint of a time when everyone—even someone as insignificant as he—could be harmed by the printers. Despite Samuel Johnson's comments that a song or epigram might be printed without the knowledge of the author, but not an entire book, and that Browne issued the alleged pirated edition as a feeler to judge public reaction without revealing his authorship in case the book

1. *Seneca's Tragedies*, trans. Frank Justus Miller, II, 163 (lines 883–884).

failed,[2] Browne's charges of piracy have been largely validated by recent editors, on the bases of the numerous errors and revisions between the 1642 and 1643 editions of *Religio*.[3]

The charm of Browne's self-effacement and his admission of the mutability of his thoughts should cause even unsympathetic readers to have confidence in so candid an author. In a time when both king and Parliament are slandered and misrepresented and when the entire society verges on death and destruction, "complaints may seeme ridiculous in private persons"; but the urgings of his friends and his love of truth have overridden his willingness to let time moderate his troubles. For an author to so disparage his work even as he introduced it would surprise, yet interest most readers. Besides, what is more inviting than a "private exercise," not to be read according to the "rigid test of reason"? Written seven years earlier, with no library available (an occupational complaint prevalent not just in the Renaissance), and representative of less mature judgment than he would command at this moment, the book before the public was admittedly imperfect in more ways than the author could acknowledge. What he was not telling his readers was how few changes this authorized version comprised, and how little substantial effect his Apology was intended to convey.

## The Gentle Controversialist

Browne clearly prefaced his work with excuses in order to avoid controversy, but the body of *Religio* suggests that he recognized himself at age thirty as innately abrasive. His attempts in the preface to disarm or deflect the quarrels his book would arouse are nullified by the first section of *Religio*, for it lists the factors that made him and his ideas argumentative.

Browne opened his memorial (I, 1) with allusions to the wariness with which the world regarded the scandalous profession of physician—an attitude that, Coleridge observed, "in nine cases out of ten is the honor of the medical profession."

2. Sir Thomas Browne, *Sir Thomas Browne's Works*, ed. Simon Wilkin, I, xx–xxi. Hereafter referred to as Wilkin.

3. *Religio Medici*, ed. Jean-Jacques Denonain, xxii–xxviii, for a summary of the textual changes. The 1955 Denonain edition is the text for quotation.

The suspected atheism of physicians, combined with Browne's scientific education on the Continent and a personal objectivity toward religious quarrels, constituted a self-portrait of a man whose judgments were questionable. Augmenting the coldness of the book's reception was the seeming arrogance of its title. Thomas Keck, the supposed author of *Annotations Upon "Religio Medici"* (1656), suggested that some readers interpreted the title of Browne's book to mean "that Physicians have a Religion by themselves, which is more than Theology doth warrant."[4]

Even though *Religio* is a personal work, it contains few references to the author's personal life. Nevertheless, a clearly distinguishable self-centeredness and self-awareness emerge. For one facet, throughout the work Browne's contemplations of his death convey his indifference to earthly memorials and even an indifference to life itself. He also obviously relished extending commonplaces on the transience of life to the level of imaginative exclamations of his own.

The greatest number of personal allusions occur in Part II of *Religio*, which, as its major subject, examines charity, a virtue Browne defined as being close to self-love. In the course of his discussion of charity, Browne contemplated his life, which he described as a "miracle of thirty yeares . . . not an History, but a peece of Poetry, . . . to common eares like a fable" (II, 11). Perhaps to clarify this already traditional point, he added, in the 1643 edition, a 155-word passage in which he developed more fully his view of his reality as a microcosm. From a study of himself—not of his exterior, but of his interior nature—he concluded that he was "something more than the great." Mere allusion to an accepted commonplace was rarely Browne's intention in *Religio*; instead, he time after time turned traditional metaphors to personal applications. "Nature tels me I am the Image of God as well as Scripture"; not to know this is not to know the "first lesson" in the "Alphabet of man." Browne continued, in the 1642 text: "Let me not injure the

4. *Coleridge on the Seventeenth Century*, ed. Roberta Florence Brinkley, 456. See Paul H. Kocher, *Science and Religion in Elizabethan England*, 239–57, for an investigation of "the forces at work to preserve and intensify" the tradition of the physician as atheist. Thomas Keck, in Sir Thomas Browne, *Works*, 49. Quoted by permission of The Huntington Library, San Marino, California.

felicity of others, if I say I am as happy as any." The audacity of other declarations in this section must have struck him as extreme, for he omitted from the 1643 version "I am the happiest man alive. I have that in me that can convert poverty into riches, transforms adversity into prosperity: I am more invulnerable than *Achilles*; Fortune hath not one place to hit me." He also omitted the statement that he was a king on earth: "I can be a King without a Crowne, rich without a royalty, in heaven though on earth, enjoy my friend and embrace him at a distance; with which I cannot behold him." He also added a qualifying "me thinkes" to his doubt that Aristotle defined sleep "throughly" and changed "I observe that men oftentimes, upon the houre of their departure, doe speake and reason above themselves" to the more moderate "it is observed that men sometimes."

After categorizing his life poetically and mythically, Browne rejected historical fact and external reality as instruments for understanding his microcosmic self. He urged that the outside world be studied from an Olympian perspective for true re-creation; the inner vision cannot be circumscribed by geometrical distances. Having moved beyond such constrained limits as the circle, the mind perceives the divine both in itself and in nature. This perception is "the first lesson," which inculcates a happiness that prevails over illusion and reality. Yet, from the security of this internal tranquility Browne perceived that separation from one's friends reawakens unhappiness. At such moments dreams are a welcome escape from a world that is itself illusory. Thus a truer reality may lie in our dreams, since in them the soul through reason and fancy is freed from the encumbrances of the senses. So free was Browne in his dreams that his happy laughter wakened him. His belief in the realities of unconscious life is epitomized by a passage added to the 1643 version, in which sleep is a part of life that parallels death; in his sleep man best "acts his nature" (II, 12).

Browne wrote that, if he could remember his dreams faithfully, he would study nothing else. He regarded them as being, in part, religious exercises—communications with God—and in part contemplations of astrological influences. The conjunction of Scorpio and Saturn at his birth was for him as influential on his character as any hereditary factor. Such a declaration placed him somewhat behind some of his contemporaries, if he was stating a literal belief in astrology, but more probably he was using astral patterns to his own ends—self-analysis. Finally, melancholy over impending death pervaded his sleep. He held that even more than in dreams the faculties of the soul are freed in the last hours of a man's life so the soul "begins to reason like her selfe, and to discourse in a straine above mortality." Sleep is not death, "it is waking that kils us." Although sleep is the limbo between life and death, it is so like death that, he confessed, he always said a farewell prayer before sleeping, since he was content to "sleepe unto the resurrection" (II, 12). His "dormative" is expressed in an almost childlike verse prayer that asks in part for blessed, not infested dreams.

### Tolerance and Faith

Despite the melancholy intimated in the preface and in the sections on sleep and death, the prevailing tone of *Religio* is neither somber nor grim. Rather, the book is the sedate statement of beliefs held by a man who is concerned about scientific and religious truths. At the outset (I, 1) Browne corrected those who would deny the characterization of Christian to him as a physician and scientist. His Christianity was a fact, and it was his through grace and reason, not by an easy acceptance; he aligned himself most assertively with the principles taught by Christ. Not only did he differentiate his Christianity from that of the naive because his was fed by the gathered convictions of his "riper yeares," but he set himself apart from the zealous and the uncharitable by his tolerance of non-Christians. He did not state explicitly that the charge of atheist or materialist or skeptic could be brought against him, but the self-awareness of his work implies an oblique acknowledgment of that possibility. While others might detect an incongruity between science and religion, he correlated them in an expression of tolerance.

Certainly, his tolerance of Roman Catholicism and pagan faiths set him off from the conservative as well as the sectarian thinkers of his time.[5] In addition, he specifically allied himself with that Protestantism which he believed to be closest to that "primitive integrity" of the Church in the time of Christ. Fittingly, he objected to the implication of protest in the name of the reformed church, but nonetheless he himself protested against the "decaied" state of Roman Catholicism—its attacks against Luther he compared to the Jews' abuses of Christ. Through his knowledge of the Roman liturgy, gained while he lived on the Continent, Browne perceived that practices of the Roman church demonstrated unities with other churches of the Christian faith and promoted similar devotion. Dissociating himself again from zealots, both Roman Catholic and Protestant, who emphasized their differences, he admitted to being genuinely moved by Roman Catholic ceremony, although he was troubled that much of it was designed to impress a credulous laity. With magnanimity he hoped for the discovery of some ground on which reconciliation of the divided factions within the circle of Christianity might be effected (I, 2–3).

Frank L. Huntley has traced the motivation for Browne's tolerance to a natural reaction against the anti-Catholicism of his stepfather, Sir Thomas Dutton.[6] Whatever his motivation, Browne carefully qualified all that he wrote. His repeated reminders that Roman Catholic ceremonies exploit the superstition of the masses and his assumption of a superiority by which he "rectified the errours of their prayers by rightly ordering mine owne" make him far from radical in his tolerance; more important, his reservations show that he fully understood the implications and dangers in what he was writing. The seriousness of his tolerance is enhanced by the naturalness with which he disowned zealousness and self-appointed reformism of all sorts.

In fact, these early sections of *Religio* are self-conscious explanations of how Browne stood, both within and without the circumference of Christianity. First, however, as if to quiet

5. Similar expressions are to be found in a letter written by James Howell to Sir Ed. B., Knight, July 25, 1635, in *The Familiar Letters*, ed. Joseph Jacobs, I, 333–37.
6. *Sir Thomas Browne*, 53.

any doubts about his loyalty, Browne clearly declared (I, 5) his Anglicanism. By elaborating his circle imagery, he encompassed the scope of his religious attitudes within the bounds of the Christian faith. The perfect circle permits breadth of view and avoids the arbitrary narrowness that serves only sectarian purposes. Browne had achieved an Aristotelian moderation: "For in everything it is no easy task to find the middle, e.g. to find the middle of the circle is not for every one but for him who knows."[7] For external authority, religious councils, and the articles of the Anglican church, Browne substituted "the rules of my private reason, or the humor and fashion of my devotion." He omitted from the 1643 version the statement that preceded these rules: "No man shall reach my faith unto another Article, or command my obedience to a Canon more," perhaps because it smacked of the very dogmatism he was opposing. On matters pertaining to his salvation he repeatedly aligned his faith with orthodoxy, which provided a rational framework on which he felt free to build his criticism of the Church. He squelched any charges that his Anglicanism was sectarian by expressing his contempt for those who would limit the origins of the Church of England to Henry VIII's reign. His attitude toward the Pope was most temperate, although he took care to note that the Pope would not return his "good language." Browne deplored the railing in the pulpit, which aroused the vulgar but in no way affected the educated, and he shunned the intolerant. Probably Browne would have agreed with Benjamin Whichcote that "nothing spoils human Nature more, than false Zeal: The *Good Nature* of an Heathen is more God-like, than the furious Zeal of a Christian," and that "our Fallibility and the shortness of our knowledge should make us peaceable and gentle: because I *may* be Mistaken, I *must* not be dogmatical and confident, peremptory and imperious. I *will* not break the certain Laws of Charity, for a doubtful Doctrine or of uncertain Truth" (Aphorisms 114, 130).[8]

Just such an aversion to absolutism prompted Browne to declare his avoidance of arguments about religion (I, 6). He

---

7. *Ethica Nicomachea*, trans. W. D. Ross, IX, 1109a24–25. All references to Aristotle are from the Oxford translation.
8. *Moral and Religious Aphorisms*, ed. Samuel Salter, 15, 17.

offered a fine piece of Baconian advice about successful argument: Argue with those above you if you want to be informed, with those below you if you want to be confirmed in your judgments. In addition, he warned the rashly zealous that the nature of truth and error may best be understood by a humble and peaceful man. He recognized reason as his best guide to truth, so he pronounced himself the servant of his reason, a decision admired by Dr. Johnson in his *Life of Browne*: "There is, perhaps, no better method of encountering these troublesome irruptions of scepticism, with which inquisitive minds are frequently harrassed" (Wilkin, I, xlvii–xlviii). Where truth itself is ambiguous, as in philosophy, he proposed to be equally paradoxical, while in matters of religious truth he would "keepe the road" ("love to keepe" in 1643) by avoiding "Heresies, Schismes, or Errors, of which at present [1642?] I hope [added 1643] . . . I have no taint or tincture." The apparent ease with which Browne admitted his inclination to paradox and then excused casually the "two or three" heresies that inhered in his "greener studies" was no protection from contemporaries who were eager to quarrel with him. He reasoned that, since heresy has the regenerative strength to be reborn again and again, no one is fully responsible for its existence.

A clear example of Browne's separation of the broad medial religious truths essential to salvation from those particular truths open to rational exploration lies in his attitude toward a literal reading of the Bible. His questioning of the Bible dismayed some of his conservative readers, but it is another key ingredient in his latitudinarianism. While he praised the Bible for its truth, beauty, and imperishability at the expense of the Koran (I, 23) in a panegyric his dogmatic contemporaries undoubtedly relished, he prefaced those praises with a statement of rationalism that might have caused consternation. He pronounced Scripture to be "but the conclusions and fallible discourses of man upon the word of God." Still thinking of the persuasiveness of the holy text, Browne pondered the obstinacy of the Jews and the Turks (I, 25) in resisting its teachings. He was "amazed" by the Jews' interpretations of Scripture and their rejection of the New Testament, but he denounced their persecution as "a bad and indirect way to plant Religion." Besides, his fellow Christians, he knew, professed some of the same views on the divinity of Christ.

Browne identified persecution with fanaticism, which leads to "wicked Heresies, and extravagant opinions." His attitude toward non-Christians was a close weaving of admiration and rejection—admiration for their fortitude under persecution, rejection of their beliefs. Although he was not free of the prejudices of his time, he refused to persecute those who differed from him. Even his refutation elsewhere of the vulgar error, "That Jews stink," may be described as "an early specimen of sympathetic racism."[9] His concrete though mild tolerance leads one to endorse W. K. Jordan's enthusiastic view that "it is refreshing indeed to reflect that England could produce thought of this quality during the height of the Laudian repression."[10]

Just as such persecution in Browne's time had only an historical veracity for support, so too the truth of martyrdom was becoming clouded. He based the relativity of who is a martyr directly on the earlier question of who is a heretic. His consistent disapproval of dogmatism and zeal mitigated his respect for the Christian martyrs. For one point, he argued, martyrdom had been abused by too many claimants; nominations of their leaders by zealous sects could not always be accepted (I, 26). Finally, he confessed that, although there were few who feared death less than he (a point on which he was resolved), he believed that he had a moral duty to preserve his life. Wisdom does not induce one to self-murder—a sly jibe at those who avidly pursue martyrdom.

Not surprisingly, Browne's tolerance extended to "those honest Worthies and Philosophers" of paganism (I, 54). Although he stated bluntly the orthodox belief, "There is no salvation to those who beleeve not in Christ," his sympathy lay with the great figures of paganism who lived unaware of "the History of *Adam*." A traditional synthesis running from Philo to Ficino held that Plato complements Moses, Socrates "con-

9. Edgar Rosenberg, *From Shylock to Svengali*, 318.
10. *The Development of Religious Toleration in England from the Accession of James I to the Convention of the Long Parliament* (1603–1640), II, 452.

firms" Christ, and the Magi of Persia and Egypt parallel the prophets of Israel. Such assumptions dissolved differences between Christian doctrine and pagan theology, so each could be understood in an allegorical sense complementary to both.[11] Thus Browne permitted a heightened dignity and priority to "men that live according to the right rule and law of reason," although the "perfectest actions of earth" must be transformed by belief in Christ before they have moral "claime unto Heaven." It is interesting that, having raised this question of who is saved, he revealed his anger with those "insolent" enough in their rationalism "to controvert the works of God, or question the justice of his proceedings." His own search for truth was characterized by humility and guided by right reason.

Aristotle, the Stoics, and the Skeptics or Pyrrhonists are examples of those who did not practice the high ideals they preached (I, 55). From the safe criticism of historical rather than contemporary hypocrisy Browne turned to the discussion of virtue and vice in men of his day. Men know good but do evil because they have a "depraved appetite," which is contradictory to the dictates of their reason. In sum, "we are all monsters, that is, a composition of man and beast." From this commonplace he concluded, somewhat contentiously, that although the way to salvation is difficult and narrow, "those who doe confine the Church of God, either to particular Nations, Churches, or Families, have made it farre narrower than our Saviour ever meant it." He added in 1643 a short section (I, 56) that establishes firmly his thinking on Christianity. In this section he denounced those who would restrict the Church to Europe. Both Asia and Africa had been reached by apostles and had produced martyrs before Christianity had penetrated Europe, so they cannot be excluded. He did not deny the concept of the Elect, but he satirized the ferocity with which each denomination or sect denied salvation to the next. Each would exclude all nonmembers from God's mercy and grace, the only avenues by which salvation can be attained. He concludes that there must be more than one Saint Peter as well as

11. Jean Seznec, *The Survival of the Pagan Gods,* trans. Barbara Sessions, 98–99.

several heavenly gates, judging by the way each sect turns the key against the other. "We goe to heaven against each others wills, . . . and with as much uncharity as ignorance."

Browne warned that some who believe themselves saved are not, because man's judgment is not reliable (I, 57). He expressed amazement at the number who were certain of salvation. He envisioned a hierarchy of saints in which, he modestly stated, he would be happy to "bring up the Rere in Heaven" (I, 58). Despite that modesty, he was "confident and fully perswaded" of his own salvation, although he would "dare not take my oath" on it. Not just a need for empirical verification caused Browne to hesitate, but a sense of unworthiness; the weighing of doubts and humility against confidence and assertiveness prevented his absolute certainty of salvation. A realization that his salvation depended on his working it out with *"feare and trembling"* and the need for "mercy and beneplacit of God" humbled him. He then indulged in a flurry of wit and paradox based on the Johannine view of time: *"Before Abraham was, I am,"* which allowed Browne to measure "in some sense" his existence back to the "Idea of God." He added, in 1643: *"Eve* miscarried of mee before she conceiv'd of *Cain"* (I, 59). Temporal reality is not to be limited to historical time or place.

This consideration of the means to salvation continues in I, 60, where Browne belittled those who maintain that faith "onely" (also added in 1643) serves as a ground for salvation. While he believed this to be true, he found scriptural evidence that the will of God acts directly to influence the fortunes of men. Above all else, he believed that no man can "boast" of his faith, because it may be "a remove from nothing." Thus, no man can have complete confidence in the strength of his faith to save him—good works must also be performed.

The breadth of Browne's tolerance resulted partly from the universality of his tastes. Perhaps it was too generous, for in the 1642 edition he almost included the devil among his forbearances but clarified any possible misunderstanding with a firm statement in the 1643 edition. His charity was general because he was "averse from nothing" (II, 1). But the succeeding passage is a rather important contradiction to this openness to all creation: "I doe contemne and laugh at . . . that great enemy of reason, vertue and religion, the multitude," which includes not just "the base and minor sort of people; there is a rabble even amongst the Gentry." Considering the nearly non-political nature of *Religio*, it is surprising to read, "Let us speake like Politicians, there is a Nobility without Heraldry, a naturall dignity whereby one man is ranked with another." The times were corrupted by the "byas" that ignored the truth that the best-ordered societies were ranked by quality, not wealth.

Charity, according to Browne, provides man with a virtue higher than his own nature (II, 2). But the motivation must be "the Will and Command of my God." To give alms "to satisfie the hunger of my Brother" is a lesser act—certainly moral and passionate, perhaps rational, but not divine.

There are many methods of practicing charity (II, 3). Of particular importance to his own custom are the forgiveness of others' ignorance and, more directly, study not for oneself, but for the good of others. In discussions of serious matters, charity maintains a discreet and peaceable tenor. On the other hand, passion throws reason off the scent of an argument. Besides, "the Foundations of Religion are already established, and the principles of Salvation subscribed unto by all," so few controversies remain that are worth the arousal of passion. The quarrels of scholars, comparable to argument over the "S. and T. in *Lucian*," are pointless but amusing. Outwardly, scholars are peaceful men, but the sharpness of their tongues and the scratching of their pens carry as far as posterity for "an Authenticke kinde of falsehood . . . that belies our good names."

Speaking from within the shelter of his faith and learning (II, 4), Browne condemned several offenses against charity. Illogical and cruel epithets against people of other nations "wound" the persons and "assassine the honour of a Nation"; those who endeavor to destroy vice also destroy virtue, for each is "yet the life of one another"; when vice is in the ascendant, the persistence of goodness in a minority enhances the value of virtue. Further, "No man can justly censure or condemne another, because indeed no man truely knowes another." He is "in a cloud" to his friends, while to God, who only knows him, he is nothing. Since we primarily measure others by ourselves, "all is but that we all condemne, selfe-love."

*Religio Medici* is an examination and an expression of the Delphic "Know thyself." Browne, therefore, declared that self-love is the center of man's consciousness. He noted subtly that, while many complained that "charity growes cold" in his time, this was true most often for those who burned with "the fires and flames of zeale; for it is a vertue that best agrees with coldest natures, and such as are complexioned for humility." Since man, unfortunately, "is his owne *Atropos*," Browne asked how can he be charitable toward others when he is so uncharitable to himself?

Browne held that there are two enigmas in love: Our desire for love is so infinite that we are never satisfied, and our self-love is so strong that those we love become ourselves (II, 6). Yet, the spiritual love that forgets physical appearance is not only friendship but also charity. Since "the greatest happinesse" is to desire salvation for others, he could not pray "contentedly" (added in 1643) for himself "without a catalogue of my friends"; so he prayed for his neighbors, his patients, his enemies. He noted that he always responded to "a passing Bell, though in my mirth and at a Taverne," with prayers and best wishes for the departed spirit. Only the devil could pray harmfully against a person. He omitted "at a Taverne" in 1643.

Browne admitted (II, 7) that earlier in his life he believed that merely to neither harm nor be harmed contained "enough of morality, but my more setled yeares and Christian constitution have fallen upon severer resolutions." He continued: "I hold [changed to 'can hold' in 1643] there is no such thing as injury" because man is "a masse of Antipathies." Beyond self-love is self-charity, which includes charity to others because it is part of one's fight against one's own sins. With severe irony Browne expressed thanks that "I have no sinnes that want a name," but he felt "indignation, anger, contempt and hatred" when he contemplated his sinful nature, and he repented of it. He added a portion on depravity, but omitted in the 1643 version an admission that his self-detestation sometimes approached self-destruction. Returning to his theme, he concluded that it is an act of charity to denounce our sins.

Just as it is self-charity to divorce ourselves from our general sins, it is compatible that we should denounce vanity and thank God that we have escaped the sin of pride (II, 8). Grammarians, linguists, travelers (especially sailors), and seekers after knowledge generally are given to vanity, Browne believed; and even though he had shared—perhaps even exceeded—their experiences, he did not think he had allowed these advantages to become a cause of pride. Thus he disowned the effort to attain any ultimate knowledge in a world of conflicting philosophies and disciplines. Fluctuations of old and new knowledge, the uncertainty of systems, and the general intellectual flux only encouraged him to maintain his Christian faith and to view all else with a skeptical eye. Only after death will ultimate knowledge be revealed.

### The Necessity for Heresy

Writing out of a dual identification of his own uniqueness combined with a realization that he spoke for other scientist–Christians, Browne declared that his rationalism and his fideism were not in conflict; he was both a good Anglican and a man of private, unorthodox contemplations. It is not surprising that his humanity and charity should entertain heterodoxies. But the reader is not prepared for the frank confession of youthful heresies, which Browne carefully distinguishes as long-condemned rather than recent errors (I, 6–8). The language, the timing, and the paradoxical interlude on the eternality of heresy, which, with the "revolution of time" reappears "like the river *Arethusa*," hardly signify controversial revelation, seeming rather to be calculated reflection on the attractiveness of the familiar cyclical pattern of human events. By aligning himself with Anglicanism, Browne freed himself for speculative daring. Nevertheless, his consideration of the various heresies explains much about the nature of his latitudinarianism.

Browne's admitted first "heresy," the mortality of the soul until "the last day" when both soul and body are resurrected, he termed a "conceit" held by all; thus he evaded controversy. The joy of seeing "my Saviour at last" gave him the patience to "be nothing almost unto eternity." [12] His second heresy, that

12. George Williamson, *Seventeenth Century Contexts*, 148,

the vengeance of God is not eternal, "but after a definite time of his wrath hee would release the damned soules from torture" grew out of the authority of Origen, who held that the punishments the soul endures are medicinal and educational. Further, Origen wrote that unlimited punishment does not await the soul, because God's love and man's free will combine in the finality of God's universal rule.[13] Browne maintained that his third heresy, prayer for the dead, "I did never positively . . . practise." He excused his propensity for these three errors on the basis that, just as he could not avoid "charitable inducements" to pray for others, so too he could find "no malice" in his avoiding despair through contemplation of a divine mercy that could forgive all. His language is markedly unsentimental; it is much like Jeremy Taylor's simple statement that prayer for the dead is "at the worst . . . but a wrong error upon the right side of charity."[14] Browne avowed that he never propagated his "bare Errors, and single Lapses" but allowed them to die, thus avoiding Lucifer's sin of tempting others to sin.

Yet, the matter of heresy lingered in Browne's mind, for he added a short section (I, 8) in 1643—perhaps in rebuttal to Sir Kenelm Digby—in which he held that, just as there are always heresies, so too "men of singular parts and humors" will always have unusual and original ideas, which need not be heretical. There are "many things untouch'd, unimagin'd" over which "a sober judgement" and "the libertie of an honest reason may play and expatiate with security." By emphasizing the endless reaches of religious speculation Browne made the important and sophisticated point that schism is the rule rather than the exception where doctrine is the concern. Thus, the "circle" of the Church is never closed; in fact, he said in an elliptical way, truth is itself disunified and fragmented, at all times partially heretical and sometimes unknowable. He did not say that divinity is also "double-faced," but he hinted that

---

175, discusses the stimulation Browne's mortalism had on subsequent debate in the century.

13. Jean Danielou, *Origen*, trans. Walter Mitchell, 277, 287. For Origen on resurrection, see *Contra Celsum*, trans. Henry Chadwick, 303, 276–81, 420, 489.

14. *The Whole Works of the Right Rev. Jeremy Taylor*, ed. Reginald Haber, rev. Charles Page Eden, V, 597.

it, too, includes unrealized truths. To the moral and religious absolutists of his day as it is to those of ours, such a position is anathema.

## An Oh Altitudo for the Soul

From his hypothesis that religious speculation and near-heresy circulate cyclically among great thinkers of all ages, Browne (I, 9) extended the breadth of his rational skepticism and imaginative wondering to an *oh altitudo* (Romans xi:33). This surprising paradox characterizes the attraction *Religio* held for the next generation; the arguments the *oh altitudo* provoked prove it was understood to be more than just rhetorical. His affinity with the Tertullian concept, "*Certum est, quia impossible est,*" might have been dismissed as patently rhetorical, but it was not so in Tertullian, nor is it in Browne. In the sermon "*De Carna Christi,*" Tertullian denounced those who cannot accept Christ's resurrection because it is contrary to natural law. To his mind, this very supernatural-ness made the resurrection credible because "philosophy does not take into account the omnipotence of God. Only the faith of the church, based on the tradition of prophets and apostles, adequately understands this." [15] Browne later invoked the all-embracing power of God as the force that supersedes man's knowledge and prompts his spiritual thought. The gravity of his position is implicit in his claim that it will "answer all the objections of Satan," a personage who, in Browne's normal reference, is not a figure of speech but the epitome of deceit and evil. While he could conceive of his sublime God as such an "answer," a later contemporary, Henry More, found such views deficient.

*The Second Derivative Property of the Mystery of Godliness is Communicability. For in that it is Intelligible, it becomes hereby Communicable. Whence it appears what Communication I mean: not such as in competible also to Magpies and Parots . . . but a Rational impartments of the matter, whereby a mans Understanding is satisfied of the real grounds of our belief. . . . And if we be ask'd a reason of our belief, and the Apostle requires us to answer, assuredly he was not conscious of any Unreasonableness of the*

15. Robert M. Grant, *Miracle and Natural Law in Graeco-Roman and Early Christian Thought*, 195.

*Christian Faith in his time. That of that witty Father of the Church, Credo quia impossibile, however, it might please the Answerer, it could never satisfie the Opposer. . . . For he that will acknowledge Impossibilities in his Religion, gives up the Cause without blowes, and yields at once all that his adversary desired, namely that his Religion is nothing but a Forgery or Foolery.*[16]

Even so, Browne relished the difficulties of having total faith. He professed his happiness that he did not witness at first hand the miracles of Christ and His disciples. Even if Browne was indulging a self-conscious twist of fancy that appealed to his ironic sense of relative truth, he was taking an intellectual (or anti-intellectual) stance that epitomizes his deepest thought. Yet all of these statements carried the stigma of impiety to his extremist readers. The flexibility of his fideism seemed extremely dangerous to the rigidly dogmatic minds of his time.

The extremities of *oh altitudo* lead to the mystical preoccupations of Browne's imagination. The limitations of reason involve a conflict with faith, and his recognition of this conflict is one of his distinctions. He sought a unity between faith and reason by being less absolute in his demarcation of natural and supernatural knowledge than some of his contemporaries. Nevertheless, he was not incoherent in his mingling of the mystical and the rational. His spiritual beliefs were intrinsically so God-centered that his natural thought became so, too; consequently, there is no dichotomy in his analysis of questions of faith and reason, particularly since he did not leave dogma to the theologians, as he claimed. Nevertheless, the extremes of his imaginative vision do serve to blur the clear progressions of any coherent argument. For how can a commitment to the mysterious produce a system of thought? There is, nevertheless, a self-consciousness about his mystical leanings that establishes a measured mode of thought: his *oh altitudo* was controlled by a knowledge of what he was allowing his rational mind to do. He always knew from whence he spoke; his voice speaks out of an intellectual awareness, at once rhetorical and poetical, skeptical and devotional.

16. *An Explanation of the Grand Mystery of Godliness*, 459 (IX, 3, i). Quoted by permission of The Huntington Library, San Marino, California.

Browne's Pyrrhonistic skepticism led him to adopt (I, 10) the Socratic dictum that man knows essentially nothing—surely no naive point of view. His conscious subservience of reason to faith and definition to metaphor signifies once again an intellectual commitment.

Even if Browne's marginal gloss to Hermes is not authentic,[17] his Latin descriptions not explicitly Platonic, and his Aristotelian definitions unexplained, his bias is distinct: he preferred to define the soul of man as the angel of man and the body of God rather than as an entelechy or the essence of actual being (*De Anima*, 412a). The metaphor that light is the shadow of God "humours" him more than the definition that light is the *actus perspicui*, visible movement (*De Anima*, 418b). The body or the shadow of the Deity seems to be Hermetic. In "The Cup of Monad" Hermes described the body of God:

With Reason (Logos), not with hands, did the World-Maker make the universal World; so that thou thus shouldst think of Him as everywhere and ever-being, the Author of all things, and One and Only, who by his will all beings hath created.

This Body of Him is a thing no man can touch, or see, or measure, a Body inextensible, like to no other frame. 'Tis neither Fire nor Water, Air nor Breath; yet all of them come from it. Now being God He willed to consecrate this to Himself alone, and set its Earth in order and adorn it.[18]

The remainder of Hermes' speech describes the commonplace mysticism of the permeation of the universe by the mind, which stands superior to the physical body. The imagery of the cup is familiar from *Timaeus* and is probably a traditional Orphic and Pythagorean symbol (Mead, I, 450–56). This unseen body of God in the universe is analogous to the Platonic world-soul, which also appears in Browne. Ficino employed both the shadow and the circle of God.[19] Although the Divine Vision is traditionally one of light, within the interplay

17. *Catalogus Translationum et Commentariorum: Mediaeval and Renaissance Latin Translations and Commentaries*, ed. Paul Oscar Kristeller, I, 152. See also Sir Thomas Browne, *Religio Medici and Other Works*, ed. L. C. Martin, 290n10.16; 291n10.19–20; 293n12.17–18. Hereafter referred to as Martin.

18. G. R. S. Mead, *Thrice-Greatest Hermes*, II, 85.

19. *Marsilio Ficino's Commentary on Plato's "Symposium,"* ed. and trans. Sears Jayne, 212, 215, 136–37.

of light and dark there would be shadow. God, in Philo's vision, has a shadow:

But God's Shadow is His Reason (Logos), which using, as it were an instrument, He made the cosmos. And this Shadow is as it were the Archetypal Model of all else. For that as God is the Original of His Image, which he [Moses] now calls [His] Shadow, so, [in its turn] that Image is the model of all else, as he showed when, at the beginning of the law-giving, he said: "And God made man according to the Image of God."—This Likeness being imaged according to God, and man being imaged according to this Likeness, which received the power of the Original.[20]

Philo's writings were part of Browne's library and that "peculiar delight" which the former felt "when a passage [in the Pentateuch] in its literal acceptance was contradictory or absurd"[21] is comparable to Browne's continuous desire for more paradoxes in theology. When Browne told his reader how "I teach my haggard and unreclaimed reason to stoope unto the lure of faith," he was being didactic, for he taught the reader how to read and to understand what he is reading. Browne's intention was not an absolute acceptance of the literalness of Scripture, for, in raising paradoxes and ironies he suggested a line of skepticism that is not displaced by the concluding emphasis on the irrational; his rational perceptions were kept alert. He would, to be sure, ultimately hold that such puzzles are not essential to one's salvation and therefore open to speculation. Thus, his mysticism and scriptural questionings are much more artistic than dogmatic, since they impart to the reader a personal excitement for the myriad of ideas and expressions that fascinated their author.

## The Contemplation of Mysteries

The self-consciousness with which Browne pursued the ramifications of the ideas his mind and imagination evoked is expressed when he set an Horatian mood (*Satires*, I, iv, 133–34)[22] for his contemplations and his readers' relaxed reactions

20. Mead, I, 236, quoting *Leg. Alleg.*, III, 31.
21. Edwyn Bevan, "Hellenistic Judaism," *The Legacy of Israel*, eds. Edwyn Bevan and Charles Singer, 53.
22. *Satires, Epistles and Ars Poetica*, trans. H. Rushton Fairclough, 58–59.

to them: "In my solitary and retired imagination (*Neque enim cum porticus aut me lectulus accipit, desum mihi*)" (I, 11). Even in such withdrawn meditation Browne was mindful that he was not alone; his contemplations were carried forth in the presence of God's wisdom, eternity, and providence (I, 11–19). While earthly time antedates man by only five days, eternal time calls forth an *O! altitudo!* God's definition, "*I am that I am*" was intended to "confound mortalitie, that durst question God"; but Browne was not deflected from his inquiries by this acknowledged inability of the human mind to comprehend eternal verities. Not even "that terrible terme *Predestination*," which he interjected after one of his elliptical "therefores," frightened him. His mild tolerance of this doctrine conflicted with his youthful heresy that God's mercy releases the damned. Even so, Browne was not surprised that "the weake" and "the wisest" are troubled by Calvin's belief that God is no respecter of persons. A reconciliation of the mercy of God and the justice of God is central to Calvin's rebuttal of his opponents. Calvin held that, since through Original Sin all men are guilty and deserve punishment, God evidences His mercy through His free grace "by giving to some what they never deserve"; He manifests His justice thus: "By not giving to all, he declares the demerit of all."[23] To those who question the arbitrariness of Calvin's system, the answer is that we may take confidence in its incomprehensibility: "Let us be content with some degree of ignorance where the wisdom of God soars into its own sublimity" (II, 236). Browne did not by any means promote Calvin's doctrines; his interest was motivated by a public concern with the harshness of the dogma and a personal fascination with conjectures he perceived when this view of God's elective powers combined with Augustinian speculation on eternity: "Those continued instants of time which flow into a thousand yeares, make not to him one moment; what to us is to come, to his Eternitie is present, his whole duration being but one permanent point, without succession, parts, flux, or division."[24]

A contemplation of the mysteries of God and eternity leads

23. *Institutes of the Christian Religion*, trans. John Allen, II, 212.
24. See *The City of God*, trans. Marcus Dods, 364 (XI, 22).

naturally to consideration of the mysteries of numbers. The
"difficulty" in the doctrine of the Trinity of denying "in a
relative way of Father and Son . . . a priority" caused him, not
to ponder the mystery of this denial, but to manipulate fanci-
fully the image of the triad (I, 12). He wondered at Aristotle's
eternal world (*De Caelo*, 284a1–2) or two eternities, the latter
taken perhaps from the aither (*De Caelo*, 270b21–24) or from
the distinction drawn between the eternal movements of
heaven and the Eternal Mover (*Metaphysica*, 1073a34–35)
—a differentiation between the visible and the invisible.
Browne's identification with Aristotle of the three-part soul—
the vegetative, the sensitive, and the rational, symbolized by
the triangle—does not correspond exactly with Aristotle's pre-
sentation of the five faculties of the soul (*De Anima*, 414a29–
31). Nevertheless, the tripartite soul may be found in Plato,
who envisioned the soul as being composed of reason, passion,
and desire or appetite (*The Republic*, 440b–441a).[25] Also in
the *Timaeus* (51d), the structure and generation of living
things follow triangular constructions. Plato's dependence on
triangular explanations prompted either Aristotle or one of
his followers to complain: "How absurd it would be if, when
one wished to show that the three angles of a triangle are equal
to two right angles, one were to assume as a principle that the
soul is immortal! For it is not appropriate and connected. As a
matter of fact, one can prove that the three angles of a triangle
are equal to two right angles quite as well without the immortality of the soul" (*Magna Moralia*, 1183b1–6). Aristotle did
say that any attempt to demand a general definition for either
a figure or the soul is absurd because no such definition can
"express the peculiar nature of anything that is" (*De Anima*,
414b25–32). Even if Browne had known of such a criticism of
an importunate fascination with numbers he would not have
disavowed his enchantment with inexplicable relationships between the divine trinity, the geometrical triangle, and the tripartite soul. The ease with which he united these concepts
verifies the high correspondence he perceived in them. Division introduces unity, which inculcates perfection, in his view.

There is, after Pythagoras, a "mysticall way" that absolves

25. All references to Plato are from *The Collected Dialogues*,
eds. Edith Hamilton and Huntington Cairns.

the complexity in these concepts. Browne reinforced his earlier warning against giving too much weight to philosophy by allowing that "there is a set of things which carry in front, though not in capitall letters, yet in stenography, and short Characters, something of Divinitie." As before, Browne perhaps overlooked Aristotle's complaint in *De Caelo* (300a15–19) that the natural world is composed of "weight and lightness" whereas the Pythagorean unit is not; nevertheless, the prestige of the Pythagorean principles in combination with the Platonic triad and the Christian trinity was widespread among scholars. Aristotle acknowledged both the Pythagorean triad (beginning, middle, and end in nature) and the number three, with probable reference to such gods as Zeus, Athena, and Apollo (*De Caelo*, 268a11–15, note 4). If Browne's vision of the mingling of number and substance falls short of that of Copernicus and Kepler, it still combines the knowledge of divinity with the pursuit of ciphers and signs in nature. Perhaps Browne was more easily fascinated by the similarities the triangular symbols evoked than he should have been. Probably, he was responding to the imaginative freedom and breadth of scope that may be deduced from mathematical definitions, for example, "the precise definition of an ellipse introduces us to all the ellipses in the world." [26] Browne's attraction to the magical numbers of Pythagoras is fitting in view of one of his purposes in writing *Religio*, which was to investigate the relationship between faith and reason. In the myth surrounding Pythagoras, Browne had found a satisfying blend of a philosophy that had originated as a formulation of religion, but had been revived as a basis for science:

However far Pythagoreanism may have broken away from religion in the direction of pure science, it never became a dispassionate scientific study of the nature of number, such as the modern mathematician's, but was always . . . on the lookout for symbolical significance. . . . But the numerous symbolical meanings Pythagoreanism discovers are seldom . . . parts of any coherent system of rational thought: they are not as a rule deduced the one from the other, but are independent discoveries. . . . When they do happen to agree, it is of course a godsend; and there is an increasing aspiration, as the scientific motive progressively outweighs the religious,

26. D'Arcy Wentworth Thompson, *On Form and Growth*, ed. John Tyler Bonner, 269.

*to force them somehow to agree and to make up a consistent and unified whole. But such an aspiration was never fulfilled without the continual turning of a blind eye. If, for instance, evenness is unlimited and bad, the number 4 ought not to symbolize justice. But 4 is also the first square number, and to be foursquare is to be fair and just. The Pythagorean does not say at this point, as the modern scientist would say: "Here are two incompatible propositions: I must give up one or the other." He refuses to surrender either, in much the same way as a modern theologian refuses to surrender either Omnipotence or Benevolence.*[27]

To Browne such a moral and scientific dualism would not have been objectionable; the divinity of numbers overrides their quantity. The abstracting power of numbers supported his endorsement of the all-embracing generality of the Hermetic formula that "this visible World is but a picture of the invisible." He would probably ask, why not both benevolence and omnipotence?

The contemplation of such mysteries prompted Browne to indulge in a touch of superiority when he weighed the "content and happinesse" gained from study as "the advantage I have of the vulgar" (I, 13). But he again rehearsed, in an addition to the 1643 version, the difficulty of attaining knowledge of either God or one's self, and even admitted that he would "honour my own profession and embrace" the advice of the Devil at Delphos in order to gain such wisdom. Like many of his scientific colleagues, he justified his research into "the obvious effects of nature" by contending that such probing " 'tis the debt of our reason wee owe unto God." Once again he attacked "those vulgar heads" who "with a grosse rusticity admire his workes." To offset any arrogance in this passage, he reiterated his sense of inferiority before God by adding a concluding sentence and poem that merely repeat these ideas. Ultimately, in either form—prose or verse—Browne's declarations are not startling; in fact, the redundancies are so evident that the reader wonders at the compunction that necessitated his ending this statement with a pious summary of his good intentions and his desire for salvation. Surely Sir Kenelm Digby's criticisms did not stimulate such protestations. This description of the intermixture of God's and man's will and of man's striving to understand and serve God is an effective ex-

27. J. E. Raven, *Pythagoreans and Eleatics*, 129.

pression of Browne's characteristic conviction of a dual love and commitment.

To a man of Browne's inclination, the glory of God is a contemplation of the absoluteness of causation. His explanation of "one first cause, and foure second causes" (I, 14) is consistently Aristotelian (*Physica*, 198a23–31). It superimposes, to be sure, a hierarchy presided over by a providential God who exists without causal motion, then angels who are immaterial, and finally a first matter, which is without form. Since God incorporates all second causes—the efficient, material, formal, and final—Browne loved to ponder this divine action in nature. For Browne, God's acting in the world "to raise so beauteous a structure as the world and the creatures thereof, was but his Art"—once again an idea that Browne could derive from his reading of Aristotle: "For the word 'nature' is applied to what is according to nature and the natural in the same way as 'art' is applied to what is artistic or a work of art" (*Physica*, 193a31–32). It seems imperative that the workings of a craftsman–God such as Browne envisioned should apply as much to the basis of his medical thought as to his mystical. Browne's pleasure at Galen's mention of the Deity only reinforces the tie between his views on the natural world and his understanding of divine causation. Since Digby substantially agreed with Browne's views here, the qualifying "sometimes, and in some things" added in 1643 to the remarks on Galen probably signifies Browne's natural moderation, a caution to the reader to avoid overgeneralization.

The existence of the divine force in nature was substantiated for Browne by the natural law, *Natura nihil agit frustra*; herein he could call on the support of Aristotle (*De Caelo*, 271a23–34; *De Generatione Animalium*, 744a36, 744b16) and of Galen. When Browne stated his preference for the study of the "little Citizens" to that of nature's prodigies, he added the Book of Proverbs to his list of authorities (I, 15). When his anatomist's eye measured the tiny beings while his imagination measured the universe, a precise regard for quantity was unnecessary because numbers are immeasurable and inexact in their meanings.

Browne, throughout I, 16, professed a natural theology in which God orders His linear creation with the care and exactitude of "an excellent Artist." The powers of Browne's First Mover extend absolute control over all subsequent sequences of cause and effect. The universality of God's hand denies deformity—a view that closely parallels Aristotle's reconciliation of monstrosity with necessity (*De Generatione Animalium*, 767b13–16). Browne closed his discussion with a conventional unification of art and nature.

The omnipotence of God's art was in Browne's mind closely allied with two avenues of Divine Providence: the "ordinary and open way," which relates to the processes of the natural world, and Fortune, a "way full of Meanders and Labyrinths," by which God acts outside our knowledge of causal factors (I, 17). Apparently Browne did not object to maintaining this dualism, for he admired the occurrences of chance in his life and in recent history. Nothing is left entirely to chance, even the "successe of that pety Province of Holland" resulted from God's mercy and direct will.[28] But he was not overly troubled by the intricate mysteries of Providence; in fact, his only qualification was the ebb and flow of life by which he rationalized the saying, "All cannot be happy at once." Thus, a cyclical movement in history may explain "in a relative way" the fluctuation of good and bad fortune, although much more than fortune is involved in these patterns. In his image of the helix and the meridian he recaptured an ancient doctrine still acceptable to his contemporaries.[29]

Causes do not "operate in a loose and stragling way," for everything is ordered by God, yet in our ignorance there is nothing "ridiculous" in praying before engaging in games of chance. Perhaps the wisest answer for Browne's time would have been that of Gerolamo Cardano: "But now I return to the question at issue; if anyone should say that my Genius was advising me, although apparently he had never yet revealed himself, I will not dispute it; yet, there must have been some

28. See Rosalie Colie, "Sir Thomas Browne's 'Entertainement' in XVIIth Century Holland," *Neophilologus*, 36 (1952), 162–71, for a study of the involvement of *Religio* in the Dutch controversy over the merits of the ancients and the moderns, and Martin, 294*n*17.35–39.

29. Williamson, 36–37, points out that Thomas Forde in *Lusas Fortunae* (1649) borrowed Browne's description in treating the mutability theme.

art by which the Genius himself had this foreknowledge. On this point, (as I have said) I leave the decision to others."[30] Browne recommended humility before the powers of chance; he disdained those who seek to influence chance for material rather than intellectual rewards, since a realization of the superiority of the latter brings wisdom. Meditation on the influences of fortune directed his mind to the controversial question of judicial astrology. While admitting the existence of numerous arguments against it, he nevertheless professed that an acceptance of astrology "doth not injure Divinity" (I, 18) because over all else man must recognize that God, not the zodiac, deserves our gratitude for good fortune and is the true and infallible cause of all events and things.

To emphasize the importance of this divine causation Browne warned against atheism, which relies too much on second causes. These atheists have listened too closely to passion and reason while ignoring the third member of the soul's triumvirate: faith (here substituted for Plato's "desire or appetite"); this triad must be kept in proper order. Admittedly, such harmony is difficult in matters of religion—an area in which there are perplexing questions that can be answered only through prayer. In the 1642 edition Browne ended his thoughts on the subject at this point, but in the authorized edition of the following year he doubled the length of this section by relating his debates with the devil. Perusal of the *Archidoxes* of Paracelsus and a reading of "the secret Sympathies of things" might have helped Satan to "disswade my beliefe" about such biblical incidents as the brazen serpent, the drenching of the altar in I Kings xviii:38, the destruction of Sodom and Gomorrah, and the supply of manna in the desert. Browne remarked that Josephus' observation of manna's abundance in Arabia in his lifetime and contemporary reports of its being gathered freely in Italy undermined the probability of a miracle. So his battle of wits with the devil was not unavailing, for his "honest endeavours" did not harm "the edifice of my faith" (I, 19)—possibly another quiet rebuttal to his critics, present or future.

30. *The Book of Chance: "Liber De Ludo Alae,"* trans. Sydney Henry Gould, 34. Reprinted from Oystein Ore, *Cardano: The Gambling Scholar.*

Self-protection seems to be his purpose again, at the beginning of I, 20, with the addition in 1643 of "or any other" to the
first sentence: "Neither had these or any other ever such advantage of me." His citations of the *Archidoxes* and the doctrine of sympathies as rational and natural explanations for
the miraculous were perhaps controversial, because by these
means he was defending physicians from charges of atheism.
Browne's compatibility with Paracelsus was based on a teleological explanation of nature; the purpose of *Archidoxes* is to
reveal "the treasure of the chief good," that is, Eternal God
as revealed in nature, so we may understand it "in a material
way." Paracelsus' main intention was to teach the laws of
medicine, and he began his treatise by reaffirming the importance of the microcosm: in curing the corporeal body the
physician allows the spiritual body "to perfect its actions therein, like civit in a pure and uncontaminated casket." The remainder of the work treats the separation of the four elements
and the nature of the quintessence. According to Paracelsus,
the extraction of the virtues of the quintessence will put in
man's hands a power that can only be hinted at, so we must
never forget that the "foundation" of this knowledge "brings
with it a faith fixed on the Creator, and a hope of His love towards us, as of an excellent father for his children."[31]

While Browne recognized that atheists—those who concentrate on second causes in nature—exist, he minimized the
impact of their beliefs. In his own case, Satanic doubts could
not do harm, for the span of Browne's faith in ultimate truth
encompassed the teleology of Epicurus, the blasphemy of the
anonymous *De Tribus Impostoribus*, and the Satanic "Rhetorick" of Machiavelli and Lucian. Browne espoused a controversial companion when he endorsed Epicurus' denial of
Providence as "no Atheism, but a magnificent and high-
strained conceit of his Majesty" (I, 20). When he expressed
equal satisfaction with Epicurus' portrait of the gods (probably in the *Epistle to Menoecus*) and the Stoic doctrine of
"fatall necessitie," he might have been recollecting the coun-
terarguments by Cicero against Epicurus. Cicero disapproved
of the Epicurean maxim, "That which is blessed and eternal

31. *The Hermetic and Alchemical Writings*, ed. Arthur Edward Waite, II, 5, 6, 36.

can neither know trouble itself nor cause trouble to another, and accordingly cannot feel either anger or favour, since all things belong only to the weak."[32] Browne's championing of Epicurus occurred at a time when the latter was still generally in disrepute. C. T. Harrison has found only two other English writers, Nicholas Hill and Francis Bacon, joining Browne in Epicurus' behalf in the first half of the seventeenth century.[33] Supporting Epicurus' ennobling of the distant gods was courageous because of the vile associations of such thinking with the writings of Lucretius, whose materialism loomed dangerously in the eyes of Browne's contemporaries.

While Browne acknowledged his doubts about the immortality of the soul and about lesser questions of scriptural validity, he was not troubled. He was least skeptical about such essential questions as immortality and was intrigued only by the—to him—harmless contradictions and ambiguities of the Bible. Browne characterized many of the tales in the Bible as fabulous; he himself "could shew a catalogue of doubts" (I, 21) not noticed by other men. Nevertheless, he steadfastly upheld the sanctity of Scripture and did so in a typically witty manner by ratifying the word of Saint Paul against that of sailors. Browne's flexibility is epitomized in his calm, somewhat facetious, literal questionings of Scripture. Despite his openness to new interpretation, Browne was certain that "these [scriptural tales] are no points of Faith, and therefore may admit a free dispute" (I, 22), an attitude that Alexander Ross was to attack severely. Even though he had been involved in an actual dispute concerning Peter's angel (Acts xii:11–16) with "a young Divine . . . the *Franciscan* Opponent," Browne's stance, amused speculation, remained unaltered. All such interpretations "are but the conclusions and fallible discourses of man upon the word of God" (I, 23).

Browne's train of thought was drawn again and again to the miraculous. While accepting the miracles of the Bible and the early Church, he doubted contemporary instances, especially those witnessed by the Jesuits, whose "daily" endorse-

32. *De Natura Deorum, Academica*, trans. H. Rackham, 47.
33. "The Ancient Atomists and English Literature of the Seventeenth Century," *Harvard Studies in Classical Philology*, 45 (1934), 20, 12.

ment of transubstantiation was also dubious, in his mind (I, 27). He added, in 1643, a short section (I, 28) in which he expressed admiration for only one authority: "Eternity, and that is God himselfe."

The claims from more recent evidences, whether of miracles or of the miraculous power of relics, did not affect his devotion, although he obviously enjoyed investigating such claims. Such questions were to be debated by other writers throughout the period, but it is especially interesting that Browne was cited by Charles Blount as late as 1693 in his *The Oracles of Reason* as an author "so justly admired as well as by Foreigners as his own Country men, upon the Account of his Knowledge in all Gentile sorts of Literature [who] does have . . . his many Doubts and Scruples" on such matters. Blount after more or less directly quoting examples from I, 19, 21, 22, and from *Vulgar Errors* concluded that "God seldom alters or perverts the course of Nature, however Miracles may be necessary sometimes to acquaint the World of his Prerogative, lest the Arrogance of our Reason should question his Power; a Crime no wise Man can ever be guilty of: Who climbing up from Cause to Cause, shall ever find the highest Link of Nature's Chain to be tyed at the Foot of Jupiter's Chair" (*The Miscellaneous Works* . . . [London, 1695], pp. 3, 12, 15–16). Blount's willingness to rest on compromises based on discretion rather than conclusiveness is further illustrated by his taking a middle-of-the-road position on original sin, preferring to be more charitable than dogmatic.

## The Worlds of the Spirit and the Soul

Since Browne's thinking on many corporeal questions is teleological and Platonic, it is not surprising that his ideas about man's soul and the world of spiritual beings are even more metaphysical.

While he upheld the "verity" of scriptural history against that of the chronicles, he qualified in the 1643 version his total acceptance of Moses' account of his own death. He was unable to dismiss oracular wisdom, despite its Satanic origin, for it served him as evidence of the spiritual world (I, 29–30).

Browne's belief in the existence of spirits and witches arose from his acceptance of the principle of plenitude—the full universe. This belief in witches has drawn more adverse commentary than any other single statement in *Religio* or, for that matter, in his entire writings. Browne's annotator, Thomas Keck, puzzled over the problem of witches: "What sort of Witches they were that the Author knew to be such, I cannot tell; for those which he mentions in the next Section, which proceed upon the principles of Nature, none have denied that such there are. . . . But for the opinion that there are witches which co-operate with the Devil, there are Divines of great note, and far from any suspition of being irreligious, that do oppose it." Keck continued with the suggestion that Nero might be an example of one who sought learning with the aid of the "Magick Arts" and "cunning men," while on the question of cohabitation with the devil there were available the judgments of authorities (Augustine, Aquinas, and Justin Martyr) which held so (p. 71). Browne's unfortunate involvement in 1664 in the trial of Amy Duny and Rose Cullender as witches motivates more modern dismay. Certainly, if the composition of Browne's library is indicative of his interests, the presence there of only one inconsequential book by one R. T. on witchcraft implies that interest was slight.[34] Moreover, Dorothy Tyler has absolved him of any responsible guilt in the Duny–Cullender trial.[35] Once again, his temperateness saved him from acting out of extreme superstition. His credulity was a weakness but not a scar. Devilish possession did not so easily win his acceptance, although he allowed for combining the traditional guardian angel (for example in Aquinas, *Summa Theologica*, I, Q, 113)[36] with the traditional distinction between white and black magic. Browne perceived a strain of science originating in "traditionall Magicke, . . . learned . . . at second hand" from the Devil's "Schollers" (I, 31), which then became the empirical principles of science, removed from

34. Malcolm Letts, "Sir Thomas Browne and His Books," N&Q, 11th series, 10 (1914), 362.

35. "A Review of the Interpretation of Sir Thomas Browne's Part in a Witch Trial in 1664," *Anglia*, 54 (1930), 178–95.

36. Trans. Fathers of the English Dominican Province is the text for quotation.

Satanic stigmas. In any event, Browne believed that man should be thankful for the knowledge inspired by good and bad angels. Thus were Aquinas' moral guardians transformed by Browne into learned informants.

Man's guardian angel mediates his position between the worlds of matter and spirit (I, 33). The biblical account of this state contains "obscurity" (I, 34), but literalist difficulties may be avoided by an allegorical reading. In his further speculation about the habitation of angels, Browne hoped he would "not offend Divinity" (I, 35), for his witty meanderings had a serious religious purpose. Just as he concluded that the "Microcosme" is not "onely a pleasant trope of Rhetorick," so too he explored the reality of all the conventional concepts, such as the chain of being and the amphibious nature of man (I, 34). Both the traditionalism and prestige of his definition hinder the modern reader in responding emphatically to the author's searching intentions. On the other hand, to describe God's creative powers as "*Omneity* [that] informed *Nullity* into an Essence" seems an inadequate defense against such critics as Digby.

Browne drew on Genesis, Plato, Aristotle, Paracelsus, Saint Augustine, Galen, and contemporary thinkers for his series of speculations about the creation of man (I, 36). Ignoring or subverting differences among his authorities, Browne centered on the making of man by God. The creation of the universe is *ex nihilo*, but man is a combination of materials infused by an immortal soul. Thus Browne combined the scriptural and scholastic attributes of God with the Platonic conception of the workman–God who creates with artistic purpose out of available materials (*Timaeus*, 68e–69e). Browne disagreed here with Saint Augustine, who denied the artisan–God (*The City of God*, xii, 23). Browne also rejected Paracelsus' belief in the homunculus, instead preferring to examine the two orthodox explanations of how soul and body combined. Traduction, the favored hypothesis, held that the soul was passed into the body in the act of conception. Browne did not believe this explanation could be denied, yet he was troubled by the doctrine of the transmission of the soul in coition. To avoid this conclusion he seemed to prefer the less approved notion—infusion

—which held that God created souls and then infused them into bodies at birth. The general theoretical questions raised by Browne were to be argued throughout the century. His skepticism about the soul's inorganic nature would still be debated in 1693 by Charles Blount.[37]

Despite his misgivings about the origin of the soul, Browne concluded that his study of anatomy had taught him proper respect for divinity. He did not ignore the Aristotelian emphasis on the rational soul's dependence on the body; his own imagery of the seed incorporates a partially material basis for the soul. He rested his case on the evidence of anatomical experiments, saying that the absence of an "Organe or proper instrument" stands as "a sensible and no inconsiderable argument of the inorganity of the soule," the latter passage added succinctly and emphatically in the 1643 edition. His thinking did not mesh into any tangible expression; instead, he committed himself to the mystery that we are men, "and we know not how."

Consideration of the inorganic nature of the soul led Browne to meditate death. He contemplated the Isaiahic metaphor, "*All fleshe is grasse,*" without any of the morbidity of the medieval moralist; instead, he clearly relished the literal truth that "we have devoured our selves, and yet doe live and remayne our selves" (I, 37). Lesser metamorphoses are unbelievable because man's soul is subject to "neither contrary nor corruption." So certain of the purity of the soul was he that, in a reversal of his earlier heresy, he declared that the souls of the dead so surely depart from this earth that ghosts do not exist. In this he surpassed in two ways the thinking of his time: first, the orthodox faith that only the souls of martyrs went immediately to heaven, lesser souls waited until Judgment; second, the literal belief in existence of ghosts. Thus he stepped outside commonly held spirit lore by declaring the existence of only evil spirits, since in his view human souls would not linger in this world after death if the heavenly life beckoned them. Such a metaphysical extension is a small gain over the general superstitions of the time, but it was enough to

37. "Anima Mundi" (1679) in *The Miscellaneous Works,* 37 ff.

be controversial. It was approved by the Danish scholar, Olaus Borrichuis, although the editor of the 1715 edition of Borrichuis' *Dissertationes* divorced the Danish writer's thought from that of the "irreligious *Religio Medici* of Browne."[38]

Browne admitted to a normal fear of death, but he had discovered that contemplation of death did not frighten him (I, 38); indeed, he confessed that in his melancholy he sometimes desired it (a sentence on this desire was omitted from the 1643 version—one of two such deletions). His attention then passed from a dignified vision of death to another of those temporal scriptural questions that fascinated him: the age of Adam at his creation (I, 39). Adam, in the accepted thought, was then thirty (a parallel with himself that he does not call to the reader's attention), "created in the perfect age and stature of man." But "every man is some moneths elder than hee bethinkes him," a statement that prefaces an imaginative view of the birth of man out of "the truest Microcosme, the wombe of our mother." Man exists in three worlds: the womb, this world, and immortal life. The philosopher's stone had taught Browne "how that immortall spirit and incorruptible substance of my soule may lye obscure, and sleepe a while within this house of flesh." The presence of the soul within the body during its earthly existence was to him much like the development of the silkworm, another example of the Divine at work in nature. The orthodoxy of the stone closely parallels his intended use of it, even if he was speaking metaphorically. Evelyn Underhill explains the traditional view in this way:

Upon the spiritual plane also they held that the Divine Idea is always aiming at 'Spiritual Gold'—divine humanity, the New Man, citizen of the transcendental world—and 'natural man' as we ordinarily know him is a lower metal, silver at best. He is a departure from the 'plan,' who yet bears within himself, if we could find it, the spark or seed of absolute perfection: the 'tincture' which makes gold. . . . This 'incorruptible substance' is man's goldness, perfect principle: for, 'the highest mineral value resides in Man,' says Albertus Magnus, 'and God may be found everywhere.' Hence the prosecution of a spiritual chemistry is a proper part of the true Hermetic science.[39]

38. Ethel Seaton, *Literary Relations of England and Scandinavia in the Seventeenth Century*, 168.
39. *Mysticism*, 142–43. See also 35–36.

Browne concluded this section in the Pembroke MS by favoring an "hermeticall" definition of death, which signifies that "in a naturall and experimentall way, man seemes to bee but a digestion, or a preparative way unto that last and glorious Elixar which lies imprison'd in the chaines of the flesh."

Browne, rather than being afraid of death, was filled with shame at the changes it works. This section, which dwells on the mutability of the flesh, closes with an exquisite piece of sardonic humor: "I might not call my selfe as wholesome a morsell for the wormes as any" (I, 40). He added another section in 1643 (I, 43) to elaborate on such ideas as the providence of God being the most potent factor in longevity. His fine image declares, "though the radicall humour containe in it sufficient oyle for seventie, yet I perceive in some it gives no light past thirtie." Thus he moderated the audacity of his earlier remarks about death; he reintroduced the omnipotence of God yet did not allow himself to moralize about old age and approaching death as Digby did in his rebuttals. Although Browne accepted Lucan's view that the seeking of earthly bliss is vanity, he could not share the Stoics' admiration for suicide. Rather than follow the example of heroic suicide Browne would choose the suffering acceptance of Job, since "it is then the truest valor to dare to live" (I, 44). Subsequently, he nearly doubled the length of this section by adding a catalogue of Renaissance complaints about the power of death, although his tone here is not as pessimistic as it might be in the work of a less paradoxical author. He gained satisfaction from the belief that death is an escape from the miseries of life; at the same time, these miseries seem less when compared with imminent death.

Thinking of man's death led Browne to speculate on the world's death. He endorsed the Christian concept of the world's end, but this is not synonymous with the view that the world is "old" or "decayed" (I, 45). He took the orthodox[40] position that "to determine the day and yeare of this inevitable time, is not onely ... madnesse, but also ... impiety" (I, 46), but he was subtly unorthodox when he wrote that "some be-

40. C. A. Patrides, "Renaissance and Modern Thought on the Last Things: A Study in Changing Concepts," *HTR*, 51 (1958), 171.

leeve" (changed from "I beleeve" in the manuscripts and the 1642 edition), "there went not a minute to the worlds creation nor . . . to its destruction" (I, 45).

Browne denied belief in a "Judiciall proceeding, or calling to the Barre" on the "last day," but he declared that, without the resurrection, "all Religion is a Fallacy" (I, 47). Such a stance enabled Browne to subscribe to Seneca's judgment (*De Vita Beata*, ix, 4)[41] that "vertue is her own reward, is but a cold principle." Nevertheless, he had practiced Seneca's "honest artifice" (*Ad Lucilium Epistulae Morales*, epistle xi, 6)[42] to pretend when alone and tempted that his "deare and worthiest friends" were with him. That artifice, however, leads to mere "morall honesty" and not to virtue for the sake of Him who "must reward us at the last." The resurrection is therefore the ultimate goal and its anticipation the truest guide in morals.

Browne's affirmation of the resurrection is one of the most famous portions of *Religio* because in it he posited palingenesis as evidence of this phenomenon. As demonstration he used the regeneration of the flame-consumed plant. But first, with regard to the resurrection of the dead, Browne declared that "to beleeve onely possibilities, is not faith, but meere Philosophy" (I, 48). Divinity is beyond reason and sense, while such a mystery as magnetism is verifiable by sense, not by reason; therefore, reason cannot serve as essential guide even in matters of philosophy.

Having relegated reason to the lowest level of evidence, he turned to the consideration of the immortality of the body as well as of the soul. Rather than deal in abstractions, he here illustrated the reality of a separation and reunification in the natural world by discussing the regeneration of plants. Similar conceptions were examined by William Drummond in *A Cypress Grove*, by a Dr. Daniel Cox, and by Henry Power.[43] Browne's belief in the immortality of the form was based on the theory of the noncorporeal form, which combines with

41. *Moral Essays*, trans. John W. Basore, II, 122–23.
42. Trans. Richard M. Gummere, I, 64–65.
43. See *The Works of William Drummond*, 117–28; Joan Bennett, *Sir Thomas Browne*, 89; E. S. Merton, "The Botany of Sir Thomas Browne," *Isis*, 47 (1956), 164; and Martin, 307*nn*46.2–5, 46.6–8; 308*n*46.15–17.

matter but survives matter because the form is of a higher nature, close to the Ideal.[44] The significance of Browne's thinking may be found in Joseph Needham's statement that the "first experiments in chemical embryology were undertaken" in Browne's home in Norwich. Although Browne's examinations were "static" rather than "dynamic," his role was clearly measurable.[45]

At the heart of Browne's thinking was the microcosmic Idea or seed. He speculated that the world cannot be destroyed by fire, since fire is but one of the four elements; perhaps, he mused, certain "Chymists" are correct in holding that the world, in that final fire, will be "chrystallized" into glass. Further, even if God did annihilate His creation, He would not destroy the microcosm—a view consistent with Browne's most serious thought. Browne resumed his consideration of seed and Idea to postulate that, "in the seed of a Plant to the eyes of God, and to the understanding of man, there exists, though in an invisible way, the perfect leaves, fruits and flowers thereof" (I, 50). Contemplation of this marvel reconciles the principles of perfection and immutability with contrary signs of corruption and destruction.

As for hell, Browne declared his lack of fear of it or of a vengeful God. He separated himself from those "slaves of the Almighty" who fear Him rather than serve Him and who do not perceive the mercy of His judgments, but see them only as punishments (I, 52). Characteristically, Browne pursued this train of thought to the paradox that "God is mercifull unto all, because better to the worst, than the best deserve; and to say he punisheth none in this world, though it be a Paradox, is no absurdity" (I, 53). He tempered his early view that none are frightened into Heaven to "I can hardly thinke there was ever any scared into Heaven" (I, 52, 1643 edition).

The ideal nature of the soul's relationship to the spirit and mercy of God existed for Browne in harmonious order (II, 9). Harmony is beauty, especially the beauty of the music of the

44. Walter Pagel, "Religious Motives in the Medical Biology of the XVIIth Century," *Bull. Instit. Hist. Med.*, III (1935), 127–28, and E. S. Merton, *Science and Imagination in Sir Thomas Browne*, 44–50, 57–59, 68–70.
45. *History of Embryology*, 133, 159.

spheres. The harmony of music is "a Hieroglyphicall and shad-
owed lesson of the whole world." His "Catholicke obedience"
(the dangerous word, *Catholicke*, even in its meaning of universal, was omitted in 1643) to harmony aroused devotion in
him, no matter what the kind of music—even "that vulgar and
Taverne Musicke." To be in harmony is to be in a state of
good health, so he dissociated himself from those physicians
who desired the spread of disharmony in order to create illness
—a perceptive jibe at another rumor of the day disparaging
medicine. From the medicinal properties of harmony, he could
with some coherence proceed to the curative powers of the
three professions, physicke, law, and divinity, each of which
complements the other in the curing of the ills Adam's fall
brought on mankind. Death, itself incurable, is the final cure.
A highly imaginative line that describes the divine effects of
harmony: "It unties the ligaments of my frame, takes me to
pieces, dilates me out of myself, and by degrees, me thinkes,
resolves me into Heaven" was unfortunately omitted in 1643.
Perhaps it was too self-centered.

Continuing the theme of harmony, Browne concluded that
man's nature is such a mixture of good and evil that each man
carries within himself the cure for his every disease. But this
therapy does not affect the moral nature of man, for a moral
infection that reaches back to the "man without a Navell" per-
sists. The thought moved him to pray: "Lord deliver me from
my selfe." Man may seek solitude, but he will never achieve
it, for each is a microcosm and loneliness is filled with the
world, the mind, the devil, and the divine—the last capable of
drawing this disunity into a transcendent unity (II, 10).

In keeping with his view of man's God-centered and microcosmic existence, Browne examined man's relationship to
society. In one of the most tortured sentences in *Religio* (II,
13), he declared: "The method I should use in distributive
justice, I often observe in commutative, and keepe a Geomet-
ricall proportion in both, whereby becomming equable to
others, I become unjust to my selfe, and supererogate in that
common principle, Doe unto others as thou wouldest be done
unto thy selfe." He confessed to atheism if his faith was to be
judged by his refusal to "honour that which the world adores."
Charity is the highest expression of Christianity; out of this

belief he endorsed the "Epitome," *"He that giveth to the poore lendeth to the Lord."* Not only could Browne say that his views on justice and virtue were good Christianity, but also good Aristotelianism (*Ethica Nicomachea,* 1130a14). Two references to his willingness to give money to charitable causes, which he cited to demonstrate his practice, do not appear in the 1643 edition.

He opened II, 14, with this proposition: "the Basis and Pillar [of charity] is the love of God, for whom wee love our neighbour." There is nothing unusual in our loving the invisible, for "all that wee truely love is this." Virtue is the greater because it is invisible. The visible progressions of love toward parents, then toward wife, later toward children are but "dumb showes." When children mature they repeat this ritual, so "a man may bee buried alive, and behold his grave in his owne issue." He would have justly claimed that his vision is empirically grounded on the real order of things. Men do indeed temper or revert to early ties as later loyalties arise; he merely described the commonest example of this progression. Characteristically, he extended his vision to a paradox that, in turn, lends originality to all that substantiates it.

The final section of *Religio* (II, 15) centers on a prayer, but much of the controversy about the section ignores the prayer and focuses on a passing, but somewhat disparaging, allusion to Copernicus' placing of the sun. Browne's inconclusiveness here and in *Vulgar Errors* about Copernicanism may possibly be explained by his usual unwillingness to become entangled in such religious disputes as those surrounding Copernicus' ideas.[46] More likely, the reference to Copernicus in *Religio* is a bit of parenthetical humor. His ultimate concern was the fleeting nature of earthly happiness—"an apparition, or neat delusion." Here, he addressed God with a reiteration of his trust in His providence and his resignation to "the wisedome [*justice* in 1642] of thy pleasure. Thy will bee done, though in my owne undoing." The last word was toned down from "damnation" in the 1642 version.

46. Gordon K. Chalmers, "Sir Thomas Browne: True Scientist," *Osiris,* 2 (1936), 60–63, and Almonte C. Howell, "Sir Thomas Browne and Seventeenth-Century Scientific Thought," *SP,* 22 (1925), 72–80.

## The Fame of Dr. Browne and His Book

Reactions to *Religio* were quick and emphatic. John Aubrey was prompted to record: "1642, *Religio Medici* printed, which first opened my understanding, which I carryed to Eston, with Sir K. D." The hastiness of Aubrey's date, if he were carrying Digby's *Observations* with him, emphasizes the urgency he felt for comprehending this book. Years later, Aubrey and Browne were to know each other well enough for Browne to contribute an item for Aubrey's *Lives of John Dee*. Dee's son Arthur was a physician in Norwich and was, according to Aubrey, "a great acquaintance" and "an intimate friend" of Browne's. Browne put Aubrey on the scent of Dee's papers, a "quaere" that Aubrey promised himself he would pursue.[47] Aubrey also credited Browne with an item in his *The Natural History of Wiltshire* (1685, although worked on from 1656 to 1691) on the Norfolk air: "Sir Thom. Browne, M.D., of Norwich, told me that their eies in that countrey doe quickly decay; which he imputes to the clearness and driness (subtileness) of the aire. Wormwood growes the most plentifully there of any part of England; which the London apothecaries doe send for." Aubrey also transcribed Browne's "Miscellany Tract V: Of Hawks and Falconry, ancient and modern" as a part of his work.[48]

There are innumerable quotations and paraphrases from Browne's writings (although not *Religio*) in Aubrey's *Remaines of Gentilisme and Judaisme* (1686–1688) where such works as *Vulgar Errors* (II, 6; VI, 4; V, 22–23); *Miscellany Tracts* I, II, VI; *Urn Burial*; and *The Garden of Cyrus* are cited on a variety of subjects that include a woman's labor, mistletoe, Candlemas Day, dubious customs and superstitions, garlands, cereal cakes, sorcery, burial customs, yew trees, funeral music, cymbals, house-leeks, and finally, staffs and sceptres.[49] In a letter to Anthony Wood on April 7, 1673, he also expressed the hope that Browne would send to him

47. *Brief Lives*, ed. Andrew Clark, I, 37, 210–11.
48. Ed. John Britton, 12, 116.
49. Ed. James Britten, 73, 89, 93–94, 109–18, 139–40, 164–67, 173.

Thomas Gore's horoscope, which he finally succeeded in acquiring.[50]

Browne's friend John Merryweather, whose Latin translation of *Religio* in 1644 was reprinted or pirated at least eight times in the next century, was identified in a posthumous work, *Directions for the Latine Tongue* (1681) as simply the translator of *Religio Medici*. He wrote Browne on October 1, 1649, that to the pirated edition of his translation, which appeared in Paris in 1644, a preface had been added

> by some papist, . . . in which making use of, and wresting some passages in your book, he endeavor'd to shew, that nothing but custom and education kept you from their church. . . . It found some demurr in the first impression at Leyden; and upon this occasion, one Haye, a book-merchant there, to whom I first offered it, carried it to Salmasius for his approbation, who in state, first laid it by for very nigh a quarter of a year, and then at last told him, that there were indeed in it many things well said, but that it contained also many exorbitant conceptions in religion, and would probably find but frowning entertainment, especially among the ministers, which deterred him from undertaking the printing. (Wilkin, I, 367–68)

The letter continues with the information that two more printers returned the book before he found Hackius, who published it. It is also interesting that earlier in this letter Merryweather gave as part of his apology for being so negligent in informing Browne of his translation that "all the time" he was in the Low Countries and France a rumor was in circulation that Browne was dead. Could such a rumor have been propagated by those opposed to his book? In the years from the mid-1640s until the end of the century Browne's work was also translated into French and Dutch. It was bandied about in the Dutch version of the ancient-moderns controversy to support the moderns. A physician-poet, John Collop, expressed high praise of Browne in his *Poesis Rediviva* (1656):

ON DOCTOR BROWN.
HIS RELIGIO MEDICI AND VULGAR ERRORS.

*Religio Medici* though th' world Atheism calls,
The world shows none, and the Physitian all.
More zeal and charity *Brown* in twelve sheets shows,

50. Anthony Powell, *John Aubrey and His Friends*, 148.

Then twelve past ages writ, or th' present knows;
What *Paracelsus* brag'd of doth disclose,
He 'twixt the Pope and *Luther* might compose,
Though gut-inspired zelots bark at him,
He hath more knowledge then their Sanhedrim.
Or the Scotch pedant a worm in every book,
To maim the words and make the sence mistook.
Dul lumps of earth not yet concocted mud,
In natures count scarce Cyphers understood.
Let these lick up the indigested phlegm
Which Cruder stomach'd *Sciolists* belch'd 'fore them:
Dog-like to vomits run and lick each sore,
Think learning to repeat what's said before,
While these can prize truths weapons by the rust,
Crawl with the aged serpent in the dust.
Shine out dispelling th' ages darker night.
Knowledge makes only Children of the light.
Folli's unmask'd, and errors bald pate shown.
Brown others errors, others write their own.

According to John Collop the world declared Sir Thomas
Browne an atheist, but Collop recognized Browne as a modern
progressive who mediated the extremes of the Pope and
Luther against the outcries of the zealots. Collop respected
Browne as a man of knowledge who revealed the errors of the
ignorant. Pedants like Alexander Ross he dismissed as worms.

Much less complimentary is "The Answer" in *Songs and
Other Poems* by Alexander Brome (London, 1661) which contains this passage:

Thou next would'st have me turn Divine,
And *Doctor* too, indeed 'tis fine,
*Physick* and *preaching* ill agree,
There is but one *Religio Medici*.
*Paul* and every other *Postle*,
(As the Scripture doth to us tell)
That had the gift of healing, did
Not cure the belly, heart or head,
By hearbs, or Potions, Purge or *Treacle*;
But by a plain down right *miracle*.
I never heard that learned *Moses*.
Whom God himself for *Prophet* chose his,
In *Egypt* was *Physitian*, though there
He kill'd as many, men as if he were.
How pretty I should shew I saith,
As in his Sums *Aquinas* saith,

With *hour-glass* in one fist, and
With *Urinall* in the other hand.
To have my Pothecary say
Such a *Ladie's* sick to day,
And straight to have my *Sexton* calling,
And ask me when he shall toll all in.
If I must needs be both then name ye
What kind of *Doctor* you would have me.
*Chymick?* alas the costly furnace,
Will quickly my small purse unfurnish,
Or *Galenist?* that wont agree
With my other trade *Divinity*.
Nor with Preachers now the mode is't,
To strive to make themselves Methodists.

(P. 173)

The satiric context used by Brome casts doubt on the wisdom of *Religio Medici*, even if the poem is to be treated as a unique exception.

John Evelyn's famous description of Browne in his diary entry for October 17, 1671, as an indefatigable collector of curiosities has conditioned readers of subsequent ages to picture an eccentric and harmless gentleman, but that was hardly Evelyn's view:

> Next morning I went to see Sir Tho: Browne (with whom I had sometime corresponded by Letters tho never saw before) whose whole house & Garden being a Paradise & Cabinet of rarities, & that of the best collection, especially Medails, books, Plants, natural things, did exceedingly refresh me after last nights confusion: Sir Thomas had amongst other curiosities, a collection of the Eggs of all the foule & birds he could procure, that Country (especialy the promontorys of Norfolck) being (as he said) frequented with severall kinds, which seldome or never, go farther into the Land, as Cranes, Storkes, Eagles &c.: & variety of Waterfoule: He likewise led me to see all the remarkeable places of this antient Citty, being one of the largest, & certainly (after London) one of the noblest of England.[51]

A fellow physician, Gideon Harvey, captured a less gracious portrait of Browne in *The Conclave of Physicians, detecting their intrigues, frauds, and plots*. . . . (London, 1683):

> Some physicasters by reputing themselves Virtuoso's, Mathematicians, Philosophers, and witty Cracks, have insinuated this Enthymeme to the Commonality, that therefore they must neces-

51. *The Diary of John Evelyn*, ed. E. S. De Beer, III, 594.

sarily arrive to the top of their profession; for since their porous
Brain was capable to imbibe such knotty Mysteries, it's not improbable, they might much easier suck up the quintessence of the
Art of Medicine. To this Category belonged that famed Doctor of
Norw. who being Posted away from his House with a Coach and
Four to a Sick Gentleman in the Countrey, an unhappy gawdy
Butterfly thwarted the Coach, upon which a halt was made, and
the Doctor with the assistance of the Coachdriver, hunted so
long, untill they had him under the broad brimm'd Beaver. Here
an harangue was to be made by his conducting Auditor upon the
admirable Structure, Shape, Organs, and colours of the Butterfly,
particularly upon the transparent yellow, of which colour a Cap
would better have fitted him than the black Velvet one. The
Butter-fly being cag'd up in a Box, and reserv'd to a further consideration, the Journey was pursu'd, at the end whereof the Doctor
found the Patient just expir'd of a Syncopal-fit, and the new
Widow accosting him with the information, that her Dear Husband had passed through many of them by the help of a Cordial,
and so probably might this, had she not, wretched creature as she
was! expected his coming to prescribe another. But whether the
Doctor, besides the Reprimand, and the want of his Sostrum, had
the Justice done him, to be sent home on foot, I know not. (Pp.
59–61)

Nevertheless, *Religio Medici* marked Browne for good or ill.
The controversies the book aroused were real and detectable.
Even in so combustible a time as the 1630s and 1640s in England, the meanderings of Browne's religious and scientific
mind did not go unnoticed and were not dismissed as trivial
or superficial. Charles Raven has commented that "the denunciations called out by so conciliatory and orthodox a treatise
. . . show how inveterately hostile were the Churches of
Western Europe to any attempt to formulate 'a religion for
the scientist.' "[52]

Nineteenth-century critics firmly established the view that
Browne idealized himself in *Religio*. Coleridge best defined
this position:

The Religio Medici . . . is a fine Portrait of a handsome man in his
best clothes—it is much of what he was at all times, a good deal
of what he was only in the best moments. I have never read a
book, in which I felt greater similarity to my own make of mind—
active in enquiry, & yet with an appetite to believe,—in short, an

52. *Natural Religion and Christian Theology*, 1. Raven believes
that Browne was "in broad agreement with the outstanding sci-
entists and theologians of his day."

affectionate & elevated Visionary! But then I would tell a different Tale of my own heart; for I would not only endeavor to tell the Truth, (which I doubt not, Sir T.B. has done) but likewise to tell the whole Truth, which most assuredly he has not done. However, it is a most delicious Book.

His own character was a fine mixture of humorist, genius, and pedant. A library was a living world to him, and every book a man, absolute flesh and blood! and the gravity with which he records contradictory opinions is exquisite. (P. 438)

In another context R. P. Blackmur has described the kind of intellectual viewpoint and excitement we find in *Religio*:

Fortunately, there exist archetypes of unindoctrinated thinking. Let us incline our minds like reflectors to catch the light of the early Plato and the whole Montaigne. Is not the inexhaustible stimulus and fertility of the Dialogues and the Essays due as much as anything to the absence of positive doctrine? Is it not that the early Plato always holds conflicting ideas in shifting balance, presenting them in contest and evolution, with victory only the last shift? Is it not that Montaigne is always making room for another idea, and implying always a third for provisional, adjudicating irony? Are not the forms of men themselves ironic, betraying in its most intimate recesses the duplicity of every thought, pointing it out, so to speak, in the act of self-incrimination, and showing it not paled on a pin but in the buff of life? . . . Such an approach, such an attempt at vivid questing, borrowed and no doubt adulterated by our own needs, is the only rational approach to the multiplication of doctrine and arrogant technologies which fills out the body of critical thinking. Anything else is succumbing, not an approach; and it is surely the commonest of ironies to observe a man altogether out of his depth do his cause fatal harm merely because, having once succumbed to an idea, he thinks it necessary to stick to it. Thought is a beacon, not a life-raft, and to confuse the functions is tragic. The tragic character of thought—as any perspective will show—is that it takes a rigid mould too soon; chooses destiny like a Calvinist, in infancy, instead of waiting slowly for old age, and hence for the most part works against the world, good sense, and its own objects; as anyone may see by taking a perspective of any given idea of democracy, of justice, or the nature of the creative act.[53]

While the specific context of Blackmur's remarks relates to the writing of original literary criticism, may we not detect in what Blackmur praises a description of the meditative wanderings of Sir Thomas Browne?

53. *The Double Agent*, 273–74.

Browne was not unindoctrinated; his mind and personality were influenced both consciously and unconsciously by so many doctrines—old and new—that an intellectual blending took place. We see him in *Religio* listening to the reflections of his own mind. The self-awareness of the work must not be minimized, for from such self-concern come the beginnings of debate. He considered himself to be a person worth knowing, even his apologetic preface entices the reader to further pursuit of his ideas. His profession, he acknowledged openly, was controversial, his scientific education and interests set him apart from other men, and his speculations about religion and Scripture marked him as a skeptic or worse. He was obviously, though unadmittedly, proud of his character. While he was not so radically dissimilar from most men as he apparently thought, this reduction in difference does not lessen the vigor of his work. Browne's contradictions, inconsistencies, and lack of order may be held against him, but his critics, such as Sir Kenelm Digby and Alexander Ross, pay the cost of their announced consistency by writing critiques that misrepresent Browne and do their authors little credit.

Neither do we hold Browne's theocentricity against him, for it was a genuine product of his mind and his age. His continuing devotion to faith and charity was not itself controversial; but his attempts to develop both faith and charity in the light of his intellectual experiences, both empirical and intuitive, led him into difficulties. Sir Thomas described himself as serene in his beliefs and indifferent to controversy even in the midst of civil upheaval; indeed, the quietness of his later life in Norwich attests to his ability to remain calm and detached in the midst of both religious and political dispute. But *Religio* caused ripples of reaction and outcry that stand out significantly in the literature of even that age of intellectual counterattack. The irony is that Browne was not primarily an attacker or even an initiator. Nevertheless, when he undertook this meditation about what he believed at age thirty he created a catalogue of insights and perspectives touching on many of the debated ideas of his century. Even if *Religio* is merely a primer in controversy in comparison with the works of Hobbes and Milton and the battles that raged around them, it nevertheless has left its mark on the intellectual history of its time.

# III.

## SIR KENELM DIGBY

### The "Compleat Gentleman" Responds

Sir Kenelm Digby was spending Christmas 1642 as a prisoner in Winchester House in Southwark when his friend, Edward Sackville, the fourth Earl of Dorset, invited Sir Kenelm to criticize "this favourite . . . , *Religio Medici.*" Digby's confinement climaxed a period that had been tempestuous for him as well as for England. He and other Royalists had been called before the Long Parliament in January 1641 to be examined concerning their alleged dealings for King Charles. As the portents of civil war increased, Digby voluntarily left in June for France. His stay on the Continent was curtailed, however, when he killed a French nobleman, Mont le Ros, in a duel over the latter's dinner toast to the cowardice of the English king. The affair forced his return to England in November 1641. While he continued his work in Royalist and Catholic causes, Digby was spied upon and finally arrested in August 1642, but released without formal charge. As anti-Catholic and anti-Royalist forces gathered strength, opposition to enthusiasts like Digby grew. The civil war was but three months old when he was again confined, early in November 1642.[1]

Imprisonment did not stifle Digby's considerable energies, for, as John Aubrey points out, "in the Times of Confusion, the Bishop of Winchester's Lodging in Southwerk, being a large Pile of Building, was made a Prison for the Royalists; and here Sir Kenelm Digby wrote his book *Of Bodies*, and diverted himself in Chymistry, and used to make artificial precious Stones, as Rubies, Emeralds, &c. out of Flint, as Sir Frances Dodington, Prisoner with him at the same time, told me."[2] John Selden recalled Digby's plight when he wrote that Digby "was severall times taken & lett go againe, att last imprisoned in Winchester house, I cann compare him to nothing but to a

1. R. T. Petersson, *Sir Kenelm Digby*, 154–64.
2. *Aubrey's Brief Lives*, ed. Oliver Lawson Dick, 98.

great fish, that wee catched & lett goe againe, but still hee will come to the Baite, att last therefore wee putt him into some great pond for store."[3]

Contemporary and later opinion varied as to the value and the veracity of Digby's thought and work. Digby as an explorer and antiquarian suited perfectly Henry Peacham's concept of the heroic figure: "that noble and absolutely compleat Gentleman Sir Kenhelme Digby Knight" (*The Compleat Gentleman* [1634], 2d ed., p. 108). Aubrey in his life of Digby reported that he "was held to be the most accomplished cavalier of his time. . . . The learned Mr. Thomas Allen (then of that house) was wont to say that he was the *Mirandula* of his age." Aubrey's account continues in less flamboyant terms: "[Digby] had also this virtue, that no man knew better how to abound, and to be abased, and either was indifferent to him." In his Life of Thomas Bushnell, Aubrey characterized Digby's reputation in this way: Bushnell "sayd he owed, I forgett whether it was 50 or sixty thousand pounds: but he was like Sir Kenelm Digby, if he had not 4d., wherever he can he would find respect and credit" (ed. Clark, I, 225, 226, 131). A friend of Digby's, John Finch, even as he admitted that Digby was a braggart, could hold his curative powers in 1653 in higher regard than those of Van Helmont—but then, this evaluation may be excusable credulity, as has been suggested.[4] Elsewhere Finch has this ambiguous commendation to offer about Digby: "The glory of our nation, Sir Kenelm Digby; a gentleman so generally accomplished that 'twere an injury to raise his applause from any particulars."[5] On the other hand, Digby, to John Evelyn, was "an arrant mountebank" and "a teller of strange things," the first remark having probably been added when the passage was transcribed on November 7, 1651. Most of Evelyn's comments about Digby pertain to his knowledge of chemistry and medicine, so it is interesting that when he reported on observing Nicolas Lefevre's course in chemistry on December 20, 1651, he singled out only Digby by name from the "divers

3. *Table Talk*, ed. Sir Frederick Pollock, 56.
4. *Conway Letters*, ed. Marjorie Hope Nicolson, 85, 312–13.
5. Historical Manuscripts Commission, *Report of the Manuscripts of the Late Allan George Finch, Esq. of Burley-on-the-Hill, Rutland*. Series 71 (London, 1913–1965), II, 502.

Curious Persons of Learning & Quality" who attended (III, 48n550, 49). Nevertheless, in describing Digby's donation of his library to Oxford, Evelyn judged it "of more pomp than intrinsic value, as chiefly consisting of modern poets, romances, chemical and astrological books."[6] While Evelyn's comments here pertained also to the Earl of Bristol's library, it is more significant that Evelyn was probably uninformed at that particular time of the actual extent and value of Digby's benefactions. Naturally Evelyn in *Fumifugium* (1661) could also call Digby, "learned" when he found they were in substantial agreement on a subject such as air pollution (p. 11).

Edward Hyde, Earl of Clarendon, remembered Digby as "very eminent and notorious throughout the whole course of his life":

*He was a man of a very extraordinary person and presence, which drew the eyes of all men upon him, which were more fixed by a wonderful graceful behaviour, a flowing courtesy and civility, and such a volubility of language, as surprised and delighted; and though in another man it might have appeared to have somewhat of affectation, it was marvellous graceful in him, and seemed natural to his size, and mould of his voice and delivery. . . . In a word, he had all the advantages that nature, and art, and an excellent education could give him; which, with a great confidence and presentness of mind, buoyed him up against all those prejudices and disadvantages, . . . which would have suppressed and sunk any other man, but never clouded or eclipsed him, from appearing in the best places, and the best company, and with the best estimation and satisfaction.[7]*

Probably the most famous single comment about Digby by a contemporary was Henry Stubbe's complaint in *The Plus Ultra Reduced to a New Plus* (1670) that Digby was "the Pliny of our Age for lying" (p. 161). In Joseph Glanvill's rebuttal, however, Stubbe himself was guilty of lying, since he used Pliny as an authority against Aristotle; on the other hand, he would use any authority against—not just Digby personally— but against the Virtuosi generally (A *Praefatory Answer to Mr. Henry Stubbe.* . . . [1671], p. 162).

Finally, the epitaph on Digby's tomb, written by Richard

6. *Diary and Correspondence*, ed. William Bray, III, 309.
7. *The Life*, I, 31–32.

Ferrar or Farrar in 1665, represents one of the more idealized extensions of Digby's reputation:

> Under this Tomb the Matchless Digby lies;
> Digby the Great, the Valiant, and the Wise:
> This Ages Wonder for His Noble Parts;
> Skilled in Six Tongues, and Learn'd in All the Arts,
> Born on the Day He Dy'd, the 'Eleventh of June,
> And that Day Bravely Fought at Scanderoun,
> 'Tis Rare, that one and the same Day should be
> His Day of Birth, of Death, and Victory.[8]

That this extravagant person should have been stimulated by *Religio Medici*, which discussed two of the bodies of knowledge—religion and science—that were uppermost in Digby's mind at all times, is not surprising. Sackville was undoubtedly recognizing Digby's interests when he referred to *Religio* as "this favourite of yours." Digby's rapid reading of Browne's work impelled his equally rapid response—composition of his *Observations Upon Religio Medici*. Although Browne's summary of his book's unauthorized publication (the preface to the authorized edition of 1643) contains no direct allusion to Digby's rebuttal, Browne's knowledge of it may have prompted his decision to acknowledge the pirated work as his own and to revise it for formal publication. Browne and Digby had exchanged letters in March 1643 on the matter of authorized publication. Browne courteously explained the private nature of *Religio* in language somewhat like that of the preface "To the Reader." He requested that Digby withhold circulation of his criticisms until the latter had read "the true and intended original (whereof in the mean time your worthy self may command a view)" (Wilkin, III, xxviii). Browne suggested that his revised edition would show "how far the text hath been mistaken" and that "exercitations thereon, will in a great part impugn the printer or transcriber, rather than the author."

In Digby's mocking reply he professed both his inability to comply with Browne's request and his unawareness that his *Observations* was being prepared for print. Efforts to com-

8. Quoted in Huntley, *Sir Thomas Browne*, 146. Aubrey printed a slightly different version with the added introductory epithets: "that Renowned Knight, great Linguist, and Magazen of Arts" in his *Miscellanies*, 6.

municate with the printer Andrew Crooke (the publisher of both the pirated and the authorized editions of *Religio*), who had delivered "something under my name" had failed. He then apologized elaborately for the unworthiness of his "slender notions" as opposed to "so smart a piece as yours." Fully conscious of his own renown, Digby indulged in extravagant expressions of modesty. He practically disowned his work as he concluded his letter with mock reticence: "My superficial besprinkling will serve only for a private letter, or a familiar discourse with lady-auditors" (Wilkin, II, xxix). Digby also mentioned the speed with which he wrote his commentary—the busy twenty-four hours that Dr. Samuel Johnson allowed was the work's main distinction and Digby's chief claim to fame.[9] Although Digby's fuller *Observations* contains relatively little comment on Browne's style, his letter to Browne includes an accurate judgment that *Religio* is "so strongly penned, as requireth much time, and sharp attention, but to comprehend it."

The excesses in language in both letters underscore the strained mixture of courtesy, modesty, bravado, and anger that seeks expression. Dr. Johnson commented acutely on these letters: "The reciprocal civility of authors is one of the most risible scenes in the farce of life" (Wilkin, I, xxii), and contemporary readers evaluated them perceptively. A note signed A. B. appeared when the letters were published. This notice was the earliest retort to Digby, for its author acknowledged —probably without Browne's approval—that readers of both *Religio* and the *Observations* would perceive the "hasty birth" of the latter, which contains to a great extent Digby's "prepared conceptions" and "digressions . . . not at all emergent from this discourse" (Wilkin, II, xxx). This note was the first of many answers that charged Digby with misunderstanding and misrepresenting the meaning of *Religio*.

A correspondent of Browne's, Henry Bates, wrote on August 28, 1647:

But it troubles mee like the fall of Phaeton, that Monsieur le Chevalier, who passes both for a wit and a judgement, should

9. Wilkin, I, xxii. Petersson, 168–69, believes that Digby misrepresented the time devoted to the composition of his book in order to make it appear to be an unimportant endeavor.

*attempt to reyne the horses of the sunne, and Schioppir on Religio Medici; I wish hee had thought on the motto of that noble family [the Earl of Dorset's], whence hee took that employment, aut numquam tentes aut perfice, or that hee had animadverted better, or had been aliud agendo, then soe nihil agendo on that piece, sure then he would have crost himselfe, blest him to have sitt up soe late to soe little purpose, and lose his sleepe, unless hee intended to make an opiate for his readers. (Wilkin, I, 354)*

Such disparagement is justified, since much of Digby's criticism of Browne is either facetious or unfair. Coleridge's evaluation of Digby's inability to recognize the true nature of *Religio* is still very much to the point: "Sir K. Digby's observations are those of a pedant in his own system & opinion. He ought to have considered the *Religio Medici* in a dramatic & not in a metaphysical View—as a sweet Exhibition of character & passion, & not as an Expression or Investigation of positive Truth" (p. 438).

Digby's work shows little sympathy with Browne's message or his style, and most of his favorable comment does not ring true; it sounds snide or superior in tone, especially when contrasted with the self-effacement of Browne. Many of Digby's most telling points are truncated, leading not to evidence or conclusions, but to advertisements for his coming attraction, the *Two Treatises*. In fact, the *Observations* can be read only as a series of incomplete and unformed jottings, pivoting around a few related points—the nature of the soul's virtue and immortality, and the relationship between the spiritual and the physical—which seemed of first importance to Digby at the time. His thinking on even these points, which lay within his sympathies, is sometimes belligerent, as befits a man imprisoned, angered, and incoherent—a man expressing himself in haste and passion.

The *Observations* reach no conclusion because they cannot. Digby made no effort to present a cogent summation—but then, perhaps his thoughts were in too much flux to be shaped to coherence. He conveyed, it is true, his vision of an all-powerful God who is tied securely to every individual soul by a chain of causes that is visible to the insight of the rational man. But only by "right reason" can men grasp the significance of the chain of relationships. Even in his most exalted passages, Digby never neglected to emphasize judicious reason.

Nor did he forget the mechanical progression of causal relations that he conceived to be the nature of man's existence. Nor did he in these contemplations of the immortal soul forgo stating his moral emphasis on the inferiority of the body and of earthly desires.

It is a curious paradox that Browne's intuitive and Platonic insights—those moments when he felt that he transcended inferior reality and perceived true reality—and his social and personal insights—those moments when he expatiated on the charities and virtues that can be expressed between men— were most disturbing to Digby. Browne's moments of transcendental insight caused Digby to complain of "aeryness"; Browne's moments of worldly advice struck him as "vulgar motions." Digby was a man temperamentally determined not to be satisfied. To him, Browne's metaphysical speculations were either too ephemeral or too earth-laden; his earthly insights were too unaspiring. So Sir Kenelm Digby was unimpressed; yet, his *Observations* cannot be dismissed as the hasty reaction of a frustrated and arrogant mind; it is valuable because it shows us the crosscurrents of two alert and investigative minds—his and Browne's.

## Bodies and Souls Redefined

Digby began his *Observations* with pleasant commendations both to his prompter, the Earl of Dorset: "The little needle of my Soule is throughly touched at the great loadstone of yours," and to *Religio*: "This good natur'd creature I could easily perswade to bee my Bedfellow, and to wake with mee as long as I had any edge to entertaine my selfe with the delights I sucked from so noble a conversation." He decided that such "perfunctory" responses were trivial, so he promised "to blot a sheete or two . . . with my reflections upon sundry passages through the whole context of it" (pp. 1–2).[10]

Before announcing his first disagreement with Browne, Digby granted that the author had "ingenuity and a well natur'd evennesse of *Judgement*," particularly when he attacked what

10. *Browne's Religio Medici and Digby's Observations.* All references to the *Observations* are to this facsimile edition and are given internally.

to Digby was bigotry and "blind zeale" (I, 6). Shortly, however, Digby expressed his doubt that Browne could fulfill his
commitment to "follow the great wheele of the Church,"
since, according to Digby, "the faith, doctrine and constitu-
tions of that *Church* which one looketh upon as their North
starre" is not the Church of England or the "other reformed
Churches" (p. 3).

Digby's most prominently stated doubts concerned what
Browne "hath sprinkled (most wittily)" about the immortality of the soul. Citing Roger Bacon's dislike for those
who are unable to think on metaphysical planes, but who
nevertheless endlessly attempt to do so, Digby allowed that
Browne's "sharpe wit" might have served well in such studies,
but his own "little *Philosophy*" was more effective for his understanding of such subjects. Digby professed that lack of
space did not permit him to "make good this assertion" except
for this note: "That I take the immortality of the *Soule* . . . to
bee of that nature, that to them onely that are not versed in
the wayes of proving it by reason, it is an article of faith; to
others, it is an evident conclusion of demonstrative Science"
(pp. 4–5). Thus Digby opposed Browne's speculation that the
soul is mortal (I, 7). For Digby, both faith and demonstration
affirm the soul's immortality. That he returned repeatedly to
the subject of the soul is not surprising, for his allusion at this
point to the composing of "neere two hundred sheets of paper"
on the "whole science of *Bodyes*" showed that he was working
on his *Two Treatises concerning the Body and Soul of Man*,
which was published in 1644.

While it is not my intention to examine the *Two Treatises*
in this study, I will discuss those portions of the work which
are germane to his views on *Religio Medici*. A brief word about
Digby's methods and his attitudes toward his material in the
later work will help to explain why he believed the author of
*Religio* was inadequate to his subject. In his preface to the
*Two Treatises* he complained against that current doctrine in
the "Christian Schooles where bodies and their operations, are
explicated after the manner of spirituall thinges" that, according to the doctrine, have Qualities or Powers about which
man knows very little, but through which bodies operate and
function. These thinkers seek to answer questions of sense, or

motion, or even magnetic attraction by ignoring physical causes or effects and by arriving instead at positions based on "miraculous, or not understandable thinges" or "hidden qualities, that mans witt cannot reach unto."

Digby's purpose was to show "from what principles, all kindes of corporeall operations do proceed; and what kind of operations all these must be." Finally turning to the question of the soul, he promised to show that its operations "cannot proceed from those principles"; and thus "cannot have a body for its source." He ended his preface by warning his readers that they must be diligent, orderly, and "painful" if they expected to share his ideas and, more importantly, if they should attack his views. He suggested that, better than their attacking the book, let them be motivated to read even a "more noble and more profittable subject" or to form "a fairer and more complete body of Philosophy, of their owne."

So Digby's charge that Browne's training and viewpoint as a physician rendered his mind inadequate to contemplate and resolve metaphysical questions is both personally and traditionally significant. He alluded to Roger Bacon for authoritative support, a reference that probably stems from Digby's knowledge of *Opus Majus*.[11] A somewhat parallel passage may indeed be found in Part I of Bacon's work, in which he wrote that one safeguard against the conceit of wishing to appear wise (the fourth "obstacle in grasping truth") is the recognition that "universal causes should be considered first. . . . For in spiritual disease the process is the same as bodily disease; physicians learn the special and particular causes of a disease through symptoms; but the latter as well the former a knowledge of universal causes precedes, which the physician has to acquire from the processes of nature. . . . For if we are ignorant of the universals we are ignorant of what follows the universals."[12] Such a reminder of the general concepts that precede all knowledge is implied in Digby's words that the physician's "fancy is always fraught with the material drugs," and his hands and eyes with the "cutting up, & . . . inspection of

11. MS Digby 235 in the Bodleian. Wilkin, II, 121, edits the passage from Bacon as a direct quotation, but the 1909 edition of the *Observations* does not.

12. *The Opus Majus of Roger Bacon*, trans. Robert Belle Burke, I, 20–21.

anatomised bodies," so that he is least able to "flye his thoughts
at so towering a *Game,* as a pure intellect, a Separated and
unbodyed Soule" (p. 4). Digby was not championing the
superiority of deduction; he was recommending that, instead
of a concentration on particular details, an understanding of
"first principles" must be uppermost in any metaphysical question. Unfortunately Digby did not explain specifically what he
meant by the first principles of the soul when he wrote that a
knowledge of them by Browne would have prevented his first
heresy, that of believing the soul dead until resurrected with
the body.

Petersson has summarized Digby's proofs for immortality in
Chapters V through VIII in *Of Man's Soul* in this manner:

To mention the more important of the thirty he presents: the soul
contains nothing corporeal, it is self-moving, it has the faculty to
compare things, it can apprehend negatives, admit contradictions,
unify particulars, comprehend collective and universal ideas, and
can perceive the infinite and eternal truth. In exactly the same way
that the soul becomes entangled with the mind in the act of apprehending bodies, so these proofs very often refer to functions
ordinarily associated with mind, not soul. Any line of demarcation
between soul and mind Digby does not attempt. But what he does
conclude about the nature of the soul is in accord with Descartes'
conception. For both men, the soul is a function of consciousness.
As Descartes explains himself through the formula cogito ergo
sum in which, as noted cogito conveys the idea of consciousness
rather than thought, Digby presents his proofs for immortality as
different aspects of consciousness. In other words, the activity of
apprehending or thinking is the soul, and Digby is content to leave
mind and soul unseparated. (Pp. 202–3)

The convolutions of Digby's Cartesianism carry this quarrel
beyond the pages of *Religio,* but it is valuable to recall at this
point some of the complex ramifications of the body–soul
question in the seventeenth century, particularly with respect
to the *Two Treatises.* When Browne's discussion of traduction (the soul transmitted by generation to the offspring) in
I, 36, prompted Digby to judge the problem "too tedious and
too knotty a peece for a *Letter,*" he summarily declared that
the soul "is not *Ex Traduce,* and yet hath a strange kind of
neere dependance of the body; which is, as it were, Gods
instrument to create it by" (pp. 15–16). Elizabethan ortho-

doxy emphasized the immortality of the soul as a sign of the miraculous nature of the soul, but it also fell back on what Browne called "the flat affirmative of *Plato*." Digby also affirmed the immortality of the soul and its transcendence of the body, but he opposed the traditional Platonic concept when he wrote, in *Of Man's Soul* (XI, 1): "The Platonic Philosophers (who are persuaded that a humane Soul doth not profit in this life, nor that she acquired any knowledge here; as being of herself compleatly perfect; and that all our discourses are but her remembrings of what she had forgotten) will find themselves ill bested, to render a Philosophical and sufficient cause of her being locked into a Body: for, to put forgetfulness in a pure Spirit; so palpable an effect of corporeity, and so great a corruption, in respect of a creature whose nature is, to know of it self is an unsufferable error." [13] Digby contended that, just as the body must exercise, so too the soul must pursue knowledge as a preparation for the next life. Those who seek "after some knowledge of nature" and "the first noble objects" will be stronger and more perfect in the next life than those who "looke no higher then to have an insight into humane action, or to gaine skill in some art, whereby they may acquire meanes to live. These later curiosities, are but of particulars; . . . [which] falleth within the reach of every vulgar capacity." He continued with the statement that one's immortal state will grow directly out of the activity and decisions one carried out in this existence. Just as passion may motivate "right reason" to be the means to her ends, so too "spiritual" judgment directs reason to those actions it deems necessary.

He decided that "we find three rootes of infinity in every action of a separated soule, in respect of one in the body: first, the freedome of her essence or substance in itselfe: next, that quality of hers, by which she comprehendeth lastly, the concurrence of infinite knowledges to every action of hers." He concluded: "What joy, what content, what exultation of mind, in any living man, can be conceived so great, as to be

13. *Two Treatises: in the one of which, The Nature of Bodies; in the other, The Nature of Mans Soul, Is Looked Into: In Way of Discovery of the Immortality of Reasonable Soules.* All subsequent references are by chapter and section and are given internally. Quoted by permission of The Huntington Library, San Marino, California.

compared with the happinesse of one of these soules? And
what griefe, what discontent, what misery, can be like the
others?" (XI, 6). The emotionalism that marks this passage is
characteristic of Digby's interpretation of the soul's immortality throughout his *Observations* and the *Two Treatises*.
While denying Browne the right to "flye his thoughts at so
towering a *Game*," Digby indulged repeatedly in just such
ecstatic resolutions. It is no wonder that the "dependance" of
the superior processes of the soul struck him as "strange." His
concern for investigating this problem led elsewhere to a nearly
Cartesian–Hobbesian explanation that the mechanical responses of the nervous system lie at the base of all mental
processes.

The primary importance of Digby's knowledge of Descartes
is its early occurrence. A letter from Digby to Thomas Hobbes
is one of the earliest known references to the appearance of
Descartes's *Discours de la methode* in England:

October 4, 1637
SIR:
   *I come now with this to make good what I promised you in my
last: which is to putt Monsieur des Cartes (whom Mydorge so
much admireth) his book into your hands. I doubt not but you
will say this a production of a most vigorous and strong braine;
and that if he were as accurate in his metaphysical part as he is in
his experience, he had carryed the palme from all men living:
which nevertheless he peradventure hath done. I shall be very glad
to heare your opinion of him: and so in hast I take my leave and
rest,*
                                        *Your true friend and servant,*
                                        *Kenelm Digby*[14]

So, it is evident that, not only was Digby a regular correspondent with Hobbes, but he was also scientifically and phi-
losophically aware of developments on the Continent and, in
this important instance, aware earlier than many of his fellow
intellectuals. Perhaps a more characteristic letter from Digby
to Hobbes is the one dated September 11, 1637, in which he
asked about premonition and foreknowledge. The instance

   14. Reprinted in Marjorie Nicolson, "The Early Stages of
Cartesianism in England," *Studies in Philology*, 26 (1929), 358,
and in Sterling P. Lamprecht, "The Role of Descartes in Seventeenth-Century England," *Studies in the History of Ideas*, 3
(1935), 189–90, 192, 220, 217.

was Digby's fall from his horse and injury some six weeks earlier. Digby wrote Hobbes that he had received a letter and a scarf from a lady in Paris, the letter dated "about the time of my fall," indicating "that she had a strong apprehension some such misadventure had hapened to me." His letter continues thus:

> What may be the reason of this foreknowledg, or present knowledg at distance? Is it that the soule being a spirit hath within itself the knowledg of all things, and so delivereth over to the fantastie a misty notion of wt. occureth to some particular that it (the fansy) is continually beating upon? Or hath the soule a power to diduce all knowledg concerning any particular object, out of the spirits that are administered to it by the senses, when she speculateth intensely upon them? Which latter I should conceive to be the way that separated soules know all that is in this world by joyning and diving into the spirits they carry from hence.[15]

Since, according to Digby, Hobbes knew more than any living man, he was asking for instruction.

The dualism between thoughts and things in Cartesianism impressed Digby, especially when he placed his emphasis on the nonmaterial. Digby was disappointed by the "metaphysicall part" of Descartes, which did not discuss immortality fully enough to satisfy him. When they talked, later in 1644, at Descartes's home in Holland, Digby—who is supposed to have been recognized on sight—implored Descartes to apply his energies to proving the immortality of the soul. Descartes replied that, while he could not promise proof of immortality, he did think it was possible to extend man's life to the reported longevity of the Patriarchs.[16]

Digby did, however, praise Descartes in *Of Man's Soul* for stating that "Reason assureth us, that when all body is abstracted in us, there still remaineth a *Substance*, a *Thinker*, an *Ego*, or *I*, that in itselfe is no whitt diminished, by being . . . stripped out of the case it was enclosed in" (IX, 3). Digby argued that, since the soul cannot be an "accident" of the body, it must be a substance in its own right. But it is an immortal substance because it is not subject to change or "locall motion" or "the primary opposition of *Rarity* and *Density*"

15. E. W. Bligh, *Sir Kenelm Digby and His Venetia*, 236.
16. [Thomas Longueville], *The Life of Sir Kenelm Digby by One of his Descendants*, 263–64.

or to "harme from contrariety." Since *"Truth* is the naturall perfection of man's soule" and the evidence for truth infinite, the soul must attain perfect truth, not in this life, but in the next, Digby concluded. It was relatively easy for Digby to identify Descartes's definition of substance with his own. Since Digby argued from what he called the "science of Morality," he had little difficulty overriding the tenuousness of his arguments.

Digby could accept out of Descartes's dualism the argument that "the bodies without us, in certaine circumstances, do give a blow upon our exterior organes; from whence, by the continuity of the partes, that blow or motion is continued, till it come to our braine and seate of knowledge upon which it giveth a stroke answerable to that, which the outward sense first received: and there this knocke causing a particular effect, according to the particular nature of the motion" (*Of Bodies,* XXXII, i). After paying Descartes high praise, Digby argued that he would emphasize even more than Descartes that motion is significant and that he would not agree that only physical response is involved. He would

goe the more common way; and make the spirits to be the porters of all newes to the braine: only adding there-unto that these newes . . . are materiall participations of the bodies, that worke upon the outward organes of the senses; and passing through them, do mingle themselves with the spirits, and so do goe . . . to the braine; unto which, from all partes of the body, they have immediate resorte, and a perpetuall communication with it.

So that, to exercise sense (which the Latines do call, sentire, but in English we have no one word common to our severall particular notions of divers perceptions by sense) is, Our braine to receive an impression from the externe object by the operation or mediation of an organicall part made for that purpose, and some one of those which we terme an externe sense; from which impression, usually floweth some motion proper to the living creature. And thus you see that the outward senses, are not truly senses, as if the power of sensation were in them: but in an other meaning, to witt, so farre as they are instruments of qualifying or conveying the object to the braine. (XXXII, 2)

John Fulton, who has called this "almost as definite a statement of the reflex theory of reaction to sensory stimuli as anything that is to be found in Descartes's *Methode*," regards Digby "as one of the early supporters of the modern conception of the nervous system."¹⁷ Digby's explanation of sensation depends finally on "a perpetuall fluxe of little partes or atomes out of all sensible bodies . . . [which] in all probability . . . can not choose but gett in at the dores of our bodies, and mingle themselves with the [vital] spirits that are in our nerves." This, then, in turn, "must make some motion in the braine" (XXXII, 4). Sir Geoffrey Keynes has noted Digby's example in XXXII, 8, of a palsied hand as an early example of interest in neurology, in this instance a condition now known as *syringomyelia*, which results from degeneration of certain tracts in the spinal cord. Digby argued against Descartes's view that movement and sensation are conducted by the "sinews" or nerves.¹⁸

Thus, while Digby rejected traduction because of the spirituality of the soul, he was constantly drawn back to the interactions of bodies—those physical actions which may indicate something nonphysical.

Even years before his responses to Browne and Hobbes were written, Digby was apparently a person worth informing about matters pertaining to such questions as traduction. Thus, James Howell, in a letter to Digby after March 2, 1624, wrote about the Spanish match:

And it may be said, that the civil actions of men, 'specially great affairs of Monarchs (as this was) have much analogy, in degrees of progression, with the natural production of man. To make man, there are many acts must precede; first a meeting and copulation of the Sexes, then Conception, which requires a well-disposed Womb to retain the prolifical Seed, by the constriction and occlusion of the orifice of the Matrix; which Seed being first, and afterwards Cream, is by a gentle ebullition coagulated, and turn'd to a crudded lump, which the Womb by virtue of its natural heat prepares to be capable to receive form, and to be organiz'd: whereupon Nature falls a-working to delineate all the Members, beginning with those that are most noble; as the Heart, the Brain, the Liver, whereof Galen would have the Liver, which is the shop and source of the blood, and Aristotle the Heart, to be the first fram'd, in regard 'tis primum vivens & ultimum moriens. Nature continues in this labour, until a perfect shape be introduced; and this is call'd Formation, which is the third act, and is a production of an organical Body out of the spermatick Substance, caus'd by the plas-

17. *Sir Kenelm Digby*, 61–62.
18. *The Life of William Harvey*, 391–92.

*tick virtue of the vital Spirits: and sometimes this act is finish'd
thirty days after the conception, sometimes fifty, but most commonly in forty-two or forty-five, and is sooner done in the Male.
This being done, the Embryo is animated with three Souls; the
first with that of Plants called the vegetable Soul, then with a
sensitive, which all brute Animals have, and lastly the rational
Soul is infus'd; and these three in Man are like Trigonus in
Tetragono; the two first are generated ex Traduce, from the seed
of the Parents, but the last is by immediate infusion from God:
and 'tis controverted 'twixt Philosophers and Divines when this
infusion is made.*

   *This is the fourth act that goeth to make a Man, and is called
Animation: and as the Naturalists allow Animation double the
time that Formation had from the Conception, so they allow to
the ripening of the Embryo in the Womb, and to the birth thereof,
treble the time Animation had; which happeneth sometimes ten
months. (I, 192–93)*

Howell then applied his analogy to the Spanish match. Howell's is the usual Aristotelian view of the three souls.

   Obviously, Digby could not accept any explanation of the
soul's presence within the body that was based on traduction
or Platonic assumption. He desired strongly to keep the soul
separate from the body's influence in order to sustain a vision
of the free soul's epistemological pursuit of heaven and infinity. He solved for himself the dilemma of Cartesian dualism
by broadening the stimulus–response mechanism to include
those modes of spiritual truth and experience which fascinated
him so.

   Later in his discussion (p. 19) Digby speculated that, better
than the philosopher's stone (I, 39), Browne presented "a
most pregnant" exemplification of the immortality of the
soul (I, 48) in the immortality of a plant that is regenerated
from its own ashes. Although he accepted the experiment as
revealing, Digby believed that its life would ultimately fail
because the original properties of the plant are lost in the
flames: "In the ashes there remaineth onely the fixed Salt, I
am very confident that all the colour, and much of the odor
and Tast of it, is flowne away with the Volatile salt." Thus,
while Digby was not as mystically inclined as Browne, he
agreed that the Idea of the plant endures so that the Form does
not die.

   Digby's exploration of the generation of plants and animals

in Chapters XXIII through XXV in *Of Bodies* developed in detail his thesis that only the careful study of "the ordinary process which we see in bodies and in bodily thinges (that is by the vertues of rarity and density, working by locall motion)" will produce answers. He agreed that much of what he intended to explain is "performed" by "so secret and abstruse" methods that "lesse heedefullness and judgment" have caused mankind to depend on mysterious explanations. Such a result is to be avoided: "They . . . are too apt to impute them to mysterious causes above the reach of humane nature to comprehend, and to caluminate them of being wrought by occult and specifike qualities; whereof no more reason could be given, then if the effects were infused by Angelicall handes without assistance of inferiour bodies: which useth to be the last refuge of ignorant men, who not knowing what to say, and yet presuming to say something, do fall often upon such expressions, as neyther themselves nor their hearers understand; and that if they be well scanned, do imply contradiction" (XXIII, 1).

Living creatures are passive or active or compounded, he continued. Many plants are similar to those bodies which carry out one constant and continuous action, although that action can be changed, for example the waterwheel at Toledo (XXIII, 3–4). But sensible living creatures, which he terms *"Automatum or le mouens,"* have parts that are independent, separate, but subordinated for the task called for, as in the case of the minting machine at Segovia (XXIII, 5–6). He noted that under plants he was not including "zoophytes or plantanimals" that have "a distinct and articulate action" in their parts. He explained the formation of a plant through a union of the vital heat in the body with air and moisture:

*This encrease of bulke and swelling of the little masse, will of its owne nature be towardes all sides, by reason of the fire and heate that occasioneth it (whose motion is on every side, from the center to the circumference:) but it will be most efficacious upwardes, towardes the ayre, because the resistance is least that way; both by reason of the little thicknesse of the earth over it; as also by reason that the upper part of the earth lyeth very loose and is exceeding porous, through the continuall operation of the sunne and falling of raine upon it. It can not choose therefore but mount to the ayre; and the same cause that maketh it do so, presseth att the same time the lower partes of the masse, downwardes.*

He then described the separation of the plant into hard, dry parts and soft, moist parts that continue to grow, branch, and bud so that, out of "these passages, strainings, and concoctions," comes "a tincture extracted out of the whole plant; and it att the last dryed up into a kind of magistery. This we call the seede" (XXIII, 7).

With respect to the generation of animals Digby posited that "our maine question shall be; whether they be framed entirely att once; or successively, one part after an other? And if this later way; which part first?" (XXIV, 1). He rejected the concept of preformation on the grounds "that it is impossible, every little part of the whole body should remitt something impregnated and imbued with the nature of it" (XXIV, 2). Finally, he introduced the example of bean growth as a possible solution to the question:

Now if all this orderly succession of mutations be necessarily made in a beane, by force of sundry circumstances and externall accidents; why may it not be conceived that the like is also done in sensible creatures; but in a more perfect manner, they being perfecter substances? Surely the progresse we have sett downe is much more reasonable, then to conceive that in the meale of the beane, are contained in little, severall similar substances; as, of a roote, of a leafe, a stalke, a flower, a codde, fruite, and the rest; and that every one of these, being from the first still the same that they shall be afterwardes, do but sucke in, more moysture from the earth, to swell and enlarge themselves in quantity. Or, that in the seede of the male, there is already in act, the substance of flesh, of bone, of sinewes, of veins, and the rest of those severall similar partes which are found in the body of an animal; and that they are but extended to their due magnitude, by the humidity drowne from the mother, without receiving any substantial mutation from what they were originally in the seede.  . . . . . . . . .

Lett us then confidently conclude, that all generation is made of a fitting, but remote, homogeneall compounded substance: upon which, outward Agents working in the due course of nature, do change it into an other substance, quite different from the first, and do make it lesse homogeneall then the first was. And other circumstances and agents, do change this second into a thirde; that thirde, into a fourth; and so onwardes, by successive mutations. (XXIV, 5)

Rejecting the concept "that the embryon is actually formed in the seede," he held that the seed is made of a "homogeneall substance" in or of the blood that has been "transmuted into the nature" of all the parts of the body. By this he did not mean "any such unconceivable quality, as moderne Philosophers too frequently talke of" (XXIV, 8–9). There is no "complete living creature" in the seed (XXIV, 10). Thus, as Petersson has pointed out, Digby's "own experiments showed him the validity of . . . epigenesis, and led him to conclude what is today regarded as substantially true: that the egg is a physico–chemical system containing only a small part of what at birth is the completed animal" (p. 195).

In Chapter XXV Digby turned directly to the religious assumptions behind the creative process:

Aristotle . . . pronunced that this effect could not possibly be wrought by the vertue of the first qualities; but that it sprung from a more divine origine. And most . . . since him, do seeme to agree that no cause can be rendered of it; but that it is to be referred meerely to the specificiall nature of the thing. Neyther do we intend to derogate from eyther of these causes; since that both divine providence is eminently shewne in contriving all circumstances necessary for this worke; and likewise the first temperament that is in the seede, must needes be the principall immediate cause of this admirable effect.

. . . . . . . . . . . . . . . . . . . . . . . . .

This latter then being supposed; our labour and endeavour will be, to unfold (as farre as so weake and dimme eyes can reach) the excellency and exactnesse of Gods providence, which can not be enough adored, when it is reflected upon, and marked in the apt laying of adequate causes to produce such a figure out of such a mixture first layed. From them so artificially ranged, we shall see this miracle of nature to proceed; and not from an immediate working of God or nature without convenient and ordinary instruments to mediate and effect this configuration, through the force and vertue of their owne particular natures. Such a necessity to interest the chiefe workeman att every turne, in particular effects, would argue him of want of skill and providence, in the first laying of the foundations of his designed machine: he were an improvident clockemaker, that should have cast his worke so, as when it were wound up and going, it would require the masters hand att every houre to make the hammer strike upon the bell. Lett us not then too familiarly, and irreverently ingage the Almighty Architecht his immediate handy worke in every particular effect of nature. (XXV, 1)

And thus you see, how the fundamentall figures (upon which all the rest are grounded) are contrived by nature; not by the worke of any particular Agent that immediately imprinteth a determinate figure into a particular body, as though it wrought it there att once, according to a foreconceived designe or intelligent ayme of producing such a figure in such a body: but by the concurrence of severall accidental causes, that do all of them joyne in bringing the body they file and worke upon, into such a shape. (XXV, 2)

Digby in XXV, 6–7, stated that he "can not choose but breake out into an extasye of admiration and hymnes of prayse (as great Galen did upon the like occasion)" when he studied the growth of the embryo into a man. The careful planning of each stage of development staggered his mind. He ended his discussion of generation, however, with a characteristic ambivalence:

I persuade my selfe it appeareth evident enough, that to effect this worke of generation, there needeth not be supposed a forming vertue or Vis formatrix of an unknown power and operation, as those that consider thinges soddainely and but in grosse, do use to putt. Yet, in discourse, for conveniency and shortenesse of expression we shall not quite banish that terme from all commerce with us; so that what we meane by it, be rightly understood; which is, the complexe, assemblement, or chayne of all the causes, that concurre to produce this effect; as they are sett on foote, to this end by the great Architect and Moderator of them, God almighty, whose instrument nature is: that is, the same thing, or rather the same thinges so ordered as we have declared, but expressed and comprised under an other name.

Chapter XXXVII, 4, presents Digby's argument that the actions of irrational animals are material and divinely caused through "the immensity of that provident Architect, out of whose handes these masterpieces issue, and unto whome it is as easy to make a chaine of causes of a thousand or of a million of linkes, as to make one linke alone." Robert Gordon Grenell interprets the originality of the *Two Treatises* to lie in Digby's refusal, despite the probability of ready criticism to agree with " 'those who hold that everything containeth formally all things.' " Digby's view is "most certainly, in its essentials, in agreement with the present day views of the physico–chemical development of the egg, and with the ideas of protagonists of epigenesis." Grenell, as does Petersson, concludes that Digby in this context may be regarded "as one of the great thinkers of his time, if not as one of the fathers of embryology."[19]

Joseph Needham also compliments Digby's "audacity" and "naturalistic tone" and points out the irony that he was more daring than William Harvey, a far more renowned scientist.[20] In his *Two Treatises* Digby objected to the "old terminology of 'qualities' in physics and 'faculties' in biology. To say, as contemporary reasoning did, that bodies were red or blue because they possessed a quality of redness or blueness which caused them to appear red or blue to us . . . appeared mere nonsense and word-spinning to Digby."[21] Needham states that "Digby has not received his due in the past; he stands to embryology as an exact science, much in the same relationship as Bacon to science as a whole" (p. 123).

Digby was also a supporter of the theory of pangenesis, which is the process by which "representative particles are contributed from all parts of the body to the generative secretions, which secretions, upon mingling, give rise to similar parts in the offspring. This is heredity explained, the resemblance of the offspring to its parents."[22] The processes of preformation and pangenesis as applied by Browne and Digby to the broad question of generation, both organic and inorganic, recall Browne's regenerated plant. While the attributes of the flaming plant disappear into the smoke, the ashes retain the "fixed Salt" for Digby and the "Idea" for Browne.

The regeneration would probably follow the steps outlined by Digby in an address to the Royal Society in 1660 on the vegetation of plants. Digby theorized: "Thus both the innate and the extern heat, do concur to enlarge this plant, by filling both the root and the stalk of it with continual new moisture: whereof the one being exposed to the Sun and Winde, must needs grow rough and hard on the out-side; to defend from outward injuries of weather, the inner-part that remaineth tender and juicy, and would else be seen nipped in its ascend-

19. "Sir Kenelm Digby, Embryologist," *Bull. Hist. Med.*, 10 (1941), 50–52.

20. *Time: The Refreshing River*, 151.

21. Joseph Needham, A *History of Embryology*, 121–22.

22. Egon Stephen Merton, *Science and Imagination in Sir Thomas Browne*, 47.

ing; and the other thrusteth down continually hard parts deeper into the Earth, whereby it remaineth firm and able to resist the agitations of the wind, without being easily eradicated." He was speaking of a newly planted seed generating, in the sun, its surface plant and subsoil roots. Later, he continued:

> There is no doubt but that a main part of the Essentiall substance of a Plant is contained in his fixed Salt. This will admit no change into another Nature; but will alwayes be full of the qualities and vertues of the Plant it is derived from. . . . If all the Essentiall parts could be preserved, in the severing and purifying of them, I see no reason but at the reunion of them, the entire Plant might appeare in its complete perfection, so one could finde a fit medium to dilate it in. Were not this then a true Palingenesis of the originall Plant? I doubt it would not be so. For speaking rigorously, I cannot allow Plants to have Life. They are not Se Moventia. They have not a principle of motion within them. It is the operation of outward Agents upon them, that setteth on feet all the dance we have above so heedfully observed, and which so near imitateth the motions of life. And if it be not a living thing, then it is all of it in perpetuall Fluxe and Change, without having any part of it enjoy a fixed and permanent Being, for the least moments space; and consequently, there can be no Resurrection of it after once it is destroyed, since it never was at any time a determinate It, or Thing; . . . So, I conceive that a new aereall body and thing is made out of the Plant that furnished matter for this new substance, and whose substantiall form is totally destroyed, and a new one produced into the World; which is accompanyed with many accidents like unto many of those that belonged to the precedent substance.[23]

So while Digby denied palingenesis in fact, he still allowed his mind to pursue the Neoplatonic principle of the eternal form that lives after its matter is destroyed. In all of his views of plants he sought their similarities with all living things and within those similarities their enduring souls. The body is merely an indistinguishable substance from within the general flux.[24] He could not solve the dilemma of the intermixing of

---

23. A *Discourse concerning the Vegetation of Plants*, 22, 78. Quoted by permission of The Huntington Library, San Marino, California. See G. E. Fussell, "Crop Nutrition in the Late Stuart Age (1660–1714)," *Annals of Science*, 14 (1958, pub. 1960), 176, for a discussion of Digby's significance.

24. Petersson, 298–301, especially his conclusions.

the material and the spiritual, but he took pride in probing the mystery with as much precision and care as he could marshal. Indicative of this carefulness is his rebuttal of Browne (p. 10): "No body ever tooke" the toad or the serpent to be ugly (I, 16) "in respect of the *Universe* . . . but onely as they have relation to us." He deliberately ignored their unity with God, which he usually emphasized.

Perhaps just such a skeptical materialism as Digby's prompted Browne to change his account of the regenerated plant from "I make good by experience" in the 1642 editions to "is made good by experience," thus removing a troublesome personal allusion. Browne's research with plants has been examined many times, but a recent article by Charles Webster on the neglect by the Royal Society, which was seeking mechanistic explanations of plant development, of his and Henry Power's studies of plant sensitivity reinforces the receptivity of the physician–botanists to the relevance of human physiology as well as invertebrate movement to plant anatomy and sensitivity. Both Browne and Power were able to incorporate the Neoplatonic concern for the spirit into their explanations.[25]

## The Chain of Causation

Before examining specifically Digby's views on salvation, it is well to discuss his notions of the nature of eternity—the place awaiting the saved souls, and the nature of providence—the avenue for eventual progression to eternity. Here Digby raised two objections (pp. 6–7) to Browne's basically orthodox definitions of eternity and predestination (I, 11). Of the first, Digby's remarks imply a misunderstanding or misreading, for he believed Browne to say that eternity is "an infinite extension of time, and a never ending revolution of continuall succession; which [Digby continued] is no more like *Eternity*, than a grosse body is like a pure *Spirit*. Nay, such an infinity of revolutions, is demonstrable to bee a contradiction and impossible. In the state of eternity there is no succession, no change, no variety. . . . All things, notions, and actions, that

25. "The Recognition of Plant Sensitivity by English Botanists in the Seventeenth Century," *Isis*, 57 (Spring, 1966), 5–23.

ever were, are, or shall bee in any creature, are actually present
to such an intellect."

Digby's reading is faulty because Browne's statement makes
a clear distinction between time and eternity at the outset.
Browne wrote: "[Eternity] confound[s] my understanding;
[while] Time we may comprehend" because it is of this earthly
existence. Rather than defining eternity, Browne wondered
at it. Eternity is without beginning or end and, like God, beyond our powers of rational comprehension. But Digby was
fully capable of explaining eternity as a timeless, placeless, and
changeless location for angels and souls. His confidence was
so great that he promised "out of the principles of Nature and
*Reason* [to] demonstrate it to belong to the lowest Soule of the
ignorantest wretch. . . . A bold undertaking," he conceded,
"but I confidently engage my selfe to it." When he should
write on these subjects he would also have "a great deale to bee
said of the nature of *Predestination* (which by the short
touches our Author giveth of it, I doubt hee quite mistakes)
and how it is an unalterable *Series* and chaine of causes, producing infalliable (and in respect of them, necessary) effects."
But, Digby declared, eternity is "too vast an *Ocean* to describe,
in the scant Map of a Letter"; besides, he feared that he had
"too much trespassed upon your Lordships patience," and he
hoped that Dorset had "not had enough to read thus far."
This retreat to complimentary omission does not help to explain Digby's views, but merely the hint of an infinity by
Browne contradicted Digby's view of eternity, while the in-
jection of souls and angels by Digby implied a concern about
separating the realms of spirit and matter.

Just as Browne's views on predestination were not rigid
enough to satisfy Digby, the latter could not accept Browne's
statement that "the Devill and Spirits have no exact Ephe-
merides" of the cryptic method of Fortune (I, 17). Digby contended that "all causes are so immediately chayned to their
effects, as if a perfect knowing nature get hold but of one
linke, it will drive the entire *Series* . . . to each utmost end"
(p. 10). He stated parenthetically that he would prove his
contention in the *Two Treatises*. Since man is ignorant of the
"necessary causes" of things, he sees "fortuitenesse" where
there is none. Digby drew on the analogy in I, 18, of *Religio—*

"*Homers* chaine," which he defined "to bee that divine *Provi-dence* and mercy. . . . And not any secret, invisible, mysticall blessing, that falleth not under the search or cognizance of a prudent indagation" (p. 11). Wilkin's note on Digby's criti-cism still seems just: He complained that Digby's reply "does not discuss the point at issue; which is, not, whether there be any 'contingency of things, in respect of themselves'—but whether devils or angels . . . foresee future events" (II, 125–126n). Richard S. Westfall has termed Digby's position as typical of the remainder of the seventeenth century:

To some extent Digby's theory approximated the Thomist posi-tion, which held that nothing happens by chance in the eyes of omniscient God. God sees everything at once in the eternal present according to St. Thomas. He knows for all time all of the chance encounters that will cross the map of history. To the Thomist, however, the great spectacle of providence is hidden forever from human eyes, which cannot see at a glance the whole of nature com-pressed into the eternal present. Digby on the other hand thought that providence operates by a mechanical necessity inherent in the original construction of the machine. Without mentioning the eternal present, he expounded providence as a succession which would be quite comprehensible to man once he understood the machine. . . . In Digby's theory God is reduced to the role of original Creator, Who made the machine and foresaw its actions but has not bothered further since it began to run.[26]

Rather than accepting the intuitive and open way of Browne, Digby reduced the question of Providence to rational verification. Digby believed that only man's reason shows him that the mercy of the First Mover descends in a "complexe of all outward circumstances" down to "every individual on earth." A hidden Providence Digby would not accept. It is interesting that the Catholic Digby willingly accepted the Protestant example given by Browne of the success of the Hollanders against the sea and by implication against Philip II.

Concerning Browne's statement that men of wisdom accept as just their lack of material fortune, since they "being en-riched with higher donatives, cast a more carelesse eye on these vulgar parts of felicity" (I, 18), Digby commented sarcasti-cally and no doubt with personal reference: "I must needs

26. *Science and Religion in Seventeenth-Century England*, 80–81.

approve our authors aequanimity, and I may justly say his
magnanimity, in being contented so cheerfully (as he saith) to
shake hands with the fading *Goods* of *Fortune*; and bee de-
prived of the joyes of her most precious blessings; so that hee
may in recompence, possesse in ample measure the true ones of
the mind" (p. 11). Digby drew a loose comparison with the
views of Epictetus, referring perhaps to such a vivid passage as
Epictetus' response to a complainer who says:
   "Oh, but my nose runs."
   "And what have you hands for, beast, but to wipe it?"
Epictetus castigated those men who do nothing more with the
faculties God has given them than an animal would do. Our
faculties are meant to sustain us, so we must use them, not "sit
groaning and lamenting, . . . blind to him who gave them, and
not acknowledging your benefactor; . . . basely turning your-
selves to complaints and accusations of God."[27]

   Digby passed over the reference by Browne in the 1642 edition (I, 17) to the "Powder–Treason" without comment. He
might legitimately have included some painful insights into
the relationship between that notorious incident and the "fortunes" of the Digby family; his father, Sir Everard, was executed for his involvement in the plot.

   Any contemporary discussion of Providence and fortune
would lead to a consideration of "judiciall Astrology" (I, 18).
Digby couched his views in such far-fetched language as to
suggest a disagreement with Browne when actually he was in
agreement, for he admired Browne's reconciliation of astrology
and divinity. Nevertheless, he doubted that this conjunction
was important. For him, the real issue was Browne's respect
for astrology, which, Digby wrote, has "no solid rules, or
ground in nature" (p. 11); astrology was "that vaine art . . .
rather folly than impiety."

   Another reason for Digby's rejection of astrology is the
speculation that it arose from the impious and misled worship
of the heavens by the heathen. The strength of these answers
by Digby is at best a change of heart, for earlier in his life,
Petersson states, Digby had carefully recorded his horoscope,
while later he attributed to astrological influences his marriage

27. *Moral Discourses*, trans. Elizabeth Carter, ed. W. H. D.
Rouse, 15–16.

to Venetia Stanley. His intellectual guide, the mathematician Thomas Allen, was considered a foremost astrologer of his time. Digby as a Roman Catholic was compelled to reject astrology as "an insolent probing into God's secrets," but generally he "avoided . . . the religious controversy" (pp. 15, 73, 36, 186).

Despite his leanings toward belief in astrology, in order to confute Browne's opinions Digby associated astrology with "a like inanity . . . Chiromancy." He moderated his denunciation by noting that Browne "and no lesse a man than *Aristotle*, seeme to attribute somewhat more to that conjecturall art of *Lynes*" (p. 12). Browne's statement (II, 2) that Aristotle "made no mention of Chiromancy" in his *Physiognomy* seems not to have affected Digby's thinking; in the most extreme interpretation, the references in Aristotle's work to the gestures of the hand as an indicator of a person's character are far removed from any application to the art of palmistry (813a10–11). Aristotle does refer, in passing, to the art in the *Historia Animalium* (493b32–494a2) and in the *Problemata* (896a37, 964a33). Digby's own interests in chiromancy are verified by the presence in the Digby manuscripts in the Bodleian of the oldest known book of palmistry in English, probably written before 1440. The editor of a recent edition of the work notes that physiognomy, not palmistry, seems to have been the subject matter of such classical writers as Aristotle and Pliny and that, while it is not improbable that Aristotle might have written such a work, "there are no good grounds for asserting that he did."[28] Even though Digby rebuked practitioners of astrology and palmistry, he raised one interesting conjecture. While considering that man's views about the "regularly-irregular motions" of the stars may have arisen from heathen worship (p. 12), he perceived a link between natural and judicial astrology.

Later in his discussion (p. 32) Digby disowned Browne's inference that if devils had foreknowledge "their labour were at an end" (I, 57). Digby argued that the nature of devils compels them to carry on their temptations: "For on the one side, it is active in the highest degree (as being pure *Acts*, that is *Spirits*,) so on the other side, they are maligne in as great an

28. *An Old Palmistry*, ed. Derek J. Price, x, xii.

excesse." Thus he surmised that devilish intention will never cease, although the devils will be "frustrate of their morall end." His absolute chain of causation remained intact because he believed that it was impossible for devils to act in any way contrary to their nature. Browne apparently changed his view from the direct one, stated in 1642, that devils "cannot divine who shall be saved" to the more open "can hardly," which is the same verb change he made in 1643 (I, 52) with respect to being "scared into Heaven."

### "Little Knotty Peeces of Particular Sciences"

There is a close relationship between the absoluteness of Digby's view of divine causation and the principle of contradiction. Browne had expressed his wonder, in the 1642 edition of *Religio*, whether God could work contradictions (I, 27). Digby's reply was short-tempered and abstruse. He noted how "scrupulously" Browne had refused to deny God the power to work contradictions. Then, twisting Browne's remarks, he concluded that Browne "seemeth to bee in averring downe rightly, that God cannot doe contradictory things." Actually, Browne wrote, "I hold that God cannot do all things but sinne"; this was changed in the 1643 edition to: "God can doe all things." Digby used Browne's earlier statement as reason to embark on a succinct, but confusing explanation. Since nonentity is one of the "termes" of contradiction, it would be "impiety not to deny [it] peremptorily" with reference to God, who is "*Selfe-Entity*, all *being* must immediately flow from him, and all not-being be totally excluded from that effluxe" (pp. 12–13). Digby's argument is Aristotelian; in *Metaphysica* (1004b28–1005a5), Aristotle reduced contraries to being and non-being and to unity and plurality. The attribute of non-being cannot be applied to God, who is the actuality of thought and life (1072b25–30) therefore an immaterial stimulus toward realization. Perhaps Browne toned down his "he could work contradictions" to "he should" in answer to Digby's sarcastic comment that "it is not amisse to sweeten the manner of the expression, and the sound of the words." As an example of God's power to work possible contradictions Browne referred to God commanding Esdras to recall time past, but Digby countered that this task although beyond the power of man, would be possible for God to perform for it would only necessitate: "Putting againe, all things, that had motion, into the same state they were in, at that moment unto which time was to be reduced backe and from thence, letting it travell on againe, by the same motions, and upon the same wheeles, it rolled upon before" (p. 13). This view of time is essentially Aristotelian (*Physica*, 220b27–29) in its emphasis on the relationship between uniform and linear motion and the continuity and divisibility of time. Whether Digby was writing of time as infinite, as did Aristotle (233a21–31), is unclear.

Thomas Keck, in his *Annotations*, offered an Aristotelian reading of his own in the light of Digby's comments. Keck declared that Digby's explanation did not resolve the question of contradiction either:

But under favour, the contradiction remains, if this were done that he mentions; for Time depends not at all upon motion, but has a being altogether independent of it, and therefore the same revolution would not bring back the same time, for that was efflux'd before; as in the time of Joshua, when the Sun stood still, we cannot but conceive, though there were no motion of the Sun, but that there was an efflux of Time, otherwise, how could the Text have it, That there was not any day, before or after, that was so long as that? for the length of it must be understood in respect of the flux of time. The reasoning of Sir Kenelme is founded upon the opinion of Aristot. who will needs have it, that Time cannot be without mutation; he gives this for a reason, because when we have slept, and cannot perceive any mutation to have been, we do therefore use to connect the time of our sleeping and of our awaking together, and make but one of it: to which it may be answered, although some mutation be necessary, that we may mark the flux of time, it doth not therefore follow that the mutation is necessary to the flux it self. (Pp. 69–70)

Digby's objection to Browne's statement of belief (I, 45–46) that the world will not "perish upon the ruines of its owne principles," since both creation and annihilation are "above nature," reverts to the complex question of the end of the world. Digby stated that Father Thomas White[29] had shown

29. See Joseph Gillow, *A Literary and Biographical History, or Bibliographical Dictionary of the English Catholics. From the Breach with Rome, in 1534, to the Present Time*, V, 578–81. A

conclusively that the world will end according to "naturall Reason." Indeed, Digby wrote, without supporting evidence, that White by an "ingenious rule" measured "in some sort the duration of it, without being branded (as our author threatneth) with convincible and *Statute* madnesse, or with impiety." While it is extremely difficult to locate which of White's speculations Digby might have had in mind, it may be possible that such views as the following, in White's *Peripateticall Institutions* (1656), illustrate the questions under consideration. White assumed that, since the universe was created permanently and purposefully and since nature is impermanent "except for the Rationall soul," this soul becomes the "End" of creation. The universe is "a kind of vast wombe" made up of "Cells" in which these souls "may be begotten and brought up." The earth is man's cell. Thus he concluded that, according to the design hypothesis, "the Quantity of the world" is proper to "the bigness and duration" needed for the number of Cells and Spirits which God intended (pp. 189–190, Book III, Lesson XVIII).

Another disagreement at this point is Digby's contention that, whereas Browne conceived of annihilation outside nature and therefore in the hands of God, annihilation cannot come from God because "The letting loose then of the activest Element to destroy this face of the World, will but beget a change in it, and that no annihilation can proceed from God Almighty: for his essence being . . . selfe-existence, it is more impossible that Not-being should flow from him, then that cold should flow immediately from fire, or darkness from the actuall presence of light" (p. 18). So he returned to the Aristotelian argument of being and not-being, the nature of contrariety. But on the more specific points of proof Digby called upon Father White and the notion of ingenuity instead of giving evidence for his own views.

Digby prefaced such vagueness of counterargument with praises of Browne for saying "there be not impossibilities

<hr>

recent discussion is to be found in Robert I. Bradley, S. J., "Blacklo and the Counter-Reformation: An Inquiry into the Strange Death of Catholic England," *From the Renaissance to the Counter-Reformation: Essays in Honor of Garrett Mattingly*, 348–70.

enough in Religion for an active faith" (I, 9) and for rejecting "all the Metaphysicall definitions of Divines" (I, 10). Digby commented that his pleasure was "No whit lesse, when in *Philosophy* hee will not bee satisfied with such naked termes as in *Schools* use to be obtruded upon easie mindes, when the *Masters* fingers are not strong enogh to untie the knots proposed unto them." But he was also dissatisfied: "When I enquire what light . . . is, I should bee as well contented with his Silence, as with his telling mee it is *Actus perspicui*; unlesse hee explicate clearly to me what those words mean, which I finde very few goe about to do. Such meate they swallow whole, and eject it as entire." Digby promised to investigate such matters as this Aristotelian concept in his forthcoming work so as "to shew by a continued progresse, and not by Leapes, all the motions of nature; & unto them to fit intelligibly the termes used by her best Secretaries: whereby all wilde fantasticke qualities and moods (introduced for refuges of ignorance) are banished from my commerce" (pp. 5–6). Wilkin's note that "Sir K. probably intended to express his accordance with Sir Thomas in rejecting it [Aristotle's definition]" (II, 123) is justifiable, since Browne was stating a preference for the "allegorical" *Lux est umbra Dei* over Aristotle's definition, which described light as the activity of a transparent medium (*De Anima*, 418b10–12). Browne's choice opposed earlier "quasi-tentacular"[30] theories that posited the eye as a transmitting as well as a receiving organ. Aristotle defined light as "the presence of fire or something resembling fire in what is transparent" (418b16). It is not a body. Visibility or transparency is due "to the colour of *something else*" (418b5–6). Digby more certainly was rejecting the Aristotelian version as "wilde fantasticke qualities." He was to state his argument more concretely (p. 15) when he challenged Browne's linking of angels and light (I, 33).

Digby judged Browne's discussion of "pure intellects" or angels to be shallow. He agreed that Porphyry's distinction between men and angels on the basis of the immortality of the latter is faulty and he credited Browne with the ability to argue skillfully on this subject—if he so desired. Since, to Dig-

30. William Cecil Dampier, *A History of Science and Its Relations with Philosophy and Religion*, 162.

by's mind, Browne did not pursue "the tenor of their [angels']
intellectuall operations," he undertook to describe them in
this way: "In which there is no succession, nor ratiocinative
discourse: for in the very first instant of their creation, they
actually knew all that they were capable of knowing; and they
are acquainted even with all free thoughts, past, present, and
to come; for they see them in their causes, and they see them
altogether at one instant" (p. 14). Although Digby qualified
his description, it is more liberal than that of his probable
authority, Saint Thomas Aquinas. Aquinas was careful to emphasize the dependence of angels on the Divine Essence and
their inferiority to God in their intellectual range; especially
angels and all "created intellects" are ignorant of the future
(*Summa Theologica,* Q. 55, Art. 1; Q. 58, Art. 2; Q. 57, Art. 3).
Digby did not mention here the relationship of angels to God,
but he, too, stressed their innate inferiority before the Deity.
Whatever his purpose, Digby ignored Browne's basic supposition that angels perceive at once the essence and form of phenomena and define their main qualities in terms of species as
well as in terms of individual or accidental qualities.

To Browne's definition of light as "a spiritual Substance and
may bee an Angel" Digby retorted that the subject was another
too broad for so short a piece. He promised that he would
prove in his projected *Of Bodies* that light is a "solid Substance and a body" rather than a "bare quality" (p. 15). Thus
Digby rejected Browne's definition of light as quality for his
own of light as corporality, with the qualification that "among
all the corporeal things, it seemeth to aim rightest at a spiritual
nature, and to come nearest unto it" (VI, 1). Light is as tangible as "fire extremely dilated" and moves freely through the
air (XI, 4). Since Digby's remarks concerning angels contradict nothing that Browne had said, it seems that Digby mainly
intended to show his familiarity with the subject and to preface his expanded remarks in his work in preparation.

Digby argued in *Of Bodies* that, while nearly everyone
agrees with Aristotle that light is a quality, he could not accept
this definition because no one agreed on the meaning of
*quality.* Even more important than the fact that contemporary
thinkers could not define the term was the contradiction in
their arguments in favor of it. He found that his contempora-

ries wanted qualities to be "reall Entities or Thinges, distinct
from the bodies they accompany," yet they wanted these
qualities to have no "subsistence or self being," which must be
the case if they are real or independent. Supporters of the argument got around the contradiction by juggling their terms and
by retreating into metaphysics, which he was not willing to
do (VI, 1). "We say then, that qualities are nothing else but
the properties; or particularities wherein one thing differeth
from an other," for example, the heat of a fire. This is how the
term *quality* is understood in "common conversation" (VI, 2).
He then proposed five arguments that explain why light cannot be a body (VI, 3): (1) Light "illuminateth the ayre in an
instant, and therefore, can not be a body: for a body requirreth
succession of time to moove it . . . ; (2) that whereas no body
can admitt an other into its place, . . . two lights may be in the
same place"; light may be in the same place with air, and light
can penetrate "all" solid bodies; (3) if light were a body, it
would necessarily be fire and give off heat; (4) light can be
suddenly extinguished; and (5) if it were a body, it would
respond to the motion of air (VI, 3). The third reason intrigued him, so he asserted that if light is fire then it must be
"fire rarified" or diluted, even though it is still just fire. He
used a comparison quite close to Donne's famous image: "If
gold beaten into so ayery a thinnesse as we see guilders use,
doth remaine still gold notwithstanding the wonderfull ex-
pansion of it," then fire may be light (VI, 4–5). If fire must be
fed by fuel or some such matter, then he doubted there would
be enough fire "to fill all that space which light replenisheth"
(VI, 6).

His objections to light being fire continue in Chapter VII,
in which he rationalized that there is nothing wrong with dis-
agreeing with Aristotle on this matter, since it is clear that
Aristotle did not look into it with sufficient thoroughness
(VII, 1). He then described a series of experiments during
which he examined the degrees of burning and light, but these
were untrustworthy, for the senses cannot be trusted entirely.
He applied the leafed-gold comparison here again, and he also
related the problem to static electricity, glowworms, and particularly to the use of fire for heating (VII, 2–6). Insofar as
he could discern the processes of light, it returns to the air

when extinguished; it does not become a powder as some contemporaries thought.

In Chapter VIII he presented a series of arguments against
light as substance. His refutation of Browne's position ignored
the commonly known basis (Augustine, *The City of God*, xi,
9) for Browne's identification of light with angels; indeed,
Digby ignored the religious imagery entirely. His objections
issued from a scientific basis—it is true that "Augustine's
theory was not favoured in the seventeenth century" (Martin,
p. 302*n*33.7–9). Once again he pleaded that limitations of
space would not allow him to substantiate his views.

Next, Digby listed "in a short note" four subjects on which
he believed Browne to be in error: the unity of the world and
the habitation of angels—both in I, 35; the "activity of glori-
fied eyes"; and "his subtil speculation upon two bodies placed
in the vacuity beyond the utmost all-enclosing superficies of
*Heaven*," stated by Browne in I, 49. Of the latter two points
Digby commented that both are contradictions "in nature,"
especially the act of seeing "in a state of rest, whereas motion,
is required to seeing" (p. 15). This explanation of perception
is essentially Aristotelian: "If there were nothing, so far from
seeing with greater distinctness, we should see nothing at all"
(*De Anima*, 419a20–22). On the question of the unity of the
world Digby again instructed Browne to read Father White's
*Dialogues of the World* (1642), which prove, according to
Digby, that the unity of the world is verified by reason, not
only faith.

The question of the unity of the world is not one that lends
itself to an easy answer, for as Digby stated in *Of Bodies*
(XVII, 1): "It belongeth not then to us to meddle with those
sublime contemplations which search into the nature of the
vast Universe, and that determine the unity and limitation of
it; and that shew by what stringes, and upon what pinnes, and
wheeles, and hinges, the whole world moveth: and that from
thence do ascend unto an awfull acknowledgment and humble
admiration of the primary cause; from whence, and of which,
both the being of and the beginning of the first motion, and
the continuance of all others doth proceed and depend." Even
here it was Thomas White, in Digby's opinion, who had best
"sailed" into this "ocean." Of course, Digby might have

pointed to Aristotle on the question of the unity of the world if he had cared to interpret Aristotle's views on "why there cannot be more than one heaven" or universe. Aristotle based his argument on the nature of circular motion and "the character and number of bodily elements, the place of each, and . . . how many in number the various places are" (*De Caelo*, 276a18–277b25). But perhaps it was to White's *Peripateticall Institutions* that Digby was most directly indebted for his argument:

Again, 'tis evident, there's but one World: For, since there's no space, by which two worlds could be separated one from the other; and quantitative bodies joyn'd together, even by that very conjunction, are one all quantity whatever must, of necessity, by continuednesse conspire into one bulk.

Again, 'tis collected, that the World is not compos'd only of minute bodies, by nature indivisible: for, since an extrinsecall denomination is nothing, but the intrinsecall natures of the things out of which it rises; and, if there were only indivisibles in the world, all the intrinsecalls would remain the same; since the same things alwaies afford the same denomination, 'twould be impossible any thing should be chang'd.[31]

H. M. Digby and Charles de Remusat have pointed out the indebtedness that Sir Kenelm owed to White for his Aristotelianism and, more importantly, the difficulty inherent in trying to separate the two men's ideas in such works as the *Peripateticall Institutions*.[32] In his statement of "design" White declared that he wrote upon Aristotle's principles and in the "way of that eminent person and excellent Philosopher Sir Kenelm Digby; 'tis, because, since, in that so justly-to-be-envy'd Book, *Of the Immortality of the Soul*, he has dissected the whole composition of Nature, from the first Notion of Body, to the very joynts and articles of an invisible spirituall Soul, and laid it before the eyes of all; any other way, then that He had traced out, I neither would nor could proceed."

White addressed his own panegyric to Digby in "the translatour's addresse" to *Peripateticall Institutions*: "Upon this

31. Thomas White, *Peripateticall Institutions*, Book III, Lesson i, 119–20. Quoted by permission of The Huntington Library, San Marino, California.

32. Digby, *Sir Kenelm Digby and George Digby, Earl of Bristol*, 152–53, and Remusat, *Histoire de la philosophie en Angleterre depuis Bacon jusqu'à Locke*, I, 296–324.

resentment, the incomparable Sir Kenelm Digby (whose Expression would I could glory so proportionably to have hit, as my Master may his Mind) began lately to teach it Our Idiom; which it so soon and perfectly attain'd, as clear evidences His to be the truly-Naturall Philosophy: What Ingenuous Courage, once throughly engag'd (and under so sure a Champion) the same advantagious Way, in the same noblest Field, could resist the temptation to follow such a Leader and such Successe, upon so necessary a Design?" (sigs. A5a–A5b, A2b).

Digby's curt reply on these points indicates that he was interested only in what he considered to be Browne's obvious errors on difficult points. Instead of explaining more clearly his four objections, particularly that about the habitation of angels—which he omitted entirely—Digby merely cautioned Browne, *Ne Sutor ultra Crepidam* (Let the cobbler stick to his last). He recalled what he believed to be a fitting title from Saint Victor's library: *Quaestio Subtilissima, Vtrum Chimaera in vacuo bombinans possit commedere Secundas intentiones* (p. 15). Even as Digby turned the barb of this mock title toward Browne, he directed it away from himself as a Roman Catholic, for he cited only half of it. The remainder contains a satirical thrust against the Council of Constance: *et fuit debatuta per decem hebomadas in Consilio Constantiensi*.[33]

Despite Digby's failure to define his views clearly, he was probably correct in chiding Browne's vagueness. When Browne, enchanted by the endless puzzles of the triangularities of the Trinity, extended the triangular soul into an endorsement of "the secret Magicke of numbers" (I, 12), Digby might with justice remark that Browne "from the abysse of *Predestination*, falleth into that of the *Trinity* of *Persons* consistent with the indivisibility of the divine nature: And out of that (if I be not exceedingly deceived) into a third, of mistaking . . . by a wild discourse of a *Trinity* in our *Soules*" (p. 7). Again, Digby did not expand his objections but merely toyed with Browne's argument by commenting that "the dint of wit is not forcible enough to dissect such tough matters." Instead of "light" there is "obscure glimmering . . . cloathed in the darke weeds of negations." Subsequently, Digby felt

33. Francis Rabelais, *The Works of Francis Rabelais*, trans. Sir Thomas Urquhart and [Peter] Motteux, I, 325.

unable to offer "any positive examples to parallel it withall." His reservation about Browne's attribution of the doctrine of correspondence to Hermes amounts to nothing more than a reminder that such ideas are "every where to be met with in *Plato;* and is raised since to a greater height in the Christian Schooles" (p. 8). Unfortunately for the critical reader, Digby did not express his own opinion of the microcosm. The synthesis of the Platonic world–soul and Neo–Pythagorean number speculation by the Neoplatonists kept the theory of microcosm central to the English view of Plato. That Ficino and Pico della Mirandola combined all these views with what they learned from cabalistic and Hermetic writings was known to both Browne and Digby. Digby's objection to Browne's allusion to Hermes was therefore nothing more than a pedantic rebuke. As Digby asserted, the "Christian Schooles" were certainly relevant, since attempts were being made to correlate the pagan spirits with the persons of the Trinity. Since this assertion is only a shallow reminder of the profound relation of Platonism and Christianity to the question, it is reasonable to conclude that the whole matter of correspondences was so commonplace to him that comment was unnecessary. Apparently he believed in correspondences; his assumption of the chain of causation from God to man and his widely known belief in sympathetic powder as a curative agent imply a system of strict correspondence.

Although Digby affirmed a rigid system of causal relations in the universe, he could not answer wholly Browne's summary of causation in I, 14: "There is but one first cause, and foure second causes of all things; some are without efficient, as God, others without matter, as Angels, some without forme, as the first matter; but every Essence, created or uncreated, hath its finall cause, and some positive end both of its Essence and operation." Digby was especially disturbed by Browne's view of the "first matter" as being "without a forme." He doubted any authority that Browne might have "to give an actuall subsistence and being to first matter without a forme." Then apparently misreading Browne with intent, Digby charged:

*Hee that will allow that [First Matter] a Reall existence in nature, is as superficially tincted in* Metaphysicks, *as an other would bee in*

*Mathematicks that should allow the like to a point, a line, or a superficies, in Figures. These, in their strict Notions, are but negations of further extension, or but exact terminations of that quantity which falleth under the consideration of the understanding, . . . no reall entities in themselves: so likewise, the notions of matter, forme, act, power, existence, and the like, that are with truth considered by the understanding, and have there each of them a distinct entity, are never the lesse, no where by themselves in nature. (P. 8)*

Here is a kind of preface to Digby's concept of "notions," which he developed further in the *Two Treatises*. This tradition appeals "to the 'notion' in contradistinction to the 'idea' as a medium of knowledge."[34] The problem is the same as that discussed by Aristotle when he began with the thesis that "knowledge" consists of an "acquaintance" with "principle, conditions, or elements." Aristotle's statement continues: "Now what is to us plain and obvious at first is rather confused masses, the elements and principles of which become known to us later by analysis" (*Physica*, 184a10–12, 22–24). In other words, knowledge of the "how and why" of a thing is necessary before understanding is possible; a study of causes will expedite the discovery of the answers (194b16–20, 24f). The analogy Digby drew between the first matter and mathematical symbols parallels the abstraction by which Aristotle distinguished the study of natural bodies and the objects of mathematics. The latter can be separated in one's mind from their physical movement without invalidating the reasoning process or falsifying one's conclusions. But when physical entities are abstracted, as is done by "the holders of the theory of Forms," errors occur because natural attributes are being abstracted (193b34–194a3).

For Digby, all of these "notions" were merely "termes which wee must use in the negotiations of our thoughts, if wee will discourse consequently, and conclude knowingly. But then againe, wee must bee very wary of attributing to things, in their owne natures, such entities as wee create in our understandings, when wee make pictures of them there; for there every different consideration . . . hath a distinct being by it self. *Whereas* in the thing, there is but one single *unity*, that

34. John W. Yolton, "Locke and the Seventeenth-Century Logic of Ideas," *JHI*, 16 (1955), 431–32.

sheweth (as it were in a glasse, at several positions) those various faces in our understanding. In a word; all these words are but artificiall termes, not reall things" (pp. 8–9). Thus he attempted to "avoid any kind of realist theory of names. . . . The 'notion' stood as intermediary between the real natures . . . and the knowing mind." The sense organs pick up a variety of reports, so "it takes many notions to embody or express one subject." The warning Digby imparted to Browne about the distinctions between the artificial and the real was developed more fully in the *Two Treatises* where, "in his extension of the Aristotelian–Thomistic theory of knowledge in conjunction with a corporealistic analysis of sensation, Digby had gone beyond any of his predecessors in the seventeenth century in the care with which he analyzed the cognitive process from object to subject," according to John W. Yolton (pp. 433, 434, 435).

Digby argued, in the first chapter of his work *Of Bodies*, that quantity is the agreed-upon basis for distinguishing a corporeal from a noncorporeal substance. Bulk or magnitude is solid, tangible, and makes an impression upon the senses (I, 1). Using an apple as metaphor, he explained that various sensuous responses tend "to give actuall Beings to the quantity, figure, colour, smell, tast, and other accidents of the apple . . . because I find the notions of them really distinguished (as if they were different Entities) in my minde. And from thence I may inferre, there is noe contradiction in nature to have the accidents really severed from one an other, and to have them actually subsist without theire substance: and such other mistaken subtilities; which arise out of our unwary conceiting that thinges are in theire owne natures, after the same fashion as we consider them in our understanding" (I, 3). We also have a tendency, he continued, to lump together distinct things. Plato's Ideas were conceived from such an error when he stated that there "was actually in every individuall substance one universall nature running through all of that species, which made them be what they were." Since this substance could be an accident of matter, Plato made them "like Angels." Averroes, Duns Scotus, as well as some of Digby's contemporaries also conceived the universal to be in "a fictitious Being" called *"Entia rationis."* Their error, Digby thought, was in finding a "unity in the thinges which indeede is onely in the understanding" (I, 4). Digby warned that "every error is a fundamentall one" that can spiral into endless mistakes, so "we should acquiesce and be content with that naturall and plaine notion, which springeth immediately and primarily from the thing it selfe." In other words, avoid "subtility" (I, 5). This warning against Plato's thinking and the overly subtle use of words and observations applied equally well to Browne's writing, as far as Digby was concerned.

In *Of Man's Soul*, Chapter I, Digby elaborated on his views of perception and understanding: The man who comprehends correctly can "draw any operation into act." In this instance Digby used the apprehension of a knife, which "in the man, hath those causes, proprieties, and effects, which are naturall unto it" (I, 1). He continued (I, 2): "And that man, by apprehending, doth become the thing apprehended; not by change of his nature unto it, but by assumption of it unto his." To prevent his readers' thinking he was encouraging them to deny reality, he gave a particular example: "What is likenesse, but an imperfect unity betweene a thing, and that which it is said to be like unto? If the likenesse be imperfect, it is more unlike then it is like unto it: and the liker it is, the more it is one with it; untill at length, the growing likeness may arrive to such a perfection, and to such a unity with the thing it is like unto, that then, it shall no longer be like, but is become wholly the same, with what formerly it had but a resemblance of." The remainder of the chapter is a discussion of the analogical powers of man. The power of the understanding reaches as far as being that which "graspeth even at *nothing*" (I, 14).

Although Browne searched for the providence of God in his study of natural causes and found "much divinity" in the investigations of Galen and Suarez, he complained of a lack of the teleological explanation in Aristotle (I, 14). Digby agreed in part with Browne that Aristotle did not devote enough thought to the First Cause, and he shared Browne's enthusiasm for Galen, but he culminated his praise by turning once again to his friend, Father White.[35] This seriocomic

35. Williamson, 158*n*1, points out that "in 1666 Parliament coupled White's book *Of the Middle State of Souls* with *Levia-*

apology for Aristotle and panegyric on Galen and White
added little of value to the argument, but Digby ended—after
complimenting Browne's "strong parts and a vigorous brayne"
and "noble & generous heart"—by comparing the strength of
Browne's lament for "*Aristotles* mutilated and defective *Philosophy*" (Digby's phrases) to that lament "in *Boccalini,
Caesar Caporali* doth for the losse of Livies shipwracked
*Decads*" (pp. 9–10). This allusion was delightfully chosen if
it was Digby's intent to impart a sense of exaggeration and
mockery, for Trajano Bocalini's anecdote of the interruption
of the orator, Rafael Volaterano, on this day of deep mourning
is rich in both qualities:

a nimble Poet, were it either out of meer compunction of mind, or
that he would purchase reputation, by shewing the whole Colledge
of Vertuosi, how very sensible he was of that loss, broke forth into
so loud lamentations, as the Orator could be no longer heard: . . .
Apollo, who was present at the Obsequies, and who upon this
mournful occasion had covered himself with a dark cloud, being
impatient to hear that noise, and that he might the better behold
his face who wept so down-rightly, by the violence of his beams
rarified the Cloud, and found it to be Caesar Caporali, who, not
caring to see the yet remaining Decads of that admirable Writer,
did with such lamentations bewail those that were lost: which
extraordinary affection caused so loud a laughter in all the standers-
by as Volaterano's Oration, . . . could not be ended by reason of
every ones great laughter.[36]

Whether the matter under consideration lay in the realm
of metaphysics or of morality, Digby held emphatically to his
belief in immutability and anticontradiction in achieving an
answer. Of Browne's second youthful heresy, the subsequent
release of the damned from Hell through the mercy of God
(I, 7), Digby asserted that to believe such is to think that God
would or could change the condition of the soul, for the soul
of the damned is by its very essence composed of pain and
anguish. Eradication of this misery necessitates a radical
change in the essence of the unsaved soul: "To make fire cease

than as atheistic, 'apparently on the ground of their common denial of a natural immortality.' "

36. *I ragguali Di Parnasso: or Advertisements from Parnassus:
in two centuries. With the Political Touchstone*, trans. Henry
Earl of Monmouth, 199.

from being hot, requireth to have it become another thing then the *Element* of fire" (p. 5). After presenting this qualitative example, his explanation became so complicated that his criticism seems more facetious than serious; yet he consistently held to the point that the elements of the soul cannot be changed even by God, a view he reaffirmed in *Of Men's Soul* (VI, 5–6).

Because the 1642 edition of *Religio* gave Chiliast as an authority (changed in the 1643 version to *Origen*), Digby referred to the Chiliasts who, he felt, shared Browne's ideas about God's mercy. Although there was no apparent link in Browne's work between the Chiliasts and later references (I, 52–53) to those who consider eternal damnation "the sentence . . . of a severe Judge," Digby made the correlation (p. 5). By *chiliasm* Digby probably meant the millennial expectations among the progressivists of his day who were spreading a gospel of reform and advancement in the name of science and society. He wrote an epistle praising George Hakewill's *An Apologie or Declaration of the Power and Providence of God* (1627), in which he showed an early inclination to support the idea of progress. Historical chiliasm—a belief in the coming millennium, when Christ would return to earth and to power, thus establishing a Paradise of saints in this world— was condemned by Origen and Augustine. Origen saw dangers implicit in the transcendence of a belief in immediate and collective sainthood over a faith in the salvation of the individual soul; Augustine foresaw a laxity in morals encouraged by the expectation of temporal blessedness. That an anticipation of the fulfillment of apocalyptic prophecy would motivate fantastic responses is understandable. The rise of what has been called the "Free Spirit," a heresy of self-deification that continued even into the seventeenth century in such groups as the Ranters, may have been a part of the association Digby had with the term *chiliasm*. However, there is no evidence of Digby's explicit awareness of these or other radical groups who probably grew to prominence after 1646 and the instituting of the Protectorate.[37]

37. See *The City of God*, 718–21 (xx, 7); Norman Cohn, *The*

Since Digby maintained so steadfastly the unchangeable-ness of the souls of the damned, it is valuable to note his thinking concerning the saved. His views on salvation developed obliquely through a series of answers concerning old age and the nature of ghosts. Browne's witty doubts about the virtues to be gained by living to advanced age run counter to Digby's conception of long life as "a mighty great blessing" in alignment with "the course of nature, and of reason." Instead of the increase in sin that Browne foresaw, "age doth not rec-tifie, but incurvate our natures, turning bad dispositions into worser habits" (I, 42), Digby conceived the years of aging to be "time leave to vent & boyle away the unquietnesse and turbulencies that follow our passions; and to weane our selves gently from carnall affections, and at the last to drop with ease and willingnesse, like ripe fruit from the *Tree*" (p. 16). With these comments Digby directed attention to the opinions of Plotinus on the subject. A perusal of *The Enneads* does not un-cover any direct relation to Digby's idea or image. Plotinus considered time to be of importance only "if in the greater length of time the man has seen more deeply . . . but if all the process has brought him no further vision, then one glance would give all he has had." Unhappiness may increase during an extended life, Plotinus admitted, but this is due more to "the aggravation of the malady," than to the passage of time. That happiness which Digby perceived in extended years was to Plotinus also one of virtue: "No: true happiness is not vague and fluid: it is an unchanging state. If there is in this matter any increase besides that of more time, it is in the sense that a greater happiness is the reward of a higher virtue: this is not counting up to the credit of happiness the years of its con-tinuance; it is simply noting the highwater mark once for all attained."[38]

Digby likened the aging process in man to that in fruit—necessary to mellow the fruit; fruit that drops prematurely from the limb will taste of the wood and be bitter. But he also

*Pursuit of the Millennium*, 13–14, 151–52; Ernest Lee Tuveson, *Millennium and Utopia*, 15–18; and Martin, 290n8.5.

38. *The Enneads*, trans. Stephen MacKenna rev. B. S. Page, 53–54 (I, v, 3, 6).

perceived that overly ripe fruit regresses to its center like "Soules that goe out of their bodies with affections to those objects they leave behinde them . . . doe retaine still even in their separation, a byas, and a languishing towards them" (p. 16). In this state spirits frequent "Caemeteries and Charnell houses," but not for the "morall" reason that Browne presented.

Browne wished primarily to establish that ghosts are not the "wandring soules of men," but "the unquiet walkes of Devils" drawn to "the dormitories of the dead, where the Devill like an insolent Champion beholds with pride the spoyles and Trophies of his victory in *Adam*" (I, 37). Against this moral description Digby opposed his thought that these are not ghosts but "carnal Soules" unwilling to be separated from their "impressions" of the body. They "lingreth perpetually," not allayed by the "impossibility . . . of their impotent desires," but hoping to live again. Surprisingly, this view parallels Plato's (*Phaedo*, 81d). Digby went on to support the belief that a body bleeds in the presence of its slayer—a clear instance of the "unquiet *Spirit*" speaking out against the shock of sudden death. Since the "*Organs* of voyce" have been "benummed" by death, the soul agitates the fluids of the body to gush on its behalf (pp. 17–18).

Some light on Digby's experience with ghosts is to be found in William Lilly's *History of His Life and Times* (1715), in which he recounts the following:

Sometimes before I become acquainted with him [Mr. Evans], he then living in the Minories, was desired by the Lord Bothwell and Sir Kenelm Digby to show them a Spirit, he promised so to do; the time came, and they were all in the Body of the Circle, when loe, upon a sudden, after some time of Invocation, Evans was taken from out the Room and carried into the Field near Battersea Causway close to the Thames. Next Morning a Countryman going by to his Labour and espying a Man asked him how he came there; Evans by this understood his Condition, enquired where he was, how far from London, and in what Parish he was; which when he understood, he told the Labourer he had been late at Battersea the Night before, and by chance was left there by his Friends. Sir Kenelm Digby and the Lord Bothwell went home without any harm, came next Day to hear what was become of him; just as they in the Afternoon came into the House, a Messenger came from Evans to his Wife to come to him at Battersea:

*I enquired upon what account the Spirit carried him away, who said he had not, at the time of Invocation, made any Suffumigation, at which the Spirits were vexed.*[39]

Digby's thinking revealed two paradoxes. The first was his obviously greater credulity concerning ghosts than about witches. Earlier in his *Observations* (p. 13) Digby laughed at Browne's reservation about witches and his important conclusion that to deny them jeopardized his belief in spirits and even in God (I, 30). By crediting Browne with ingenuousness in his lack of evidence for witches, Digby presented himself as a sophisticated modern enjoying his skepticism and declaring his desire for "stronger motives" before agreeing. Digby has probably been praised more for his forward-looking view here than for anything else he had to say in his *Observations*. But it must be noted that he did not declare his disbelief in witches; he claimed only that he lacked evidence of their existence, and—most important of all—that he did not need to believe in them in order to believe in God and spirits. He added that he doubted "as much of the efficacy of those magicall rules . . . as also of the finding out of mysteries by the courteous *Revelation of Spirits*" that Browne proposed (I, 31). Although Browne combined the principle of plenitude with this curious dependence of belief in Satan and his agents in order to retain belief in God, neither Digby nor Alexander Ross in their objections raised this important contemporary argument.

The second paradox in Digby's views of ghosts is deeper and more significant than the first. He clearly exalted the soul over the body, and this superiority formed the basis for his belief in spiritual immortality. Now he spoke, not of immanent separation, but of a spiritual yearning by the soul for the body. Nevertheless, he stated a very important qualification in order to forfend charges of contradiction and impiety. These wandering souls are "carnal"; they have not attained the level of virtue and immateriality needed for passage into and, indeed, anticipation of the next and higher life. A soul that was dealt a violent separation from its body was released unprepared for the afterlife. In *Of Man's Soul* (XII, 5), he stated that pun-

39. William Lilly, *History of His Life and Times*, 23. Quoted by permission of The Huntington Library, San Marino, California.

ishment in the afterlife is meted out justly: "It followeth by
the necessary course of nature, that if a man dye in a disorderly
affection to any thing, as to his chiefe good, he eternally remaineth by the necessity of his owne nature, in the same affection: and there is no imparity, that to eternall sinne, there
should be imposed eternall punishment." This statement is
not precisely contradictory to others he made on less esoteric
subjects in *Of Bodies*. There the concept of cohesion between
bodies is generally explained on the basis of a "cementing
fluid": "Suppose that such a liquid part is between two dry
parts of a dense body, and sticking to them both, becometh in
the nature of a glew to hold them together; will it not follow
. . . that these two dense parts will be as hard to be severed as
the small liquid part by which they stick together is to be divided?" (XIV, 8). Thus, when the soul has been unwillingly
or violently separated from the body, the intense attraction
or "sympathy" felt by the soul for its body is expressed through
the only available fluid—blood. So in this instance of extended
connection between soul and body, the soul remains much
more carnal than the higher and purer soul of mind and
knowledge.

Digby's views here parallel his famous experiments with
sympathetic attraction, particularly with "the weapons salve,
or the sympathetike powder." In *Of Bodies* he defined attraction as that motion "which is ordinarily said to be done by the
force of nature to hinder *Vacuum*," but he warned against
personifying nature's abhorrence for a vacuum into the fallacy
of supposing that vacuity has a *"Being"* (XVIII, 1–2). "Their
contiguity and their heavynesse" cause bodies to adhere to one
another (XVIII, 2–3). He warned also that those who credit
certain actions, such as the "magneticall," to "the Divels assistance" are open to the criticism that "mans wickedness hath
been more ingenious than his good will" and that man mistakes that which is helpful to him for that which is harmful.
To do so is to "wrong . . . almighty God." To deny sympatheti-
cal effects is to "renounce all human fayth," since many have
experienced them. The body, being usually hot and moist, is
attracted to "a solide warme body" and to "any medicative
quality or body . . . better than any surgeon can apply it"
(XVIII, 9).

These views about sympathetic powers parallel one of the most fascinating sections in *Of Bodies*. At the conclusion of Chapter XXVI, in which Digby supported Harvey's theory of circulation against that of Descartes, Digby conjectured that, since it seems possible that human beings could live forever in their condition, "if all hurtfull accidents coming from without might be prevented," and since it is clear that man propagates himself, then:

it is cleare, that what maketh him dye, is no more the want of any radicall power in him, . . . [then] it must be some accidentall want, which Galen attributeth chiefly to the drynesse of our bones, and sinewes &c. . . . ; for drynesse, with density, alloweth not easy admittance unto moysture: and therefore, it causeth the heate which is in the dry body, eyther to evaporate or to be extinguished: and want of heate, is that, from whence the failing of life proceedeth: which he thinketh can not be prevented by any art or industry.

And herein, God hath expressed his great mercy and goodnesse towardes us: for seeing that by the corruption of our owne nature, we are so immersed in flesh and bloud as we should for ever delight to wallow in their myre without raysing our thoughts att any time above that low and brutall condition: he hath engaged us by a happy necessity, to thinke of and to provide for a nobler and farre more excellent state of living that will never change or end.

In pursuance of which inevitable ordinance; man . . . hasteneth on his death by his unwary and rash use of meates, which poyson his bloud: and then, his infected bloud passing through his whole bodye, must needes in like manner, taynt it all att once. For the redresse of which mischiefe, the assistance of Physike is made use of: and that, passing likewise the same way purifyeth the bloud, and recovereth the corruption occasioned by the peccant humour; or other whiles gathering it together, it thrusteth and carveth out that evill guest by the passages contrived by nature to disburden the body of unprofitable or hurtfull superfluities. (XXVI, 10)

John Browne wrote an intriguing anecdote about sympathetic medicine in his *Adenochoiradelogia: or, an Anatomick-Chirurgical Treatise of Glandules and Strumaes, or Kings= Evil=Swellings. Together with the Royal Gift of Healing* (1684):

Being in the Society of many Persons of Quallity, I had this remarkable following Observation from an eminent Person of this strange Cure. A Nonconformists Child in Norfolk, being troubled with Scrophulous Swellings, the late deceased Sir Thomas Brown

of Norwich being consulted about the same, His Majesty being
then at Breda or Bruges, he advised the Parents of the Child to
have it carryed over to the King (his own Method being used in-
effectually:) the Father seemed very strange at his advice, and
utterly denyed it, saying, The Touch of the King was of no greater
efficacy than any other Mans. The Mother of the Child adhering
to the Doctors advice, studied all imaginable means to have it over,
and at last prevailed with her Husband to let it change the Air for
three Weeks or a Month; this being granted, the Friends of the
Child that went with it, unknown to the Father, carried it to
Breda, where the King touch'd it, and she returned home perfectly healed. The Child being come to its Fathers House, and he
finding so great an alteration, enquires how his Daughter arrived at
this Health, the Friends thereof assured him, that if he would not
be angry with them, they would relate the whole Truth; they
having his promise for the same, assured him they had the Child
to the King to be touch'd at Breda, whereby they apparently let
him see the great benefit his Child receiv'd thereby. Hereupon the
Father became so amazed, that he threw off his Nonconformity,
and exprest his thanks in this method; Farewel to all Dissenters,
and to all Nonconformists: If God can put so much Virtue into
the King's Hand as to Heal my Child, I'll serve that God and that
King so long as I live with all Thankfulness.[40]

The political ramifications of the gift are as great, it seems, as
the medicinal.

Digby complimented as "extreame handsomely said" (p.
18) Browne's description of dying as "to be a kinde of nothing
for a moment, to be within one instant of a spirit" (I, 38). But
the relationship of the saved soul to its body is of an entirely
different order. Digby approached the nature of the resurrected body by another of his contentions that Browne lacked
the ability to cope with such time-consuming questions:
When Browne avoided "higher, or more abstruse *Principles*,"
and wrote instead about thoughts that "occurre in ordinary
conversation with the world, or in the common tracke of study
and learning, I know no man would say better" (p. 27).

Having reduced Browne's thinking to the trivial, Digby,
through a mixture of sincere and facetious praise of Browne's
ingenuity, declared Browne's contention (I, 48) that every
particle of the body is reunited with the soul in heaven to be
a "grosse conception" (p. 28). Digby was not surprised that

40. John Browne, *Adenochoiradelogia*, 187–89. Quoted by permission of The Huntington Library, San Marino, California.

Browne "should tread a little awry, and goe astray in the
darke." With mock courtesy he conceded that perhaps Browne
had little time to give to the "unwinding of such entangled
and abstracted subtilties." Digby admitted that Browne's
"naturall parts are such as he might have the chaire from most
men I know" and credited him with "much wit and sharp-
nesse" (p. 27), then launched into a lengthy rebuttal of
Browne's views on physical resurrection. Having deemed the
conception of the reuniting of all the particles of the body
"grosse," Digby granted that those who call themselves Christians must accept just such a belief. To emphasize this paradox Digby asked Dorset if he saw the preparations for war
near Oxford with the eyes "wherewith many yeares agone you
looked upon *Porphyries* and *Aristotles* learned leafes there?"
(p. 28). Following a brief panegyric on the excellency of His
Lordship's body, Digby incorporated the atomic theory of
"perpetuall flux" to explain "how that which giveth the
numericall individuation to a *Body*, is the substantiall forme.
As long as that remaineth the same, though the matter be in a
continuall fluxe and motion, yet the thing is still the same"
(p. 29). The only absolute forms are human souls, but since
they are absolute and unchangeable they unite with matter to
"maketh againe the same man. . . . Nay, hee is composed of the
same Individuall matter; for it hath the same distinguisher and
individuator; to wit, the same forme, or *Soule*. Matter considered singly by it selfe, hath no distinction; All matter is it
selfe the same; we must fancie it, as we doe the indigested
*Chaos*; It is an uniformely wild *Ocean*." Nature does not provide exact examples to illustrate "matter without forme (which
hath no actuall being)," but Digby thought that "enough is
said to make a speculative man see" that God's power to unite
the soul to its same body is such that

*if* God *should joyne the* Soule *of a lately dead man (even whiles
his dead corps should lie entire in his winding sheete here) unto a
Body made of earth taken from some mountaine in America; it
were most true and certaine that the body he should then live by,
were the same Identicall body he lived with before his Death, and
late Resurrection. It is evident that samenesse, thisnesse, and that-
nesse, belongeth not to matter by it selfe, (For a generall indifference runneth through it all) but onely as it is distinguished and
individuated by the Forme. Which, in our case, whensoever the*

same Soule doth, it must be understood always to be the same
matter and body. (Pp. 30–31)

Thus he asserted that the individual soul is the identifying
agent in eternity. The source of the bodily atoms is irrelevant,
since the soul is the form, the distinguisher and individuator.

Digby might have provided a fascinating speculation about
Browne's refusal (added in 1643 to I, 21) to "question who
shall arise with that ribbe [Adam's] at the Resurrection."
Henry Hammond discussed the matter of bodily resurrection
in the following manner in his *A Practicall Catechisme* (London, 1646):

> s.   *But what kinde of bodies shall those be after they be raised?*
> c.   *Spirituall bodies, I Cor. 15.44. 1. In respect of the qualities
> spiritualized into a high agility, rarity, clarity, and such as will
> render them most commodious habitations for the soul, made
> partaker of that divine vision: 2. In respect of the principle of life
> and motion, which in naturall bodies is some naturall principle,
> but in these is the Spirit of God, which shall sustain them without
> eating or drinking, & c.*
> s.   *What is the practicall beleef of this?*
> c.   *Endevouring toward these excellencies here, mortifying,
> and subdueing the carnall principle, and making it as tame, and
> tractable, as may be, and altogether complying with the spirit.
> 2. Raising up our souls, i. e. labouring, that they be, and continue
> in a regenerate state, and not burying them in that worst kind of
> grave, the carnall affections, and lusts, which is the most dangerous
> death imaginable.*[41]

Digby questioned the inclusiveness of Browne's vision of
the universal reuniting of all species by the voice of God. With
characteristic bias Digby complained: "This language were
handsome for a *Poet* or a *Rhetorician* to speake. But in a
*Philosopher*, that should ratiocinate strictly and rigorously, I
can not admit it." His stronger objection was that he could
not recognize "subsistent forms of *Corporeall* things," with
the exception of man's soul. Corporeal things are created by
the "action and passion of the Elements among themselves."
Out of these "conflicts . . . new formes succeed old ones" (p.
31). He was to examine more of these mysteries in the *Two
Treatises*. The exactness of Browne's correspondences between

41. Henry Hammond, *A Practicall Catechisme*, 28–29. Quoted
by permission of The Huntington Library, San Marino, California.

spirit and matter carried him beyond Digby and Alexander Ross, especially when he evoked the Divine Voice in this action. Once again Digby refused to apply a poetic or rhetoric reading to *Religio*—something he freely did when writing twenty-five pages on "an indissoluble Riddle" in Spenser.[42] It seems that Digby needed to know he was reading an allegorical intention before he recognized the poetic method.

Perhaps Digby's reason for not allowing Browne to indulge in symbolic explanations was his high standard for poetry and a feeling that symbol should be reserved for poets' use. Digby's views on poetry appear in his discussion of discourse in Chapter III of his work *On Man's Soul*. He there defined "an art" as "a collection of generall rules, comprehending some one subject, upon which we often worke." Grammar, then, is "the scope of which art, consisteth first, in teaching us to deliver our conceptions plainely and clearely . . . next, in making, our discourse be succinct and briefe, . . . and lastly, in sorting our wordes, so as what we say, may be accompanied with sweetnesse; both in common, in regard of the eare, by avoyding such harsh soundes as may offend it; and in particular, in regard of the custome of the language wherein we speake, and of the persons to whom we speake" (III, 7). Logic gives us the reasons by which we speak, grammar the words, and rhetoric the "life and motion" through action and gesture (III, 8). Finally, poetry itself "is not a governour of our Actions, but by advantagious expressing some eminent ones, it becometh an usefull directour to us. . . . The designe of it is, by representing humane actions in a more august and admirable hew, then in themselves they usually have: to frame specious Ideas, in which the people may see, what is well done, what amisse, what should be done, and what errour is wont to be done: and to imprint in mens mindes a deepe conceite of the goods and evils, that follow their vertuous or vitious comportement in their lifes." The preparation of the poet is demanding and comprehensive: "But unto such a Poet as would aim at those noble effects, no knowledge of *Morality*, nor of the nature and course of humane actions and accidents must be wanting: he

42. *Observations on the 22. Stanza in the 9th Canto of the 2nd Book of Spencers Faery Queen. Full of excellent Notions concerning the Frame of Man, and his rational Soul*, 25.

must be well versed in History; he must be acquainted with the progresse of nature, in what she bringeth to passe; he must be deficient in no part of *Logick, Rhetorick,* or *Grammar*: in a word, he must be consummate in all arts and sciences, if he will be excellent in his way" (III, 9). He concluded his discussion of discourse by looking back with pride at the orderliness of his procedures and at the capability of his "well ordered" thoughts to reveal "hidden thinges" in both his readers' understanding and in their knowledge of the natural and physical world (III, 14).

Digby objected strenuously to the "wilde fansie" (p. 13) of Browne's vision of a universal spirit. Especially unacceptable to Digby was the speed with which Browne passed "from naturall speculations to a morall contemplation of *Gods Spirit* working in us" (p. 14). Digby ignored the careful qualification with which Browne stated his views: "There may be (for ought I know) an universall and common Spirit to the whole world" (I, 32). Also troubling to Digby was Browne's inference that this spirit exists in the "reality of nature"; Digby preferred to limit the existence of this spirit to only "our understanding." He perceived that, instead of offering substantiation, Browne invoked "his suddaine poeticall rapture," which prompted Digby to wonder "whether the solidity of the *Judgement* bee not outweighed by the ayrienesse of the fancy." He concluded his comments with the snide statement that Browne's ingeniousness could not be doubted, but "how deepe a *Scholler*" he was must be left to more skillful judges. Digby dismissed Browne's invocation of the universal spirit with the pedantic note that Browne misunderstood the Hermetic philosophers if he expected to find their doctrine in that source. He believed Browne to have too freely transformed a metaphysical concept into a real entity. His remarks do not show the foundation for his objections, although it is clear that he was troubled by Browne's pluralism.

### God's Grace and Man's Virtue

If the mystical vision of an omnipresent power did not satisfy Digby's rational occupations, what view of God did he substitute? The reader's understanding of his conception of

God grows out of a long discussion of the nature of virtue and grace. Digby's God is as supreme and all-embracing as Browne's. But Browne (I, 47) had maintained a dichotomy between "morall honesty," which he defined as the Senecan advice to pretend, when alone and tempted, that his "deare and worthiest friends" were with him, and virtue, which he defined as acting in remembrance of Him who "must reward us at the last." Digby disowned the value of "being vertuous for a rewards sake" and swore his support to "being vertuous, . . . out of an inbred loyalty to vertue." He recognized the "noblenesse, and heroikenesse of the nature and mind from whence they both proceed" and perceived—with reference to the "Journeys end"—a compatibility between "morall honesty" and virtue, since they "both meete in the period of Beatitude." With this pronouncement he turned to the beatific state, which he believed occurs through the "grace and favour" of God, but he admitted disagreements about the "steps" by which "his grace produceth this effect." With a promise to Dorset not to trouble him with a long discussion, Digby shifted his attention to the effect grace has upon us in this life, on that basis to study "what hinges they are that turn us over to *Beatitude* and *Glory* in the next" (p. 20).

Digby then summarized the various viewpoints that people have toward God's rule. First, there are those who believe that God is a "Judge, that rewardeth or punisheth men, according as they cooperated with or repugned to, the grace hee gave" (pp. 20–21). This God can be pleased or angered, kind or indignant. Next, there are those "that flye a higher pitch" who "conceive that Beatitude, and misery in the other life, are effects that necessarily and orderly flow out of the nature of those causes that begot them in this life, with engaging God Almighty to give a sentence, and act the part of a Judge." These persons label the portrayal of God as judge "metaphoricall" and intended to "containe vulgar mindes in their duties." Digby cast his lot with "these more penetrating men, [who] are vertuous upon higher and stronger motives (for they truely and solidly know why they are so) doe consider that what impressions are once made in the spirituall substance of a Soule, and what affections it hath once contracted, doe ever remaine in it till a contrary and diametrically contradicting

judgement and affection, doe obliterate it, & expell it thence"
(p. 21). In describing the sensibilities of the soul as it seeks to
divorce itself from the carnalities of the body, he explained the
power of contrition as proportionate to the "purely spirituall"
quality of the soul. The sensitive perceive what they have lost
through "momentary trifles, and childrens play" (p. 22); when
they are aware that they could have gained eternal reward
through using "their right senses" and through obeying their
reason. The only release from the madness of sin or from re-
morse is gained when the soul escapes from "this *Prison* of
clay and flesh" through an understanding of such "intellectual
goods as *Truth, Knowledge,* and the like." Assisted by these
goods, the soul attains the level where it rejects the pleasures
of this world and perceives "the contemptible inanity in them,
that is set off onely by their painted outside." Most important
of all, the soul reaches the stage at which it longs "to bee in the
society of that supereminent cause of causes, [containing] the
*Treasures* of all beauty, *Knowledge, Truth, Delight,* and good
whatsoever." The soul becomes impatient with its "absence
from him" and comes to "hate" its bodily life as "cause of this
divorce." Digby concluded that such a soul attains a happiness
in anticipation of its liberty from the body that exceeds the
understanding of any "heart of flesh" (p. 23).

According to Digby, the love the soul has for "that infinite
entity" is so great that, "since the nature of superiour, and
excellent things is to shower downe their propitious influences
wheresoever there is a capacity of receiving them, and no
obstacle to keep them out (like the Sun that illuminateth the
whole ayre, if no cloud or solid opacous body intervene) it
followeth clearly that this infinite Sun of Justice, this im-
mense Ocean of goodnesse, cannot chuse but environ with his
beames, and replenish even beyond satietie with his delight-
some waters, a soule so prepared and tempered to receive
them."

Finally, Digby applied this correspondence between divine
and human excellence to Browne's views of virtue. The man
who practices virtue for its and reason's sake

is almost invulnerable. . . . On the other side, the hireling that
steereth his course onely by his reward and punishment, doth
well I confesse; but he doth it with reluctance; he carrieth the

Arke, Gods Image, his Soule, safely home, it is true, but hee
loweth pitifully after his calves that hee leaveth behind him among
the Philistians. In a word he is vertuous, but if hee might safely,
hee would doe vitious things. (And hence bee the ground in nature, if so I may say, of our Purgatory). (Pp. 24–25)

Digby concluded this portion of his observations with a simple
analogy of two maids, one ill and one healthy: The sick girl is
tempted to eat "ashes, *Chalke*, or *Leather*" to cure her "little
sprinkling of the green sicknesse," but she rejects the purga-
tives, knowing that they will later increase her discomfort; the
healthier girl is never attracted to this strange diet. Her hale
good looks contrast with those of the sickly one, with her "depraved appetite" and constant "danger of a relapse." Despite
the superficiality of this analogy, Digby's summation of the
susceptibility of the virtuous to vice except for their fear of
exposure is similar to that in Ben Jonson's "Epode," which
points up the paradox that the meanly virtuous are chaste
only through necessity, since they know that "man may securely sinne, but safely never." Digby ended this convoluted
discussion by substantially agreeing with Browne who also
contrasted "a naturall inclination and inbred loyalty unto
vertue" with a natural frailty that yields to "easie temptation."
Browne concluded that the basis for all virtue is the resurrection, by which "our ashes shall enjoy the fruits of our pious endeavours." It is clear that Browne perceived within the human
conscience a desire for both virtue and vice. Digby separated
those who are virtuous for virtue's sake from those who are virtuous for reward's sake but joined the two groups by declaring
that both ways of life result in beatitude. Despite this declaration of equal reward for both motivations, Digby elaborated
his argument in order to emphasize his abhorrence of the
carnalities of life.

Digby developed his thoughts on beatitude and life's goals
in a highly personal way in his dedication to his son, Kenelm,
in the *Two Treatises*. He used the turmoil and the chaos of the
time (he was writing from exile in Paris) as a backdrop for
presenting the book to his son as an instruction in how to arm
himself against the worst that might happen. The dedication
expresses thanks to his namesake for being of the mind and
education to understand the difference between the temporal

and the superficial, the eternal and the divine. Man thus learns self-government through knowledge and attains the "end . . . of all mans aymes . . . Beatitude: that is, the most happinesse, that his nature is capable of. . . . Now the way to be sure of this, is eyther infalliable authority, or evident science." Those who follow only authority are dependent on others, but then, not everybody has the wit and judgment to be independent. He who would try, however, should read this book. Extending the concept of self-government through two traditional analogies, the statesman and the horseman, Digby cautioned that one need not specialize in the minutiae of horsemanship in order to be a fine horseman. Instead, "a complete brave man, must know solidely that maine end of what he is in the world for: and withall, must know how to serve himselfe when he pleaseth, and that it is needfull to him," of what the divine, the metaphysician, the natural philosopher, the mathematician, and others have to offer to his purposes. Digby then characterized the writing of the *Two Treatises* as being just such an act of self-government.

Digby's advice becomes more poignant in the knowledge of the death of this eldest son four years later. Clarendon's account is justifiably well known: "The earl with near an hundred horse (the rest wisely taking the way to London, where they were never inquired after) wandered without purpose or design, and was, two or three days after, beset in an inn at St. Neots in Huntingtonshire, by those few horse who pursued him, being joined with some troops of colonel Scroop's; where the earl delivered himself prisoner to the officer without resistance: yet at the same time Dalbeer and Kenelm Digby, the eldest son of Sir Kenelm, were killed upon the place; whether out of former grudges, or that they offered to defend themselves, was not known."[43]

Digby followed his discussion of the goal of the beatific vision, which parallels Browne's emphasis on the resurrection, by speculating on Browne's concern (I, 54) for "those honest Worthies and Philosophers" who may have been damned because they lived before Christ's incarnation. Digby conjectures that if these men "followed in the whole *Tenor* of

43. *The History of the Rebellion and Civil Wars in England,* ed. Bulkeley Bandinel, VI, 97–98.

their lives, the dictamens of right *Reason*, but that their Journey was secure to *Heaven*" (p. 25). He referred the reader back to the passage on the virtuous soul as an illustration of "what temper of minde is necessary to get thither." Nevertheless, Digby complained that, although the avenue of right reason presents itself to man, most men are too susceptible to "*Passion* and terrene affections" to be easily led to beatitude by "nature and reason in their best habit"; so the teachings and example of Christ must lead most to salvation. Christ's crucifixion "taught us how the securest way to step immediately into perfect happinesse, is to be crucified to all the desires, delights, and contentments of the *World*" (pp. 26–27). Digby therefore concluded that Christ's "last act" taught man what "course is best; whereas few are capable of the *Reason* of it" (p. 26).

On the surface it might appear that Digby's stance was not much different from the emphasis on salvation through Christ as expressed by Browne, but Digby continuously emphasized the disavowal of this world in the knowledge of the "*Reason* of his incarnation," whereas Browne viewed living according to the dictates of reason as simply a "naturall" act of the human species, not worthy of further rewards. Browne necessarily ended on the paradox that all salvation is through Christ alone. Digby's rational basis for virtue, with its emphasis on the "perfectly judicious man" who is able to rise above the worldly, is—ironically—more earth-bound that Browne's, which dismissed earthly virtue as inconsequential where eternal rewards are concerned. Both writers compromised somewhat the absoluteness of orthodox salvation through Christ, but Digby's rationalism is the greater compromise.

In order to abbreviate his earlier discussion of virtue Digby delayed his definition of grace. He apparently forgot about the matter until some rereading of his "loose papers to point them" disclosed the omission. He then added a postscript (pp. 43–44) on the matter of grace, in which he explained that he did not mean to "conceive it to be a quality, infused by *God Almighty* into a Soule." This explanation was apparently too superficial to satisfy either his theological or philosophical scruples, so he redefined grace "to be the whole complex of such reall motives (as a solid account may be given of them) that incline a man to vertue, and piety; and are set on foote by Gods particular *Grace* and favour, to bring that worke to passe." An example of this would be the sensual man who suffers some calamity that softens his heart and stirs his mind. While in this impressionable condition he encounters a book or sermon that reminds him of his mortal danger and lifts him to contemplate higher things. After his renouncing of sin he associates with the pious, who are able to change him even more conclusively to "a course of Solid V*ertue*, and *Piety*." Digby concluded that "These accidents of his misfortunes . . . were ranged and disposed from all Eternity, by G*ods* particular goodnesse and providence for his *Salvation*; and without which hee had inevitably beene damned; this chaine of causes, ordered by G*od* to produce this effect, I understand to bee *Grace*." After Digby's repeated denunciations of the fleshly and his frequently embellished references to the goodness of the Deity, the simplicity and ease of this anecdote is surprising and, indeed, gratifying.

The general context for Digby's analysis of grace and virtue is the subject of charity—the main topic of Part II of *Religio*. Digby prefaced his examination of Part II by comparing it to an "*Ocean* of *Error*, . . . infinite, and . . . bearing no proportion in it" (p. 32). After labeling Browne's introductory remarks "affected," Digby charged that Browne lowered "divine *Charity* [to] a generall way of doing good" that only as an afterthought is directed toward fulfilling the will of God. Although Browne had denounced the prejudices of the multitude (II, 1), Digby turned the author's words back on him by placing Browne with the vulgar: like them, Browne viewed God as judge, rewarder, or punisher. Digby could then complain of the de-emphasis of God's will in Browne's view of charity; at the same moment he ridiculed any references to the commands of God as "in a narrow compasse." Unfortunately, Digby's definition of charity does not clarify this disagreement in any concrete way: "W*hereas*, perfect *Charity*, is that vehement love of God, for his own sake, for his goodnesse, for his beauty, for his excellency that carrieth all the motions of our Soule directly and violently to him; and maketh a man disdaine, or rather hate all obstacles that may retard his journey to him." He concluded with a mixed metaphor in which the

face of God both "warmeth us to doe other good" and over-
flows "the maine streame . . . in a multitude of little Channels"
(p. 33). Thus Browne's conception of a natural virtue that
supersedes private ends and is indifferent to all but God's will
was replaced in Digby's view by an urge on the part of man to
be with God—an urge so strong that man will hate evil and
love good.

He could neither "commend" nor "censure" Browne (p.
34) for wishing he could pass on his knowledge as a legacy to
his friends and for suspecting that patrons support learning
and the arts as much out of fear of revengeful authors as a desire for immortality (II, 3). At best, Digby could only allow
these matters pass, perhaps with a smile.

A more serious instance of Browne's concern for earthly matters, Digby believed, was Browne's desire to "engrosse" the
griefs of his friends so that "by making them mine owne, I may
more easily discusse them" (II, 5). Digby derogated such a
desire as contrary to good judgment. He cited Epictetus, who
held—according to Digby—that grief for another only "dis-
ordereth the one, without any good to the other" (p. 34). Perhaps Digby had in mind a statement such as, "But it is not fit
to be unhappy on the account of any one, but happy on the
account of all; and chiefly of God, who hath constituted us
for this purpose." Epictetus argued essentially that grief is an
affront to God because it allows the mourner to be affected by
happenings outside his powers (p. 188). Digby objected to the
suggestion that the feelings of men should be like those of
angels "that doe us good, but have no passion for us." He considered Browne's kindness for men too extreme, especially
when he thought that Browne compared his filial love to that
love which God has for the soul. Digby took this statement and
subsequent ones by Browne that dealt with the "three most
mysticall unions: two natures in one person; three persons in
one nature; one soule in two bodies" as evidence that Browne
was "a right good natur'd man"—but, by implication, slightly
blasphemous. Digby apparently misread Browne's first statement about the union of the divine and the human in Christ.
Browne, there, was first comparing his love for his friend to his
love for virtue itself and, second, his love for his soul to his love
for God. He did not intend the correlation that Digby drew.

Nevertheless, Digby felt it necessary to remind Browne that
Saint Augustine "retracted" his extreme grief for a friend, on
the ground that it resembled more the *"Rhetoricall* declama-
tions of a young *Orator,* then . . . the grave confession of a
devout *Christian."* Digby asked, darkly, "What censure upon
himselfe may wee expect of our *Physician,* if ever hee make
any retraction of this discourse concerning his *Religion?"* (p.
35). Browne added two moderating phrases, "I thinke" and
"mee thinkes upon some grounds" to the section in 1643, but
not to the portions that Digby found so extreme.

Browne's point (II, 8) that the pursuit of philosophical
knowledge leads to skepticism provided Digby with substantiation for his preconception that the dissatisfaction offered by
skepticism "is the unlucky fate of those that light upon wrong
*Principles"* (p. 35). Once again Digby cited Father White,
who this time provided a chain of *"Theorems* and demonstra-
tions of *Physickes"* that link as continuously as the principles
of mathematics. When Browne admitted that he humbly
shared Solomon's complaint "of ignorance in the height of
knowledge," Digby retorted that Solomon never complained
in this manner—although he did, according to Digby, lament
the futility of earthly knowledge, such as the names of plants,
when one should be attending to "divine contemplations and
affections" (p. 36). Once again Digby emphasized the values
of the next life, yet Browne's reservations about the vanity of
pursuing that knowledge which will be revealed to us after
death elicited Digby's mild disagreement. While Digby agreed
that all will be opened to us after death, he did not accept this
as a reason to forgo study in this life. There is "great advantage" and "contentment" in earthly study, for it protects
against deception. He maintained that "the salt of true *Learning,* the bitter *Wood* of *Study,* paineful meditation, and orderly consideration [cure] ignorance, folly and rashnesse" (p.
37). By *study* he did not mean penetration of the subtleties of
"clamorous *Schooles"* but pursuit of "solid and usefull notions"—not "windy vanities." Above all, he declared, the ha-
bitual pursuit of truth in this world will foster an "inclination"
toward further study in the next life. Whether the particular
"vanitie" is indulgence in liquor, tobacco, or women, each man

must "make his tast before-hand" and must cultivate and support his own choice. That one man's choice is not another's is exemplified by Digby through a juxtaposition of the apocryphal account of Archimedes' death and the vanities of "playne *Country* Gentlemen" for their husbandry (p. 38). Digby thus, by an irregular route, reaffirmed that "earnest affections" to knowledge in the next life must be initiated in this. Rational knowledge is man's "surest proppe" here and now and "perfecteth a man in that which constituteth him a man." Digby closed his disquisition, "confident" that all his readers would support him in requesting Browne to "keepe his *Bookes* open, and continue that *Progresse* he hath so happily begun" (p. 39). Digby's good-natured advice capped a generally humanistic appeal to uphold the study of earthly knowledge.

No reader, seriously or mildly interested in *Religio Medici,* can resist comment on Browne's views on procreation (II, 9). Digby was only the first of many. He addressed his comments directly to Dorset in a facetious tone that veiled a hope for agreement against Browne's "wish that wee might procreate and beget Children without the helpe of women or without any conjunction or commerce with that sweete, and bewitching *Sex.*" Even Plato sacrificed to the Graces and Mahomet made intercourse "the essence of his *Paradise.*" Browne "setteth marryage at too low a rate, which is assuredly the highest and devinest linke of humane society" (p. 39), while writing of Cupid and beauty like "the Learned *Greeke Reader* in *Cambridge* his courting of his *Mistris* out of *Stephens* his *Thesaurus*" (p. 40). Browne had married by 1641, yet the first sentence of this section (II, 9) began in 1642: "I was never yet once, and am resolved never to be married twice," which he then changed in 1643 to: "I was never yet once, and commend their resolutions who never marry twice"—an evasion of the truth about his new acquaintance with married life. He did change "*wish* that we might procreate like trees" to "*be content* that" [my italics], perhaps in response to Digby's remarks. Browne may also have eliminated from II, 9, a statement that Aristotle condemned "the 4th figure" in logic (*Analytica Priora,* 41b) because of Digby's syllogistic rebuttal.

Digby's continuous, entirely orthodox, and in no way sur-

prising emphasis on the higher nature of the next life seems to
have blinded him to a true understanding of Browne's style,
personality, and persuasiveness. Clearly, Digby did not comprehend how Browne's personal references to his equanimity
and to the "miracle" of his thirty years (I, 41; II, 11) could in
any way "conduce to any mans betterment" (p. 19), which
was, in Digby's mind, Browne's purpose for writing his book
(or for that matter any writer's purpose for writing any book).
On the basis of Browne's self-indulgent remarks, Digby concluded that the story of Browne's life would make a "notable
*Romanze.*" Margaret Bottrall has pointed out the irony that,
although slightly amused by Browne's idiosyncrasies, Digby
disapproved of them, yet he himself wrote for private con-
sumption a tale of his adventurous and highly idiosyncratic
courtship of Venetia Stanley.[44] Huntley explains Digby's disapproval on the basis that Digby was himself too conceited to
comprehend Browne's intention: to list his "own attainments
. . . to derogate himself in the praise of his Creator." Huntley
comments that Digby's personality "stands between the *Religio Medici* and [his] grasp of it" (pp. 141–42).

The intolerance with which Digby judged Browne's personal allusions is matched by the retort he offered (p. 40) to
Browne's love of such paradoxes as "There is no man bad, and
the worst, best" and "There is no man alone . . . though in a
Wildernesse" (II, 10). Digby found no value in such statements; he dismissed them as "*aequivocall* considerations, [not]
pertinent to the morality of that part where he treateth of
them." Such criticism sounds more like crabbed ill humor than
anything else, but no doubt such expressions rooted in an inability to admire the beauties of paradoxical truths other than
those produced by his own insights. As Coleridge said, Digby
should have seen the *Religio* "as a sweet Exhibition of character & passion, & not as an Expression or Investigation of
positive Truth" (p. 438). The greatest paradox of all is that
while Digby thought he was contemplating absolute moral
truths when he studied metaphysical problems, he dismissed
Browne's imaginative aphorisms as irrelevant and equivocal.

---

44. *Every Man a Phoenix*, 32–33. Digby's romance has been
published as *Private Memoirs of Sir Kenelm Digby*.

## Conclusions for a Long Night's Work

Digby concluded his *Observations* by gradual stages that suggest a series of afterthoughts. First, he found Browne's concluding prayer (II, 15) weak, "not winged with that fire which I should have expected from him upon this occasion" (p. 41). He disagreed with two thirds of Browne's ingredients for the happy life. In 1642 Browne prayed: "Blesse mee in this life with but the peace of my conscience, command of my affections, the love of my dearest friends, and I shall be happy enough to pity *Caesar*." Digby commented that a peaceful conscience and discipline over the emotions are not so important to the "perfect *Christian*"; instead, "Love onely that can give us *Heaven* upon earth, as well as in *Heaven*; and bringeth us thither too" is of importance. As he had earlier, in his objections to Browne's views on charity, Digby restricted the object of this higher love to God alone and disputed Browne's customary reference to the importance of the love of friends. Perhaps this rebuke motivated Browne to change his prayer in the 1643 edition to "the love of *thy selfe and* [my italics] my dearest friends." Having corrected Browne's temporality, Digby conceived the author's "intended *Theame*" as being that the love of God is "this transcendent and divine part of *Charity* that looketh directly and immediately upon God himselfe; and that is the intrinsecall forme, the utmost perfection, the scope and finall period of true *Religion*, . . . I have no occasion to speak of any thing, since my *Author* doth but transiently mention it; and that too, in such a phrase as ordinary *Catechismes* speake of it to vulgar capacities." The latter remarks probably refer to Browne's definition of charity (II, 14): "To love God for himselfe, and our neighbour for God. . . . Thus that part of our noble friends that wee love, is not the part we embrace, but that insensible part that our armes cannot embrace." Despite the simple beauty of this expression of Platonic love, Digby questioned both the proportion of Browne's argument and the commonness of his language.

Digby's second conclusion is an apology to Dorset for "how sleightly, upon so great a suddaine" he studied Browne's book and how audaciously he ventured "to consider any moles in that face which you had marked for a beauty." Digby justified his criticisms by defining the limitations he followed: "I offer not at *Judging* the prudence and wisedome of this discourse; Those are fit enquiries for your Lordships Court of highest appeale; in my inferiour one, I meddle onely with little knotty peeces of particular Sciences" (p. 42). Digby excused his special interests as too limited and too mediocre to be of importance to Dorset, whose "imployments are of a higher and nobler *Straine*; and that concerne the welfare of millions of men." Digby rated his book as close to those "low in ranke . . . low in their conceptions, and low in a languishing and rusting leisure," the last a reference to his comfortable imprisonment. In a strained analogy Digby described his own remarks as being as inconsequential as the complaints of an individual husbandman about his land when compared to the opinions of his ruler. So Digby apologized again for his "demurrer unto a few little particularities in that Noble discourse" (p. 43). Digby clearly intended to close his *Observations* with a request for a peace, without which "a generall ruine threatneth the whole *Kingdome*." That the long night's work was finished is shown by his speculation about the day, for after signing the 22nd, he parenthetically conjectured that it may be the 23rd, "for I am sure it is morning, and I thinke it is day." Thus the work was to end on a pleasant note of personal allusion. But the work was not to end, for Digby, having done some rereading, discovered that he had forgotten to complete his discussion of grace; so a final note was added. This afterthought was discussed earlier.

## A Divine Materialism

Sir Kenelm Digby distrusted both the intuitiveness and the worldliness of Sir Thomas Browne—the latter because Digby preferred man to concentrate on the spiritual values that are executed in the service of a watchful God; the former because he sought what he considered to be rational explanations for the immortality of the soul—the absolute chain of causation and the power of grace. Like Browne, Digby is a supremely transitional figure. Nearly a mechanist in his emphasis on an intelligible causation open to the rational mind, Digby yet expressed faith in eternal grace and reward.

Most of Digby's *Observations* are ephemeral and truncated. In them, he too often chastized Browne's inability to deal with metaphysical questions when he himself failed to deal with them adequately. Suspicious of metaphorical concepts, Digby nevertheless often neglected to define concretely his own views. He merely assumed that the test of reason and the truth of faith coincided in those beliefs which he held. Yet Digby's arguments are not deceitful, for he honestly sought naturalistic evidence to substantiate his metaphysical beliefs. By rejecting or tempering Platonic idealism or Hermetic mysticism in Browne, Digby appeared to uphold more materialistic explanations; but at the same time Digby thought Browne's charity and love of friendship too worldly and material in another sense. He moderated the heights of imagination and paradox in Browne by terming them flighty and unrealistic, then elaborated Browne's social and moral values into a nearly absolute servitude of man to a loving God. Actually, Browne and Digby were very close in their emphasis on the primacy of God and His will, but Digby would not recognize this near agreement. He must have thought the twistings and turnings of Browne's teleology ill-defined at best and "vulgar" at worst. While Browne wondered at the divine hand in human affairs, Digby rationalized its existence and moralized on its effect. Digby's system was too rigid and too mechanical to allow for the Janus-like Browne, who enjoyed paradox and contradiction. Digby searched for tangibility and reliability in his universe, so he expected the same qualities in *Religio*.

# IV.

## ALEXANDER ROSS

### The "Perpetual Barker" Responds

What explicit response Browne's Preface, "To the Reader," with its plea that his work not be subjected to "the rigid test of reason," might have drawn from Sir Kenelm Digby we shall never know. But Alexander Ross, in his *Medicus Medicatus* (1645), did not neglect Browne's overture. In a dedicatory epistle to Edward Benlowes, at whose request Ross "endeavoured . . . to open the mysteries of this Treatise, so much cried up by those, whose eyes pierce no deeper than the *Superficies*; and their judgements, then the *outsides* of things," Ross took issue immediately with Browne's alleged attempt to evade close scrutiny. Browne had cautioned the reader that "there are many things delivered Rhetorically, many expressions therein meerely Tropicall, and as they best illustrate my intention; and therefore also there are many things to be taken in a soft and flexible sence, and not to be called unto the rigid test of reason." To this request for reserved judgment Ross retorted: "Expect not here from mee *Rhetoricall* flourishes; I study matter, not words . . . as I suspect that friendship, which is set out in too many *Verball Complements*; so doe I that Religion, which is trimmed up with too many *Tropicall* Pigments, and *Rhetoricall dresses*. If the gold be pure, why feares it the Touch-stone? The *Physician* will trie the *Apothecaries* drugges, ere hee make use of them for his Patients bodie; and shall wee not trie the ingredients of that Religion, which is accounted the physick of our soules?"[1] Then Ross rounded out his introduction with complimentary remarks to Benlowes and with excuses that begged indulgence for his own work: the lack of adequate time, books, and quiet to do his task at its best.

1. *Medicus Medicatus*, sigs. A3–A4. Quoted by permission of The Newberry Library, Chicago, Illinois. Subsequent references will be given internally.

Benlowes and Ross held much the same opinion of Browne's moderation and his lack of partisanship in the struggles of the established orthodoxy against Roman Catholic and Puritan encroachments. It was Benlowes' disapproval of tolerance for Catholics that prompted him to request that his friend answer both Browne and Digby. The need for rebuttal was largely sectarian and political in motive, for Benlowes' interest in contemporary theoretical and scientific questions was slight and unenlightened. Benlowes himself attacked the Pope in his Latin poem *Papa Perstrictus* later that same year.[2] So Ross also may have been "perfectly aware that he is in an intellectually antagonistic world,"[3] for he wrote as one defending a sanctified position that had been brutally assaulted.

Born in 1590–1 in Aberdeen, Scotland, and educated at the university there, Ross enjoyed the patronage of Edward Seymour, Earl of Hertford, and thus became Master of the Free School at Southampton and one of the chaplains to Prince Charles prior to the civil war. He eventually became Vicar of Carisbrooke in the Isle of Wight and died in the parkhouse at Bramsell in Hampshire in 1654. He left a considerable fortune accumulated from patronage and from the sales of his books. According to Anthony à Wood, "among the many rich legacies" in his will were: "200 livres to the senate of Aberdeen, to remain for ever towards the maintenance of two scholars that shall be born in the town of Aberdeen, and educated in Grammar there, 50 l. to the town of Southampton, for the better maintenance of the schoolmaster, 50 l. to the poor housholdkeepers of All-saints parish there, 50 l. to the public library at Cambridge, 5 l. to that of Oxon., & C. Andrew Henley . . . was his executor, who had his library . . . wherein, mostly in the books, he found, as I have been credibly informed, about a thousand pound in gold."[4] Thomas Denne, who studied Latin and Logic under Ross and died in his house in 1648, recommended *Medicus Medicatus* to Henry Oxinden "because it is

2. Harold Jenkins, *Edward Benlowes (1602–1676): Biography of a Minor Poet*, 149, 109, 151.

3. Foster Watson, "Alexander Ross: Pedant Schoolmaster of the Age of Cromwell," *Gentleman's Magazine*, 279 (1895), 473.

4. Wood, *Athenae Oxonienses*, ed. Philip Bliss, II, 241–42; Watson, 472; and John Bowle, *Hobbes and His Critics*, 17–18.

generally applauded,"[5] but Thomas Hobbes, referring to Ross's attacks on *Leviathan*, wrote in 1654: "And yet here we must complain of want of sufficiencie or ingenuitie, to acknowledge the truths, or confute the errors of that book, which till it is done, we shall not count the Author an Heretick. On this side the sea, besides the dirt and slander cast on him in Sermons and private meetings, none hath put any thing in Print against him, but Mr. Rosse, one who may be said to have had so much Learning as to have been perpetually barking at the works of the most learned."[6]

### Tolerance Subverted

At the beginning of his work Ross established his attitude: he repeated, then disregarded—obviously with sarcastic intent —Browne's desire for a temperate assessment: "We must be bold to let him know, that our reason is not given to us in vaine: shall we suffer ourselves to be wilfully blind-folded?" (p. 1). Although Ross's complaint might have been justifiable, his attack was not. That Ross's avowal of rationality was not merely one of objectivity or tempered judgment appears in his remarks that compare Browne's "stupidity" to a triad of analogies: the parable of the tares, the proverb "All is not gold that glisters," and the subversion of the Trojan horse. Aligning himself with the perceptive "*Laacon,*" Ross rhetorically answered his own questions about "the *traps* and *snares* laid in our waies" (pp. 1–2). The rationale offered by Ross is in no way rigid in Browne's sense. Rather than examining Browne's private remarks with too close an eye for consistency—a rational criterion that might otherwise be considered commendable although somewhat inappropriate to Browne's random impressions—Ross scrutinized *Religio* according to his own subjective preconception, rational only in a selfish sense of personal conviction.

Ross's mind is shown as much in what he did not comment

5. *The Oxinden and Peyton Letters, 1642–1670,* ed. Dorothy Gardiner, 76.

6. "The Epistle to the Reader," *Of Liberty and Necessity,* ed. Baron Cay V. Brockdorff, sigs. A7b–A8a. See Bowle and Samuel I. Mintz, *The Hunting of the Leviathan,* for studies of Ross's *Leviathan Drawn Out With a Hook.*

upon as in what he considered worthy of attention. He passed over the first sections of *Religio*, in which Browne stated his purposes and declared his Anglicanism, but I, 3, which opens by designating the danger inherent to those pledged to pressing differences of opinion, drew his comment. Browne's tolerance for divergent opinions and Ross's anger aroused by that tolerance comprise the first general area of disagreement worthy of examination.

Although Browne did not specify the Roman Catholic church as he examined the common basis of faith that should bridge the arbitrary barriers separating devout Christians, Ross never doubted that the hated Roman Catholics were meant. Naturally, Ross overlooked Browne's cautions against extremism and condensed his point about a common faith to this: "He tells me that between us and the Church of Rome there is one faith." So stated, the subtlety of Browne's oblique argument is lost and the expansiveness of his appeal negated. Thus Ross construed, at least for his reader's sake, that Browne "will have us beleeve with the *Romanists*" on six dogmatic positions that Ross interjected, knowing that the points would be unacceptable to most of his conservative readers: priests as equal mediators with Christ, transubstantiation, prayer to saints, the equality of papal authority with scriptural, the acceptance of the Apocrypha, and the adoration of images. Despite the sternness of Ross's damnation of any compromise with Catholicism, a flicker of ironic humor leavens his comments in the stipulation that Browne would have those of "one faith" accept enough dogma to "merit both of congruity and condignity, yea supererogate." Ross closed his first series of criticisms with a strained pun: "If our faith be all one . . . this may be indeed *religio Medici*, the religion of the House of *Medicis*" (p. 2). Clearly, Ross was treating Browne's work with ridicule, not with objective analysis.

Ross next paraphrased Browne in such a way as to have Browne stating that he was "not scrupulous in defect of our Churches to enter Popish Churches, and pray with Papists; for though the Heathen temples polluted the Israelites, yet the Popish impieties are not such as pollute their temples, or our prayers made in them." Even though Ross's summaries distort Browne's tolerance almost into intolerance, they still leave

Ross matter to criticize. He listed a number of observations that vary in their misapplication to Browne's thinking: a series of scriptural examples disprove the necessity of praying in church; praying with papists "is . . . a confirming of their Idolatry"; mixing with Roman Catholics "is a scandall to the weaker brethren, and woe to him by whom scandall cometh"; such conduct "argues notorious dissimulation . . . and we know what *Simulata Sanctitae* is," Ross hinted darkly; praying with Catholics necessitates echoing their words; the "Popist Churches, being actually imployed about Idolatry" are worse than the heathen who worshipped the sun and the moon, which are, at least, God's creations, rather than images made by man (pp. 3–4). Then Ross listed four categories of idolatry: "1. *Hermeticall*, which is the worship of Images: 2. *Poeticall*, the worship of deified men: 3. *Physicall*, the worship of the great *Platonick* animall, the world, or the part thereof: 4. *Metaphysicall*, the worship of Angels, or other created spirits" (p. 4). He concluded that Catholics practice all except the third of these.

Picking out Browne's declaration of religious sentiment in the presence of any devotional object, Ross offhandedly commended Browne's frequent remembrance of Christ, then pointedly reminded him that these objects are not the true source for the recognition of Christ's presence, for His legacy is "his *Words* and *Sacraments*." In fact, the sight of idols such as a crucifix should "excite his indignation." We must react as Moses and "*ezechia*" did before the golden calf, for is not silence "a secret consent . . . wherein God is dishonoured?" (pp. 4–5). Ross ignored Browne's temperate acknowledgment that, while such religious objects reflect sincere commemoration, they are employed many times for their emotional appeal to the masses. To Ross's mind, Browne's candid admission of religious stimulation by contact with the trappings of the Roman church far overrides Browne's own condemnation of the encouragement of superstition such symbols might have among the vulgar.

Next, Browne's criticism of the prejudiced for their mockery of "a solemne Procession," which caused him to weep "abundantly," drew Ross's conjecture that the mockers were playing the "part of Democritus." Ross asked who has the greater blindness, "He that laughs at the folly of superstitious Processions, or he that weeps out of a preposterous devotion?" (p. 5). Addressing Browne directly, Ross commended his weeping if it was out of pity for the processioners, but he expressed doubt, based on Browne's words, that such was the case; he charged Browne with lacking "the heart and Christian courage to reprove such Idolatry" (p. 6) and suggested that Browne weep for himself because he had made others' idolatry his own. The frankness of Browne's confession of faith was wasted on Ross. To the latter, tolerance suggested a gullible piety, dangerous in its ramifications. In contrast to Browne's penetrating self-analysis, Ross spoke ex cathedra.

The contemporary reader of Ross's animadversions would probably not have been surprised at the author's passing over Browne's generalized remarks in the first two sections of *Religio* in order to concentrate his opening attack on the details of tolerant behavior described in I, 3. Browne was treading dangerous ground when he became so specific. Actually, his moderation would not have been so unusual in the 1630s, but in 1642 it was ill-timed and generative of conflict. The decade preceding Ross's attack had seen the publication of many more deliberative and perceptive discussions of the dangerous authority of the Roman Catholic church than Browne's personal impressions reveal. That vested interests, whether clerical, social, or political, were feeling the strain imposed by the spread of moderate thought may be intimated by Ross's alarm. Social and political tolerance of Roman Catholicism in England had become dangerous. The missionary activities of the Jesuits and their rise to prominence at court during the 1630s had intensified the opposing pressures, which erupted in the civil conflict of the 1640s. An increase in conversions in high places, the identification of the Roman church with French and Spanish policies distasteful to some Englishmen, and the open presence of sympathies with Rome in church and court contributed to the mounting bitterness among Puritans and conservative Anglicans and Presbyterians.

Questions of the laity's responsibility to religious authority were also in Browne's mind in the early sections of *Religio*. In I, 5, Browne stated his preference to follow the dictates of reason and his own "humor and fashion" rather than any ex-

ternal authority. As for his attitude toward the Pope, Browne
extended more charity to the prelate than he expected to receive, though he denounced the outcries of the vulgar against
Rome. Such relativism could make little appeal or sense to
Ross and those to whom he spoke.

Here Ross again passed over with no comment much that
Browne wrote, preferring to attack that portion which is charitable to that feared enemy, the Pope. Ross listed his objections
to Browne's position: (a) Christ refused temporal power, so
how can the Pope both follow Him and be a temporal prince?
(b) the terms by which we address the Pope are no worse than
those used by Christ against Herod and the rabbis; (c) the
language Browne termed "popular scurrilities" is the same
used in Scripture to describe the Pope; (d) we may " 'suffer
without reaction' in particular wrongs, but not when Gods
glory is in question. . . . To suffer God to be wronged, and not
to be moved, is not charity, but luke-warmness or stupidity."
Finally, Ross cited examples showing that "we give the *Pope*
no other language, then what he hath received of his owne
party" (p. 7) and then concluded with a long list of charges
against various Popes who "have justly deserved these titles, if
you look on their flagitious lives, and hereticall doctrine" (pp.
7–8): "What duties of good language do we owe to *Zephe-
rinus* a *Montanist*, to *Marcellinus* an *Idolator*, *Liberius* an
*Arian*, *Anastasius* a *Nestorian*, *Vigilius* an *Eutychian*, *Ho-
norius* a *Monothelite*, *Sylvester* a *Necromantick*; *John* the 23.
that denied the resurrection, and others? What shall I speak
of *Sylvester* the second, *Benedict* the ninth, *John* the 20. and
21. *Gregory* the seventh, &c. who gave themselves to Sathan
and Witchcraft? I will say nothing of their Apostasies, Idola-
tries, Whoredomes, Blasphemies, Cruelties, Simonies, Tyran-
nie, &c." (p. 8).

Such embellishments only serve to cap earlier allusions in
the passage. Ross's citations of Christ's rejection of a temporal
kingdom and of Christ's driving the moneychangers from the
Temple were commonplaces of the time. His panorama of
heretical Popes reveals a learned but peculiar perspective on
controversies within church history. Yet much of what he introduced lacks direct relevance to Browne's ideas. They had

become mere stalking-horses for Ross's charges on the dubious-
ness of papal authority. Nevertheless, with his sense of the
imperative, he addressed Browne directly as if to suggest an
intuitive knowledge of a mind that maintained such a sup-
posedly rash tolerance. He directed Browne to read the writings of Saint Bernard and those "who have sufficiently demonstrated the forgery" (p. 6) of *The Donation of Constantine*.
By coupling the spirituality of Saint Bernard and the worldliness of Constantine, Ross established, perhaps unconsciously,
the poles of his polemic. He did not elaborate beyond these
allusions but veered off to continue on his erratic way. Yet
Saint Bernard's position that a spiritual leader must be
schooled in the monastic virtues—not in war or politics, which
are better left to the Christian prince[7]—reinforces the dichotomy Ross supported. A typical Ross maneuver is the inter-
jection of *The Donation*, which had become an embarrassment to the Catholic position, since it implied forgery.

Ross's catalogue of heretical Popes includes fourteen men
who have, ever since their reigns, aroused controversies of one
kind or another. While Ross could not prove Browne guilty of
any of their supposed heresies, he could taint Browne with
guilt by association in vaguely relating him to all of them.

Section I, 6, of *Religio* opens with Browne's declaration of
abstention from religious disputes: "I could never divide my
selfe from any man upon the difference of an opinion, or be
angry with his judgement for not agreeing with mee in that,
from which perhaps within a few dayes I should dissent my
selfe. I have no Genius to disputes in Religion, and have often
thought it wisedome to decline them." Browne's humorous
advice on the futility of argument was wasted on Ross, who
attacked Browne's lack of enthusiasm for proselytism. Every
Christian, Ross believed, must argue fiercely, for "not to dispute against an Heretick, is not to fight against an enemy." He
attacked the single-mindedness with which Browne sought to
"follow the great wheele of the Church" and with a burst of
allusions condemned those who would always follow the
"broad way." What if "this *Wheele* is sometime out of order,"

7. Hayden V. White, "The Gregorian Ideal and Saint Bernard
of Clairvaux," *JHI*, 21 (1960), 343.

(p. 9) as was Judaism in the time of Christ, or Christianity, with the rise of Arianism, in the time of Athanasius? Ross's admiration for Athanasius is paradoxical in the light of the charitable behavior the latter afforded individual heretics. He closed this passage with an apocalyptic gesture reminding Browne of Christ's prophecy that at His return He would find little faith upon earth—implying, according to Ross, that the "great wheele" may always be untrustworthy (p. 10). Thus, the reactionary Ross showed himself always quick to disparage the middle way. The inconsistency between Browne's espousal of the Church's teachings in preference to individual religious conclusions and his questioning of the Church's grasp on the truth was not investigated by Ross. Instead, he was content to appear as one of the true believers who in times of crisis insist that their way is the only way.

Later in his examination of *Religio*, Ross allowed no room for latitude to admit the possibility that "those honest Worthies and Philosophers which dyed before [Christ's] In- carnation" (I, 54) might have been redeemed, despite their ignorance of Christ. Ross was absolutely certain that salvation is only through Christ. The only amelioration of the ancients' eternal lot is that "it will be easier for them . . . in the last day, then for *Jewes* and *Christians*, who have knowne their Mas- ters will, and have not done it" (p. 63).

Ross had no sympathy for Browne's magnanimous opinion (I, 56, another new section added in 1643) that the Christian Church existed in Africa and in Asia. While Ross did not summarily deny that there were some Christians in those places, he held that the evidence offered by Browne did not give "stabilitie or permanencie to the Church there" (p. 63). Ross then embarked on a list of the heresies associated with the Eastern church, which represented for him "rather *Scele-tons*, then the body of *Christ*" (p. 64). Most of the sects men- tioned were, in Ross's opinion, either more heretical than the Roman Catholic church or Romanist themselves. By such reasoning, Ross could object to Browne's liberal avoidance of sectarian conflicts in the England of the 1640s and at the same time condemn Browne's religious breadth with just the kind of intolerance that Brown decried.

### Strictures on the Body and Soul

Ross's complaints against Browne were not limited to his allegedly naive tolerance. He also found Browne's thinking defective on particular points of faith, for example, on the immortality of the soul.

Browne's admission of three youthful errors (I, 7) drew ample discussion from Ross, who advised the reading of Plato's *Timaeus* and *Philebus* and of Aristotle's *De Anima* on the soul's immortality, since Browne had doubted that philosophy had provided any proof. It is ridiculous that Ross should advise Browne to read Plato, but he did. He attacked, not the heresy of mortalism directly, but instead the minor point that philosophy has not disproved mortalism. He seems to have been more intent on improving Browne's knowledge of Platonic and Aristotelian proofs than on warning against the danger of heresy. He listed seven evidences of the soul's immortality:

1. *The soule is of an heavenly and quintessentiall nature, not of an elementary.* 2. *The soule is a simple substance, not compounded of any principles; therefore can be resolved unto none. . . . 3. As the soule hath neither matter nor forme in it, so neither are there in it any contrarieties: now all generation and corruption are by contraries. This is the reason why Philosophy denieth any generation or corruption in the Heavens, because they are void of contrarieties. 4. It is a Maxime in Philosophy, Quod secundum se alicui convenit, est ab eo inseparbile; therefore life is inseparable from the soule, because it lives by it selfe not by another, as the body doth, or by accident, as the souls of beasts do. 5. Mens soule have subsistence by themselves, not by their composita, as accidents, and the formes of beasts have; which is the cause of their decay. 6. The soule hath a naturall desire to immortality, which if it should not enjoy, that desire were given to it from God in vaine. . . . 7. If the soule perish it must be resolved to nothing; for it can not be resolved unto any principles, as not being made of them: if some thing can be resolved unto nothing, then some thing was made of nothing; but Philosophy denies this; therefore it must needs deny that, of the corruption of the soule, and consequently, it holds the soules immortality.* (Pp. 11–12)

Ross's description of the properties of the soul is distinctly Aristotelian, although the list he compiled does not match precisely the doctrine of Aristotle. Both the conception of the superiority of the heavens and the view that generation and decay take place through contraries may be found in a single passage in *De Caelo* (270a13–23), but the transference of these remarks wholesale to the nature of the soul overstates the point. While Aristotle denied in part that the soul is indivisible, he did explain the soul in terms of its parts: the nutritive, the appetitive, the sensory, the locomotive, and the intellective. Thus, the soul is in some mysterious manner compounded although Aristotle did not term it such.

Ross's remarks about the soul come primarily from Aristotle's view on the intellective faculty of the soul—the presence of the mind. It is this component that is as superior and as independent from the body as Ross would state the entire soul to be. The soul, in Aristotle, is closely related to its body, although the union is an unequal one: "If, then, we have to give a general formula applicable to all kinds of soul, we must describe it as the first grade of actuality of a natural organized body. That is why we can wholly dismiss as unnecessary the question whether the soul and the body are one. . . . Unity has many senses (as many as 'is' has), but the most proper and fundamental sense of both is the relation of an actuality to that of which it is the actuality" (*De Anima*, 412b5–10). The soul, to Aristotle, was not as free from matter or from the body as it was to Ross. In fact, Aristotle believed that "the soul is inseparable from its body, or at any rate that certain parts of it are (if it has parts)—for the actuality of some of them is nothing but the actualities of their bodily parts" (*De Anima*, 413a4–6). The only transcendent feature of the soul is the mind (the thinking and the judging faculty), which "cannot reasonably be regarded as blended with the body: if so, it would acquire some quality, e.g. warmth or cold, or even have an organ like the sensitive faculty" (429a21–26).

Ross thus endowed the soul with higher powers not precisely found in Aristotle's analysis. This heavenly essence of the individual soul, with its priority over body or matter —so important to Ross—cannot be found with certainty in Plato's *Timaeus*. Although the accepted connotation of a macrocosmic–microcosmic relationship is there, Plato spoke more directly of a world–soul (34b–35a). Despite Ross's confident statement that the "soul hath neither matter nor forme," Plato and Aristotle did not so argue. Plato's proposition is that the soul, although susceptible to the diseases of the body (*Timaeus*, 86b; *The Republic*, 611b–e), rises above them, with only the body being left to die while the soul passes through the cycle of reincarnation. Plato's myths on the immortality of the soul were either ignored by Ross or disparaged whenever Browne showed fondness for them. Ross's contention that the "soule hath a naturall desire to immortality" approximates Plato (*Timaeus*, 90) when he presented the soul as yearning for a spiritual existence in the superior realm of true reality transcending the mutable—thus inferior —material world. Although *Timaeus* substantiates the view that the soul through its unity with the world–soul subsists independently of the body (30a), there are difficulties involved in defining the Platonic ideal in relation to the Christian concept of the individual soul. It is questionable that the spiritual essence, passing back and forth from this world to the next and then returning to join another body, is identical with the immortal soul in which Ross believed. So, too, Aristotle's contention that the soul is inseparable from the body to which it gives life could do little to reinforce Ross's religious view.

Since the Platonic myths did not appeal to Ross, he suggested *Philebus* as a possible explanation of spiritual immortality. This late dialogue examines more directly the question of pleasure, so the nature of the soul arises significantly during a discussion of the mixture of pleasure and intelligence in life, in which the possibility of "limits" is raised. The work presents the conception of a cosmic order, governed by reason, within which a cosmic soul—much like that described in *Timaeus*—coexists with bodily elements fragmented from the physical universe and spiritual elements corresponding to the world–soul (*Philebus*, 30a–b). So Ross's case for immortality and the separation of the body and the soul in the afterlife is based on qualitative differences, not directly on mythic or supernatural accounts. That his motives were scientific or philosophic rather than religious and ethical is dubious. Ultimately, his explanation of immortality is a preconception based on faith and Scripture and merely affixed to the Greek accounts. Biblical evidence would have been held by him as the supreme authority while Platonic myth would have been dismissed as invalid. But he attempted to discuss the soul as a philosophical entity rather than as an instrument of salvation or rebirth. Further reading shows that belief in an eternal system of reward and punishment confirmed his emphasis on the soul's immortality, so no appeal to a Platonic quest for true justice was needed. In fact, Ross's next answer to Browne dismissed any protestations about our unworthiness to be immortal; they were, he wrote, only the wishful doubting of the sinful who would prefer to escape immortality because it signifies "torments, rather than sleep or rest" (p. 13).

Ross was offended by Browne's acceptance of Origen's belief that God in His infinite mercy will "release the damned soules from torture" (I, 7). Ross reminded Browne that Saint Augustine had shown "how pernicious this opinion . . . is, for . . . it destroyes Gods justice" (p. 13). Augustine had extended Origen's argument to its ultimate conclusion: "Which opinion, if it is good and true because it is merciful, will be so much the better and truer in proportion as it becomes more merciful. . . . And yet they dare not extend their pity further, and propose the deliverance of the devil himself" (*The City of God*, XXI, 17). Ross argued that God's mercy is "regulated by his owne wisedome, not by our conceipts." Scripture instructs us in the boundaries of God's temperament, so if some are made melancholy by the thought of eternal fire, they must think instead of eternal bliss (p. 14). Ross was not swayed by Browne's expansive conception of God's mercy, but a contemporary, George Rust, writing on Origen's opinion, expressed his belief that, if God truly created nothing in vain and if He pronounced what He created as being "good," then in His foresight some release must have been planned for the damned as well as the saved. Leading into a corollary in Origen's thought that the damned will be released so they may try again to fulfill the aim God had set for them, Rust explained that even the end of the world does not mean eternal death or eternal punishment.[8] Rust's (and Origen's) argument, based on the "gracious providence of God, or the necessity of the Nature of things," would probably have caught

8. A *Letter of Resolution Concerning Origen and the Chief of His Opinions*, ed. Marjorie Hope Nicolson, 80–81.

Browne's liking, since his main concern was a merciful release
from eternal torture, the eternal fire that Ross maintained is
ever necessary.

Browne's third error, in Ross's judgment, was a charitable
inclination toward prayer for the dead. Ross's answers are
commonplaces: Such prayer is "needlesse" for the saved and
"fruitlesse" for the damned; such prayer reveals a belief in
purgatory, which is "injurious to the bloud of *Christ*" because
He "purged us"; such prayer has no scriptural basis. Primitive
Christians did not pray to or for the martyrs but "rehearsed"
their names "that they might not be obliterated by silence,
and that posterity might know that they were in blisse." Ross
therefore surmised that prayer for the dead is another of those
superstitions which have "crept by degrees into the *Church*"
(pp. 15–16).

Browne's preference for "Platonick" and "allegorical" descriptions (I, 10) rather than "Metaphysicall" ones did not
please Ross, who preferred to define the soul as "first *act* and
*perfection* of the body" (p. 17) over Browne's fancies about
the soul being man's angel or the body of God. Ross first dismissed as "absurd" the theory that "*Soules* and *Angels* are of
the same *Species*, . . . seeing the one . . . subsist without bodies,
so are not the other: the one are *intellective*, the other *rationall*
substances" (p. 18). In other words, angels are capable of
understanding without having to resort to organic reasoning,
as man's soul or mind must do. Ross thus incorporated intellect in an Aristotelian sense, although Aristotle was speaking in part in a Platonic sense: "It was a good idea to call the
soul 'the place of forms,' though (1) this description holds
only of the intellective soul, and (2) even this is the forms
only potentially, not actually" (*De Anima*, 429a26–29). Ross
was here brushing against Platonism himself, even though
more directly he was thinking of the distinction made by
Aristotle between the active intellect and the passive intellect.
The latter is "potential" and is "in time prior to actual knowledge, but in the universe as a whole it is not prior even in
time." The former is "actual" and "is identical with its object"
(430a20–21). Aristotle's discussion is elliptical and only superficially parallels Ross's dichotomy between souls and angels.

Ross continued with his argument that if the understanding

intellect subsists without substance, then angels must differ
not only *"specifically"*—that is, as to species, but also *"numerically"*—that is, quantitatively or in particularity—from
the souls of men (p. 18). If Ross had attended to Browne's
discussion of angels in I, 33, he would have found the distinction there in Browne's statement that angels "have knowledge
not onely of the specificall, but the numericall formes of indi-
vidualls." Ross's desire to assert the immortality of angels
continued throughout his career, for in his *Leviathan Drawn
Out With a Hook* (1653) he attacked Hobbes's efforts to
reconcile angels with the materiality of all created things.
Ross's citation of "the Schooles" in support of his case seems
strange in the light of his bias, but Protestant writers on
angels sometimes used Catholic authorities for support of
their statements. The degree of Ross's concern may well be
measured by the strength of his retorts to Browne, who
showed little inclination toward corporeal interpretations of
spiritual beings. Ross usually followed scriptural authority
faithfully, but he deviated sharply in his disagreement with
Browne's statement that angels know of the affairs of men,
according to Luke xv:10. Ross retorted that such omnipotence
is only God's. He continued his argument, in the Thomistic
mode, that the knowledge angels have is dependent upon
God. He then embarked on a rebuttal to Browne's liking for
the metaphor that termed light a "spirituall Substance, and
may bee an Angell." What kind of "a skipping Angell will
*ignis fatuus* make? The Chandlers and Bakers trades are
honourable; those can make lights, which may in time become
Angels; those wafers, which in time become gods" (pp. 42–
43). In preferring the material explanation for the nature of
light, he also ignored Augustine's identification of light with
angels (*The City of God*, xi, 9). To be sure, Browne, from his
theocentric stance, would have agreed with Ross's traditional
stipulation that all knowledge goes back to God.

Ross's ire was also aroused by Browne's rejection of his
master Aristotle and the Schoolmen. The unseen Body of God
posited by Browne (I, 10) was analogous to the Platonic
world–soul, against which Ross objected so frequently. Use of
the metaphor, God's body, compelled Ross to argue that God

is incorporeal, for if He contains matter "there must be in him a *passive possibility*, and quantity also, and distinction of parts, all which *essentially* follow the matter" (p. 18). If God and our souls are compounded of elements, he continued, then "God must be after our soules, and must be subject to some cause; for every compound hath a cause of its composition." Would it not be better, Ross asked, to reject this "strange God" and "admit the *metaphysicall* definition of the soule, to wit, *actus primus corporis naturalis organici potentia vitam habentis*" (p. 19), which is Aristotle's proposition that "the soul is the first grade of actuality of a natural body having life potentially in it" (*De Anima*, 412a27–28). Ross, in his disdain for a metaphorical description, once again cast his support to a semicorporeal but Aristotelian one. Aristotle needed to determine whether the souls "belong to the class of potential existents, or is it not rather an actuality? Our answer to this question is of the greatest importance" (402a25–27). Rejecting the theories of his predecessors, Aristotle identified matter with potentiality, form with actuality; thus, the soul "must be a substance in the sense of the form of a natural body having life potentially within it" (412a20–21). But there are two kinds of actuality, "that of knowledge as possessed," which would be the actuality of the soul, and "the actual exercise of knowledge," which would refer to the body (412a21–23). The need for the qualification "first actuality" means that the soul is the form of a body that has life and "organs" or organization (412b1–5). Later, Aristotle settled the question of the relationship of the body and the soul by returning to his conceptions of matter as potentiality and form as actuality: "Reflection confirms the observed fact; the actuality of any given thing can only be realized in what is already potentially that thing, i.e. in a matter of its own appropriate to it. From all this it follows that soul is an actuality or formulable essence of something that possesses a potentiality of being besouled" (414a25–28). Ross closed his attack on Browne's Platonism with this slur: "You were as good speak out in plaine terms with *Plato*, and tell us, that the world is a great animal, whereof God is the soule" (p. 19). Probably, Ross was alluding here to *Timaeus* (30c): "In the likeness of what animal did the creator make the world?" Ross conveniently ignored Plato's rejection of a model based on any one animal, since the world encompasses all creatures.

Browne's discussion of traduction and the union of the soul and the body in I, 36, provoked another long rebuttal by Ross, who listed ten reasons against the belief that the soul and the body are conceived together. Ross contended that the soul is immaterial, self-existent, immortal, noble, spiritual, nonseminal and nontransmutable. These qualities are confirmed by the authority of the Church, the ancients (Aristotle and Apuleius), and Scripture. These qualities of the soul affirm that it is separate from the body and superior to it, Ross believed (pp. 46–47). Although Ross cited particularly *De Generatione Animalium* as support, Aristotle's explanation of the union of the soul and the body is not entirely consonant with Ross's viewpoints. For example, the soul, although independent of matter, is transmitted seminally: "Has the semen soul, or not? The same argument applies here as in the question concerning the parts. As no part, if it participate not in soul, will be a part except in an equivocal sense (as the eye of a dead man is still called an 'eye'), so no soul will exist in anything except that of which it is soul; it is plain therefore that semen both has soul, and is soul, potentially" (*De Generatione Animalium*, 735a5–8). So, too, the embryo has soul potentially, but not actually. Ross called on Aristotle's authority with particular reference to the fact that "the Intellect" enters "into the body from without" (p. 47). There is little about the soul or the mind in *De Generatione Animalium*, although Aristotle did speak directly of "the Reason": "It remains, then, for the reason alone so to enter and alone to be divine, for no bodily activity has any connexion with the activity of reason" (736b27–29). Nevertheless, it is clear that epigenesis forms the center of the Aristotelian theory of generation and embryology.[9]

We have already seen Aristotle's conception of the mind in *De Anima*, but to return to it here will not be irrelevant. To Aristotle the mind "seems to be an independent substance

9. I am indebted throughout my discussion to Walter Pagel, *William Harvey's Biological Ideas*, 235–37.

implanted within the soul and to be incapable of being destroyed" (*De Anima*, 408b18–19). Seemingly, the mind combines with the soul, but the mind "cannot reasonably be regarded as blended with the body: if so, it would acquire some quality, e.g. warmth or cold, or even have an organ like the sensitive faculty: as it is, it has none" (429a24–26). Thus, the mind or intellect never actually combines with the body, although the soul and the body do merge in some living sense: "The body cannot be the actuality of the soul; it is the soul which is the actuality of a certain kind of body. Hence the rightness of the view that the soul cannot be without a body, while it cannot *be* a body; it is not a body but something relative to a body. That is why it is *in* a body, and a body of a definite kind. It was a mistake, therefore, to do as former thinkers did, merely to fit it into a body without adding a definite specification of the kind or character of that body" (414a17–24). Ross deviated from this exact description, preferring a God who creates first the body then the soul, later in the same order lets the body die then reclaims the soul. By this explanation Ross escaped the—to him—pitfalls of both traduction and pre-existence. The temper in which Ross approached this entire question is shown by his citation of Psyche in Apuleius as an example that the "soule is not infused, till the body be first framed" (p. 47). Later (pp. 78–79), Ross used the same argument to counter Browne's marvelous phrase, "something that was before the Elements" (II, 11).

As for the puzzling question of the "tincture and impression of reason" which Browne detected in the "monstrous productions . . . of man with beast" (I, 36), Ross answered that more reason is found in an elephant than in these monsters. Further, reason is not transferred in the seed of man, but "infused into the body, when it is articulated"; otherwise, if the soul of man were "transfused into beasts" the offspring would be "capable of salvation and damnation, of faith and the Sacraments, and the other mysteries of Religion"; the impossibility of this phenomenon occurring bears its own denial (pp. 47–48). Noticeably, Ross did not deny the possibility of humans and animals reproducing. He had earlier rejected Browne's claim that there "is a kind of beauty" in monstrosity

(I, 16), saying that, instead, it was "their monstrosity and irregularity that makes them remarkable," thus drawing attention but not "delight" to them (p. 24).

When Browne declared that the body is not the "instrument . . . of the soule, but rather of sense" (I, 36), Ross countered that the sense is dependent upon the body, rather than the reverse. Finally, Ross stated that Browne should not have expected to "find in the braine the organ of the rationall soule," for, as Browne said, this absence argues for the "soules inorganitie"; however, Ross in agreeing with Browne on this point was not disturbed by the similarity of the human and the animal cranium because "mans braine differs *specifically*," that is, in species. Ross concluded that the brain is indeed the "seat of reason" because the senses and the fancy or imagination originate there and are then used by the rational soul as it sees fit (p. 49). There was apparently for Ross no mystery in this relationship.

Ross reaffirmed through biblical example the doctrine of the transcendence of the soul in answer to Browne's mortalistic speculation (I, 39) that the soul may remain for a time in the grave with the body. Ross held that Scripture and not the philosopher's stone should be Browne's guide in this matter (p. 51). But it is evident that Ross misread the passage, for he thought that Browne was denying immortality by stating that the soul sleeps within the house of flesh. What Browne meant is clearly shown by his allusion to "those strange and mysticall transmigrations that I have observed in Silkwormes." Browne was here speaking of the presence of the soul within the body during its earthly existence, followed by the casting off of the bodily at the time of transcendence.

Ross's numerous objections to Browne's theory of the regenerated plant (I, 48) may serve as a summary of his views on form and matter, soul and body. Browne held that the form of the plant could not be destroyed and that the plant would grow again out of its ashes. Ross answered that, if the form of the plant remains, then it has not been "consumed" by the flames; any philosophy that tells us that matter is eternal while form perishes is deceiving us. If the plant is regenerated, then "Art and Nature is all one, both being able to introduce, or rather, educe a substantiall forme" (pp. 55–56). If the plant survives the fire, then the "radicall moisture and naturall heat" that are necessary for the survival of the form were not consumed by the fire, but instead "lurkes within the ashes." If the plant survives, the "effect is nobler than the cause"; if the cause has been removed, then "there may be a naturall regresse." The form that "actuates, distinguishes, denominates, defines, & perfects the matter" must still be in the ashes, like "in the *Masse, Christs* bodie under the accidents of bread." From such beliefs it is too easy to pass on to transubstantiation and the Phoenix. Even if the form is in the ashes, it is ashes, not form (p. 56). Finally, "the appetite of the matter is taken away; for to what can it have an appetite, seeing it retaines the forme of the plant?" He concluded, "Your revived plant will prove more *artificiall* than *naturall*" or "nothing but an *Idea*, or a delusion of the eye through a glasse held over a flame. . . . A sallet of such plants may well tantalize you, they will never fill you" (p. 57). So Browne's mystical Idea received short shrift from the materialistic Ross, who attacked him from nearly every direction, since self-contradiction obviously did not perturb him.

Ross's explanations of the nature of the generation and the decay of plants generally follow Aristotelian assumptions. The "forme" of the plant that endures the flames would be essentially the soul of the plant. In Aristotle, plants are alive in so far as they "possess in themselves an originative power through which they increase or decrease in all spatial directions" (*De Anima*, 413a25–28), in other words, living plants have a nutritive soul that creates growth. This growing process is explained by the heat of which Ross speaks. The loss of this vital heat which is tempered by cooling moisture, results in death and decay (*De Respiratione*, 479a8–10, 33–b3). The intermingling of form and matter is explained in terms of soul: "We must maintain, further, that the soul is also the cause of the living body as the original source of local movement. . . . But change of quality and change of quantity are also due to the soul. Sensation is held to be a qualitative alteration, and nothing except what has soul in it is capable of sensation. The same holds of the quantitative changes which constitute growth and decay; nothing grows or decays naturally except it feeds itself, and nothing feeds itself except what has a share of

soul in it" (*De Anima*, 415b22–28). Even the spontaneous
generation of plants arises from some combination of form
and matter: "The same holds good also in plants, some coming into being from seed and others, as it were, by the spontaneous action of Nature, arising either from decomposition
of the earth or of some parts in other plants, for some are not
formed by themselves separately but are produced upon other
trees, as the mistletoe" (*De Generatione Animalium*, 715b26–
716a1). Even Ross's allusions to the mixture of Art and Nature were drawn from Aristotle—perhaps such an explanation
of orderly causation as this one in the *Physica*, 199a23–33,
199b14–33:

> By gradual advance in this direction we come to see clearly that in
> plants too that is produced which is conductive to the end—leaves,
> e.g. grow to provide shade for the fruit. . . . It is plain that this
> kind of cause is operative in things which come to be and are by
> nature. And since "nature" means two things, the matter and the
> form, of which the latter is the end, and since all the rest is for the
> sake of the end, the form must be the cause in the sense of "that
> for the sake of which. . . ."
>
> Moreover, among the seeds anything must have come to be at
> random. But the person who asserts this entirely does away with
> "nature" and what exists "by nature." For those things are natural
> which, by a continuous movement originated from an internal
> principle, arrive at some completion; the same completion is not
> reached from every principle; nor any chance completion, but al-
> ways the tendency in each is towards the same end, if there is no
> impediment. . . .
>
> It is absurd to suppose that purpose is not present because we
> do not observe the agent deliberating. Art does not deliberate. If
> the ship-building art were in the wood, it would produce the same
> results by nature. If, therefore, purpose is present art, it is present
> also in nature. The best illustration is a doctor doctoring himself;
> nature is like that.
>
> It is plain then that nature is a cause, a cause that operates for a
> purpose.

Ross extended the Aristotelian comparison between art and
nature to a facetious attribution that art is ephemeral and
immaterial, thus no substantial effect can come from it. The
plant itself, that is, the form, is not consumed by the fire, but
no true plant can be regenerated from ashes. Ashes are ashes,
the material-minded Ross declared.

Although both Browne and Ross drew on the concept of the Aristotelian "form" and used the same philosopher's classification of "species," the latter could not accept the former's reunion of the form and the body in mystical terms. The exactness of Browne's correspondences between spirit and matter carried him beyond Ross, especially when he invoked the Divine Voice in this action. Ross's final view denied material regeneration, since he held that the plant of Browne's experiment would be "*artificiall*" rather than "*naturall*." Browne had omitted from the 1643 edition a moderately traditional distinction based on the concept of "accidental" qualities.

## The Attack on Intuition and Metaphor

Ross's hesitation to accept the possibility of a regenerated plant grew out of his conception of the world of nature. For example, he attacked at some length Browne's definition of nature as "that streight and regular line" (I, 16), preferring "the principle of motion and rest" (*Physica*, 192b13–15). Ross's first charge was that Browne had not redefined nature but had overthrown a clear definition for a mystifying metaphor. Ross directed his reader's attention (p. 20) to Aristotle's caution in *Topica* (139b34–37) that metaphors should be avoided because of their obscurity, but he neglected to mention Aristotle's further warning that "it is possible, also, to argue sophistically against the user of a metaphorical expression as though he had used it in its literal sense"—an argumentative technique Ross rarely neglected to apply. Of course, Ross wrote, we know that Browne delighted "in such fancies" as "light . . . the shadow of God: I think *Empedocles* . . . would please you well, who defines the sea to be the *sweat* of the earth; and *Plato* defines the *Poles* to be the little feet, on which the *great animal* of the world moves it selfe. Such definitions are good for women and children, who are delighted with toyes; wise men search into the causes and natures of things" (p. 21). Ross's knowledge of Empedocles was probably based, not on the fragments themselves, but on Aristotle's criticism in *Meterologica* (357a24–27): "It is equally absurd to suppose that anything has been explained by calling the sea 'the sweat of the earth,' like Empedocles. Metaphors are poetical and so that expression of his may satisfy the requirements of a poem, but as scientific theory it is unsatisfactory." "The earth's sweat" is marvelously concrete by any poetic standard, so Ross had chosen a fine example only to discredit it. Empedocles joined Plato, in Ross's eyes, as invalid and obscure; the poetic rightness and genius of both went unrecognized in his inflexible literalness.

Ross's argument against Browne's definition of nature as a line is thoroughly Aristotelian and nearly metaphorical in itself, since he ridiculed the comparison through one between "the ten Plagues" and "the ten Commandements" (p. 21). A line has "quantity," which nature does not have, an idea that possibly refers to Aristotle's arguments in *Physica* (193b31–194a6), which distinguish the mathematical from the physical and the abstract from the concrete on the basis of quantity and quality: " 'Odd' and 'even,' 'straight' and 'curved,' and likewise 'number,' 'line,' and 'figure,' do not involve motion; not so 'flesh' and 'bone' and 'man'—*these* are defined like 'snub nose,' not like 'curved' " (194a3–6). Ross then inquired why Browne could not see that nature is "a circular line," as revealed by the shape of the world, the stars, and the heavens, by the process of generation and corruption, and even by the circulation of the blood (pp. 21–22). The primacy and naturalness of circular movement is shown in *De Caelo* (269a19–21): "For the perfect is naturally prior to the imperfect, and the circle is a perfect thing. This cannot be said of any straight line." Huntley comments that "Ross overlooks Browne's context and full intention" when even "Browne's immediately following sentence concerns the 'revolution' of the Sun; and the whole context is one of God the geometrician who can divide a line by a stroke of his compass but who sometimes chooses 'a circle or longer way.' "[10] Next, Ross merely suggested that "Nature is not a settled course, but in the workes of Nature there is a settled and constant course; if you speake properly, and like a Philosopher" (p. 22). Ross did not agree with Browne's metaphor that "Nature is the hand of God, and

10. Frank L. Huntley, "Sir Thomas Browne, M.D., William Harvey, and the Metaphor of the Circle," *Bull. Hist. Med.*, 25 (1951), 245.

an instrument" or with Browne's statement that man must never forget God's power, for "to ascribe his actions unto her, is to devolve the honor of the principall agent upon the instrument." Ross believed Browne carried his arguments too far: "It is not the fire, but God that rosts your meat" (p. 23). Ross, in his antipathy for the Platonic metaphor of God as the soul of the world and hierarchical ruler, aligned himself against a teleological argument that in another context would probably have called forth his agreement. The remainder of Ross's argument about nature as motion, "doe not you know, that the forme actuates the *compositum,* and restraines the extravagancie of the matter" (p. 24), parallels Aristotle's definition in *Physica* (193b2–8):

> Thus in the second sense of "nature" it would be the shape or form (not separable except in statement) of things which have in themselves a source of motion. (The combination of the two, e.g. man, is not "nature" but "by nature" or "natural.")
>  The form indeed is "nature" rather than the matter; for a thing is more properly said to be what it is when it has attained to fulfilment than when it exists potentially.

For Browne to deny this definition, Ross concluded, would be like a physician's denying the processes of "generation and corruption, composition and mixture in Nature" (p. 24). Little of Ross's criticism is either original or justified; for the most part it grew out of a personal prejudice against metaphor and toward circularity.

Ross's literalness is demonstrated when a series of witty problems suggested by Browne (I, 21) prompted Ross to answer with his usual lack of humor the question of whether there is a right side of a man. Ross stodgily located the right side of man by praising the positioning of the liver there. Since Nature has declared the right hand the "honourable" one, Ross warned Browne piously that he should "endeavour to know Christs right hand from his left, that, in the last day, you may stand there with joy amongst his sheep" (p. 36). In putting his complete stock in the honor of the liver, Ross opposed his master, Aristotle, who stated that it is on the right side (*De Partibus Animalium,* 669b36–670a1), but who also said: "But no one could ever deem the liver to be the primary organ either of the whole body or of the blood" (666a25). But this is precisely what Ross held, so his view apparently reverted to the Galenic view that "the liver must be the earliest organ."[11] No anatomical evidence was necessary for Ross. Browne's shift of his "bundle of curiosities" to *"Pantagruels Library"* epitomizes the difference between him and a literalist like Ross who answered all questions soberly. Among his contemporaries, the frivolous questions about Adam and Eve, especially about the rib, were not taken seriously by most commentators, according to Arnold Williams.[12]

Finally, the conflict regarding the nature of heaven and hell defines the particularity of Ross's thought. The nature of angels and the meaning of Judgment must also be considered in this context. Ross perceived "divers errours" in Browne's discussion of such matters (I, 35). First, when Ross discovered that Browne called heaven the "immateriall world," he countered that Browne had confused the *"celestiall* world with the *intellectual."* Only the latter is "immateriall, and had its being in the divine intellect, before it was made." Browne's having called the "great Sphere *the first movable"* was an error, since if the heavens are immaterial, as Browne wrote, then "they are not movable." No immaterial realm could be the abode of the "bodies of the *Saints,* after the resurrection. . . . If the heavens have not matter, they have not quantity and parts." They are "simple, as spirits, [not] compounded substances of matter and forme." Their matter is not "as the elementary world," which is subject to "generation and corruption" (p. 43). Ross next disagreed with Browne's assigning the habitation of angels to "every where where is his essence" for they would then be omnipresent, which is not true. Finally, Ross reminded Browne that the creation of angels as "ministering spirits to the heires of salvation" does not intervene them between man and God so as to shadow God's glory; instead, man should love God even more for having created them (pp. 44–45). Ross argued dogmatically that Browne's assertion that generation and creation are based on contrarieties is not true, because creation has no "subject, without which contrarieties cannot be in nature" (p. 45).

Much of what Ross said here about the nature of the heav-

11. Joseph Needham, *A History of Embryology,* 127.
12. *The Common Expositer,* 90.

ens and Heaven is elliptical but essentially Aristotelian in basis, for Aristotle had said, "It is equally reasonable to assume that his [heavenly] body will be ungenerated and indestructible and exempt from increase and alteration, since everything that comes to be comes into being from its contrary and in some substrate, and passes away likewise in a substrate by the action of the contrary into the contrary. . . . For it is in contraries that generation and decay subsist" (*De Caelo*, 270a13–23). Thus, the heavens are eternal, changeless, and perfect. Aristotle defined "heaven" in three senses—the first, "the substance of the extreme circumference of the whole, or that natural body whose place is at the extreme circumference" is deemed "the seat of all that is divine" (*De Caelo*, 278b10–22). This description parallels most nearly what Ross judged heaven to be. This divine entity, Aristotle went on, moves continuously in a circle for an infinity of time (279b1–4, 281b26). Materially, the heavens are neither light nor heavy (269b30–31), and they apparently do not incorporate the properties of earthly and sublunarly bodies.

Ross made a distinction between generation and creation in his final comments. To him, creation is not susceptible to the action of contraries; thus, the creation of the universe differs materially from the natural act of generation and decay. In this, Ross was probably thinking of the *creatio ex nihilo*. When he spoke of the heavens as spirits he was distinctly separating them from the material world. Although Aristotle did not use these terms, he did remove the heavens from generated matter and he did conceive the heavens to be alive, as when he conceived of the heavenly bodies "enjoying life and action" (292a20–21).

Although Aristotle was still the standard authority in the universities, surely few men of the time were so fundamentally aligned with and committed to his philosophy as was Ross. "To him Aristotelianism was a live philosophy, which he applied to what he observed. Thus he was inevitably and hopelessly on the wrong side as regards most of the new ideas of the day."[13] Francis R. Johnson compares Ross's views to those of the Southern legislators who combatted the teaching of evo-

13. Richard Foster Jones, *Ancients and Moderns: A Study of the Background of the "Battle of the Books,"* 125.

lution: "His arguments opposing the new scientific ideas revealed a complete ignorance, not only of the elementary principles on which all science is founded, but also of the essential features of the very theories he was attacking. . . . But Ross was the last voluble champion of bigoted Aristotelianism in an age that was moving rapidly away from the old scholastic philosophy. The very violence of his defense of the old ideas was symptomatic of the hopelessness of a losing cause."[14]

Ross introduced a traditional line of objection to Browne's location of heaven and the destruction of the world (I, 49). Concerning the latter, Ross doubted "that this sensible world shall be destroyed in the substance thereof: its qualities shall be altered, the actions, motions, and influences of the *Heavens* shall cease; because then shall be no generation or corruption, and consequently, no transmutation of elements." Having assured his reader that the world as such will not be ultimately destroyed, he admitted that, even if it were destroyed, "yet it will not follow, that therefore above the tenth *Sphere* there is not the Heaven of glory" (p. 58). Thus he explicitly differentiated between the material world, subject to change and the immutable heavens and particularly Heaven, where "blisse and happinesse" prevail and God is wholly present (p. 57). By making this reversal, he implied that perhaps the immutability of the universe in Aristotelian terms does not encompass the moral heavens. Here, then, the terms "heaven" and "heavens" do not overlap as they do earlier in the work. Both scriptural and ecclesiastical tradition certify the reality of heaven and the fact that it is not "everywhere," but is "locall," a place where Christ has "gone to prepare a place for us." Not even the "*Gentiles*" were ignorant of such a place (pp. 58–59). Ross directed Browne to Chapter LIV of Tertullian's *De Anima* for proof that the Gentiles, including especially Plato, knew of Hell.[15] As Westfall has pointed out, Ross "for all his extravagant diction . . . had put his finger on the central issue—the relative authority of natural philosophy and inspired divinity" (p. 21).

14. *Astronomical Thought in Renaissance England: A Study of English Scientific Writings from 1500 to 1645*, 277–78, 282.

15. "On the Soul," *Apologetical Works*, trans. Edwin A. Quain, *The Fathers of the Church*, X, 296–97.

Ross treated Browne's location of heaven as an interesting and even vital question; but the matter of hell drew forth a series of angry retorts. Ross thought that Browne could not understand "how . . . fire is the essence of hell, . . . nor . . . conceive a flame that can prey upon the soule." Browne had stated that the flames of hell must refer to that hell "to come" and not to "this present Hell" (I, 50). Ross rejected these questionings by summarily stating that "the fire of Hell is corporall" (p. 59) and that the soul "may be affected and afflicted" in various ways: it can be "united to the fire, and shut up as it were in a prison there"; "it shall retaine the experimentall knowledge of those paines, which it suffered in the body"; "it is the *principium* and originall of the senses, which shall remaine in the soule as in their root"; and finally, because the fire symbolizes God's "indignation," it is not any more impossible for the fire "to worke upon a spirit, then for the materiall humours of the body to worke upon the soule" (p. 60). Thus Ross used teleological speculations to dismiss Browne's rational questions.

Naturally, Ross was disturbed when Browne placed hell within the conscience of man, rather than beneath the earth (I, 51). This inner hell he thought he rejected by a traditional argument, however circular: "Wee believe *Hell* to be under earth, because it stands with reason and Gods justice, that the wicked should be removed as farre as might be from the presence of the Saints, and the place of joy, which is above." Besides, those who are in hell do not aspire to heavenly virtue, so it is "fitting that their eternall habitation should be within the earth." The terms for hell in Hebrew, Greek, Latin, and English further signify that hell is "low, and in darknesse." Both Scripture and the ancients (Tertullian,[16] Juvenal, Virgil, and Homer) speak of hell as beneath the surface of the earth (pp. 60–62). The striking imaginativeness of Browne's view, nearly

16. A marginal gloss points correctly to Chapter XI of Tertullian's "Apology," but Ross neglected to mention that Tertullian's further argument supports Browne on the worthiness of those great ancients to attain heaven. Ross ignored the point of the passage; he merely used "the abyss of Tartarus" reference. See "Apology," trans. Sister Emily Joseph Daly, *The Fathers of the Church,* X, 38–41.

all of which had been added in the 1643 edition, is wasted on the literal-minded Ross, defender of orthodox images.

## The Literalism of Faith

Ross repeatedly fell back on a literal interpretation of Scripture as his final authority. This was true for general issues, such as the nature of the Judgment Day, as well as for specific points of interpretation.

Browne had doubts about the literalness of a Judgment Day: "I cannot dreame there should be at the last day any such Judiciall proceeding, or calling to the Barre, as indeed the Scripture seemes to imply, and the literall commentators doe conceive: for unspeakable mysteries in the Scriptures are often delivered in a vulgar and illustrative way, and being written unto man, are delivered, not as they truely are, but as they may bee understood" (I, 45). Such remarks prompted Ross to deprecate reading Scripture "*mystically*." The Church from its beginning has believed that Christ as judge will deliver sentence: "A *mysticall* and un-knowne way of tryall, will not stand so much with the honour of *Christ*, as an open and visible, that all may see and witnesse the justice of the *Judge*." Ross reaffirmed that the "literall sense" of the Bible, the "consent" of the Church, and reason hold that, since the creation was not a "*mysterie*," neither shall be the "consummation." Ross then continued his graphic re-hearsal of the last day: Christ was judged "visibly . . . by sin-ners," so He will judge them openly, especially since the saints "shall see their desire upon their enemies" and the wicked shall suffer so much the more if their punishment is meted to them openly. Finally, Ross expressed his suspicion that a view like Browne's leads to conceiving of the final punishment itself as mystical rather than sensible, a view "which is indeed to overthrow all Religion, and open a wide gap for impiety and security" (pp. 52–53). Clearly, Ross was not convinced by Browne's "bare word" but held to the old dispensation.

In the course of his discussion Ross also cited the infamous Faustus Socinus who, according to Ross, held "that eternall death, and eternall fire prepared for the wicked is only *mysti-call*, and signifieth nothing else but the *annihilation* of the

wicked for ever, without sensible paine" (p. 53). According to
H. John McLachlan, Socinus in arguing against the common
conception of Christ's atonement for our sins held that re-
pentance, not punishment, is the nature of God's forgiveness.[17]
Browne, too, may have come under the influence of Socinianism through his Oxford tutor, Dr. Thomas Lushington, and
"had to be protected from that association by his surviving
well-wishers."[18] Ross was able by these few words to draw an
affinity between Browne and one point of Socinian thought.

Browne's conjectures (I, 46) about the ambiguity of "those
prognosticks of Scripture"—so called in the Pembroke MS—
about the second coming of Christ and the revelation of the
Anti-Christ were answered in a matter-of-fact way by Ross.
Of the second coming he wrote that the omens cannot be mistaken, because they signify the final destruction of Jerusalem
and they will be greater in "extent and number" than any
previously beheld. Then, echoing Matthew xxiv:37–39, Ross
warned that mankind will be caught as unprepared for this
final cataclysm as it was for the Flood (pp. 53–54). From his
stance on the subject of the Anti-Christ Ross renewed his attack on the Pope, citing both scriptural and theological authority that all descriptions of the Anti-Christ fit the Pope.
It would have been interesting to have heard Ross's response
to a marginal manuscript note, omitted from the published
editions, referring to those who "laboure to prove the Pope
Antichrist from theire names making the number of the
beast." Echoing his earlier attack he listed some of the Pope's
defamers such as Wycliffe, the Waldenses, Huss,[19] and others

17. *Socinianism in Seventeenth-Century England*, 15.
18. Frank L. Huntley, "Sir Thomas Browne and His Oxford
Tutor; or Academic Guilt by Association," *The History of Ideas
Newsletter*, II (1956), 50. See McLachlan, 108–10, on Lushington. McLachlan also points out that Ross treated Socinianism in
his *Pansebeia* (1653) in "a bald and more or less garbled account"
and dismissed it as " 'but renovations of old Heresies' [p. 367],"
251.
19. John Wycliffe, *Three Treatises*, ed. James Henthorn Todd,
includes "Of Antichrist and his Meynee," in which Wycliffe accused the clergy of following the law of the Pope rather than the
law of Christ. Adolf von Harnack, *History of Dogma*, trans. Neil
Buchanan, VI, 136–49, surveys the conflict between the hierarchical system of the Roman Church and the espousal of the "law

who identified the Pope and the Anti-Christ (pp. 53–55). For Ross the biblical portents of both the second advent and the Anti-Christ were clearly delineated for all to understand and to be forewarned by.

Ross had earlier complained of Browne's attitude toward Christ and had implored him to follow the example of the Bible. Bypassing the famous *oh altitudo* apostrophe, Ross took Browne to task for exulting that he "never saw Christ nor his Disciples" or had been "one of Christs Patients" out of the possible fear of having his "faith . . . thrust upon me" (I, 9). Ross capitalized on these statements by resurrecting the traditional prejudice against physicians: "Was it because he or they, by curing all diseases freely would have hindered your practice? . . . The poore *Hemoroisse* got more good by one touch of *Christs* garment, then by all the physicks she had received from those of your profession."[20] After listing some of the biblical persons who desired greatly to see Christ, Ross compared Browne's presumption to Peter's faith when he attempted to walk on water. He then offered this prayer on Browne's behalf: "*I beleeve, Lord, help my unbeliefe*" (p. 17).

Later, Ross corrected Browne's speculations about the miracle of the brazen serpent. If Browne believed that this miracle was a mere "*Ægyptian* tricke" (I, 19), then he was as deceived as the devotees of that second-century snake cult, the Ophits, who worshipped the miracle of the snake itself. Ross facetiously remarked that perhaps the Egyptians learned of the snake's powers from Moses rather than vice versa. Besides, Ross explained, the power of sympathy works through "a hid vertue, having alwaies a naturall substance for the subject of it": the brass figure of the serpent could therefore have no sympathetic powers. The attraction of sympathies and antipathies may be found in such living things as rhubarb and rhododendron. The imaginative power of Moses' feat lay, not

---

of Christ," with its implications of the "invisible church," by such groups as the Lollards, the Waldenses, and the Hussites.

20. Joan Bennett, *Sir Thomas Browne*, 58, comments that "no Christian reader of the seventeenth century could have genuinely misunderstood what Browne meant." She denounces Ross's statement as a "cheap jibe [which] betrays the dishonest controversialist."

in the image of the serpent, but in the image of the erected
cross. Ross then undertook to answer Browne's doubts about
the miracles of Elias, Sodom, and the manna by citing the
sanctity of the biblical text and by offering such solutions as:
Elias could not have started the fire with bitumen, as Browne
suggested, because he would have been seen; the miracle of
the manna lay in its quantity—exactly enough for everyone—
and its quality of resisting putrefaction (pp. 28–32). In another context, Paul H. Kocher comments on the difficulties
that arise from Ross's explanations of the Bible:

> Ross of course stayed close to the literal meaning of the words of
> Scripture and argues that this was the only one applicable. With
> regard to the theory of accommodation [offered by John Wilkins]
> he retorted rather cogently that it would have been as easy and as
> intelligible to the people for the Holy Ghost to say that the earth
> moves as to say that the sun moves. The Bible, he argued, never
> tells a palpable lie about any fact in the physical world. Neverthe-
> less, Ross was considerably embarrassed by his inability to stick to
> the letter of the text in some passages like those describing the
> windows of heaven, the four corners of the earth, and the flatness
> of the earth. Even he had to admit that the Fathers had erred
> there. (P. 198)

Although none of Browne's scriptural speculations seem controversial, Ross denounced them as "impious and ridiculous"
(p. 30); thus Browne's "honest endeavours" were overridden
by literalism and caustic bad humor.

Ross objected to five of Browne's series of "niceties" (I, 22):
(a) The curious fact that no horses were found in America
although other less "necessary" animals were, might be explained by the existence of the "Strait of *Anien*, between *Asia*
and *America*"; (b) the length of Methusalem's life is certified
by both the Bible and the Church; (c) Scripture is also
"plaine" on the hanging of Judas, and no mistake has been
made in the translation (see Martin, p. 297n23.26–30); (d)
why should not the Tower of Babel have been built on the
plain, since the Bible says, "Men must build where they can,
not alwaies where they would." Browne's rational quibble
about the plain being an inappropriate place to escape another
flood held little charm for Ross; (e) " 'Tis not materiall,
whether it was a messenger, or *Peters* tutelary *Angell* that was

supposed to knock at the door; for the word signifieth both";
nevertheless, he was in doubt about the full meaning of this
passage (Acts xii: 13–17). He seemed reluctant to accept that
an angel was sent as a messenger "from man" (pp. 36–39).

Surprisingly, Ross did not interject any objections about
Browne's view that the Flood "seemes not to mee so great a
miracle, as that there is not one alwayes," even though his
view on the world-wide extent of the Flood appeared during
a great quarrel on the subject. Ross's chagrin would have increased immensely if he had seen this elaboration of Browne's
doubt about Judas' fate, which appears only in the Pembroke
MS: "That Judas hanged himself tis an absurdity & an affirmative that is not expressed in the text, but quite contrarie to the
words & their externall construction; with this paradoxe I remember I netled an angrie Jesuite who had that day let this
fall in his sermon, who afterwards upon a serious perusall of
the text, confessed my opinion, & prooved a courteous friend
to mee a stranger, and noe enemy" (Martin, 262n23.25–35).

To Browne's speculation that miracles have ceased (I, 27)
Ross agreed, since Scripture confirms this view (p. 39). He
agreed with Browne on the Thomistic definition of miracles
as the "extraordinary effects of Gods hands," but disagreed
with Browne's statement that "there is not one Miracle greater
than another." Some miracles have greater "effects" than
others, for example, the creation of the world versus the creation of man's body. He laughed a bit at Browne's "mannerly"
proposition that "God can doe all things; how he should work
contradictions, I do not understand, yet dare not therefore
deny." Ross stated emphatically, in return, that God cannot
work contradictions because His "object . . . is *possibile abso-
lutam.*" There are actions "repugnant either to his wisedome,
goodnesse, or power" such as suffering, dying, or creating another God. On these points Ross was much more confident of
his knowledge than was Browne, who vacillated, unable to
confirm or deny. Ross considered it "a breach of good man-
ners" to believe that God would do anything not suitable to
His nature. He concluded that "his power and will make but
one God, yet they are different attributes *ratione*; for the will
commands, and the power puts in execution" (pp. 40–41).

## The Certainty of Providence

The certainty with which Ross discussed the nature of God is reflected in a number of objections that he raised to Browne's views on God.

Questions about God's knowledge arose when Ross objected to Browne's description of God's wisdom: "Hee is wise, because hee knowes all things; and hee knoweth all things, because he made them all; but his greatest knowledg is in comprehending that he made not, that is himselfe" (I, 13). According to Ross, the order is just the reverse: "God knoweth all things, because he is wise, for his wisedome is not like ours; ours is got by knowledge and long experience, so is not Gods, whose wisedome and knowledge is co-eternall. . . . We know first the effects of things and conclusions by *discourse*, and then come to the knowledge of the *principles*, . . . but God knowes the principles and causes of all things *simplici intuitu*, and immediately, being all in himselfe; the effects and conclusions hee knowes in the causes and principles" (pp. 19–20).

This argument is essentially that of Aquinas, who contrasted man's division of the different kinds of knowledge, according to the different objects of knowledge, whereas "God knows all these by one simple act of knowledge" (*Summa Theologia*, Q. 14, Art. 2, ad. 2). While man gains knowledge through his rational examination of causal relations, God "knows the effects in the cause" (Art. 7, ad. 2). Ross added that God does not know things because He made them, but "hee made them, because hee knew them; . . . he knew them from eternity, he made them in time, and with time" (p. 20). Aquinas wrote: "The knowledge of God, joined to His will is the cause of things" (Art. 9, ad. 3), and "for whatever is, or can be in any period of time, is known by God in his eternity" (Art. 15, ad. 2). Ross also read into Browne's statement the supposition that Browne limited God's knowledge to only that which He has made. To oppose Browne's assessment, Ross listed four attributes that are within God's knowledge: "himselfe, . . . those notions of oure mindes which we call *entia rationis*, . . . non-entities, and . . . evill" (p. 20). Aquinas dealt with the last in Art. 11, ads. 1–4, in which he accepted Augustine's definition of evil as the privation of good and then concluded that, because God knows good perfectly, He must also know evil, the opposite of good. Therefore, evil is much inferior to good, since it can "neither be defined nor known except by good."

For an explanation of *entia rationis* and *non-entities* we must look elsewhere. *Non-ens* or *non-being* was discussed by Aquinas (Q. 16. Art. 3, ads. 2), when he defined *non-being* as having "nothing in itself whereby it can be known; yet it is known in so far as the intellect renders it knowable. Hence the true is based on being, inasmuch as not-being is a kind of logical being, apprehended, that is, by reason." Since *ens* is being, or that which is, *ens rationis* is that which has existence only as an object of reason. The latter concept is associated with the philosophy of Duns Scotus, who defined it as "that which has being in the understanding which considers it, and which can have no being outside the understanding; it posits nothing in the actual thing and it is not itself an actual thing, but it is none the less formed or apprehended by reason."[21] Although Scotus' division of *ens* and *ens rationis* is not entirely compatible with Aquinas' identification of being and non-being, Ross did not regard their difference as important, since his point was solely that God's wisdom is sufficient to allow Him to know both. Browne's general argument that man's mind does not operate as directly as that of God, whose will and mind act at one instant in a mysterious way that man can only contemplate, Ross chose to ignore. The contrast between Ross's heavily philosophic language and Browne's mystical phrasing illustrates their differences in attitude and approach. Ross wrote of God perceiving intuitively the "principles" or primary truths that men call wisdom; this process encompasses more than God can create, for God did not create Himself, *entia rationis*, non-entities, or evil. The basic discussion here is not controversial, and for the most part Ross's catalogue of scholastic explanations seems largely mis-

21. *Selections from Medieval Philosophers*, Vol. II: *Roger Bacon to William of Ockham*, trans. and ed. Richard McKeon, II, 451.

placed, since at best Browne was interested only in "Contemplations Metaphysicall."

Ross ignored the beginning of Browne's analysis of Fortune, "that serpentine and crooked line, whereby he [God] drawes those actions that his wisedome intends, in a more unknowne and secret way" (I, 17); instead, he turned to the possibly more concrete statements (I, 18) as " 'Tis not a ridiculous devotion to say a Prayer before a game of Tables," and "judiciall Astrology . . . doth not injure Divinity." Ross declared the first a "profanation"; the second statement required lengthier treatment because he interpreted such approval of astrological influences as compliance with the devil, which is contrary to "Councels, Canon, *civill* and *municipall* Lawes, and *Gods Word*." He thought it would be better to declare "in plaine termes" that Mercury and Jupiter have no influence over wealth and wit, that "the Stares were made to be signes, to measure time, to warme and illuminate, . . . promotion comes neither from *East* nor *West*, but from the Lord" (pp. 25–26). To confute Browne's position, Ross cited scriptural evidence of God's influence in the world, then listed the many ways to obtain wealth. As a finishing blow, he asked Browne if he considered Jupiter the cause of all of them, for Browne had made it seem that praying to Jupiter made unnecessary prayers to God. Ross borrowed his conclusion from *The City of God*—without giving credit: "You were as good tell us of the goddesse *Pecunia*, of the god *Æsculanus*, and his son *Argentarius*, worshipped among the *Romans*, for being the authors of *mony*, brasse and silver, that if they dispose wealth on us, wee will thank the Supreme giver for it, not them, as to call *Mercury* and *Jupiter benevolent aspects*, because they dispose us to be wealthy and witty" (pp. 26–27).[22] Ross, conscious of his magnanimity, stated that if there were any truth in astrology he would recognize it, but all laws,

22. *The City of God*, 126–28 (IV, 20). Augustine argued that virtue and felicity exist in themselves, so it is senseless to implore the various deities for these qualities; instead, practice virtue and receive felicity. He listed Pecunia, Aesculanus, and Argentinus among the gods worshipped, and asked wittily why, if Aesculanus (brass) begot Argentinus (silver) did not the latter beget Aurinus (gold).

sacred and secular, "condemn" astrology. All fortune emanates from a benevolent God, he concluded; Browne would
surely agree, if it were put to him so bluntly.

Later in his analysis (pp. 68–70) Ross objected rather
strongly to Browne's statements about chiromancy and palmistry. Browne had merely wondered if facial markings might
not indicate in some way "the motto of our Soules" (II, 2).
Ross reminded Browne that Christ warned against deceptive
appearance; we must "judge righteous judgement." While
Ross did not deny that "sometimes the face proves *index
animi*," as in Julian the Apostate and Esau, any effort to pre-
dict behavior from such signs is a "superstitious folly." Ross
also cited Juvenal's sixth satire, on women,[23] as evidence of
the folly of those who superstitiously seek the secrets of fortune. He then listed five more objections: the markings of
the body are more often "by accident, then by nature"; learning changes the future of men, for example, Socrates; man
has free will over his "morall actions"; the grace of God "doth
quite transforme nature"; men perceive the foolishness of believing "that *Jupiter* must containe himselfe within his owne
line, and not encroach upon the line of *Venus* or *Mercury*"
in one's palm. Instead, according to Ross, men should "follow
him, who only hath the seven Stars in his right hand," that
is, God or Christ. Again Ross asserted the power of the Christian God as a rebuttal to any contrary explanations of the
meaning of life—even facetious explanations like Browne's.
Ross showed himself to be in line with the customary religious
opposition to superstitions that encroach on teleological
answers to the nature of man's existence.

Browne's chancing, on three occasions, to ponder the nature
of atheism and doubt drew angry retorts from Ross. Browne's
ironic observation that there are no atheists (I, 20) provoked
a listing of fifteen instances from Saint Paul, Virgil, Cicero,
Homer, and others to show that atheists do indeed exist (pp.
33–34). Ross was especially angered by Browne's view that
the "doctrine of *Epicurus*, that denied the providence of God,
was no Atheism, but a magnificent and high-strained conceit
of his Majesty." To Ross, Epicurus and all who believe "the
world to be casually and rashly agglomerated of small *atomes*"

23. *Juvenal and Persius*, trans. G. G. Ramsay, 129–30.

are atheists (p. 33). Ross's objection was as much moral as
scientific, for pronouncing anathema on the libertine Epicurus
would have been strongly satisfying to him. He held that denying God's providence or any of His attributes is as atheistic
as to deny His very essence. Perhaps on this basis Ross would
have termed Galen an atheist; his main purpose was to associate atheism with men of the medical profession.[24] Ross went
on to declare that any who believe that religion is man-made
"to keep people in awe" are atheists. God's providence reaches
to the very hairs of our head, he stated. So a literal acceptance
of a personal God did not allow Ross to share Browne's speculation that such minute concern by the Deity about man may
not do Him honor. Ross directed his reader to Book One of
*De Natura Deorum* for collaboration of his charges of atheism
against Epicurus, Democritus, and six others. So closely were
Ross's examples drawn from Cicero that he even cited (p. 34)
that author's comparison of Epicurus' overthrowal of the
temples of the gods by argument with Xerxes' doing it by
force.[25] Browne's identification of the "fatall necessitie of the
Stoickes" with the "immutable Law" of the will of God could
only mean, to Ross, that no matter what man does, good or
evil, it is done by "an *inevitable necessity*" to which "even
*Jupiter* himselfe was subject." Ross admitted that he would
not have expected to have heard this heathen belief, which he
associated with the Turks, from a "Christian Physician till
now" (p. 35). Undoubtedly the universe pictured by Lucretius would have been a horror to Ross: "To say again that for
the sake of men they [the gods] have willed to set in order
the glorious nature of the world and therefore it is meet to
praise the work of the gods calling as it does for all praise,
and to believe that it will be eternal and immortal, and that
it is an unholy thing ever to shake by any force from its fixed
seats that which by the forethought of the gods in ancient

24. Richard Walzer, *Galen on Jews and Christians*, 11–13,
23–37, points out that Galen set a limit on God's powers; He will
do only the best of the possibilities open to Him and there are
certain things "impossible by nature"; God will not intervene
miraculously.

25. See Cicero, trans. H. Rackham, On Democritus, 33, 73,
115, 117, 197; On Epicurus and Xerxes, 111; also see 3, 5, 61, 63,
113, 375.

days has been established on everlasting foundations for mankind, or to assail it by speech and utterly overturn it from
top to bottom; . . . is all sheer folly." [26]

Another point of disagreement was Browne's classing as
atheists those who deny the existence of witches (I, 30). Ross
questioned that there is "such a strict relation between *witches*
and *spirits,* that hee that denies the one, must needs deny the
other?" Surely, he argued, spirits exist without witches (p. 41).
Apparently Ross did not unite the levels of the Great Chain
of Being in the stricter manner of Browne and others who felt
that the denial of any level, in this instance witches, was a
denial of the whole. Although a curious dependence on belief
in Satan in order to retain belief in God existed in the seventeenth century, Ross did not raise this point in his objections.
It is interesting that Ross did not bother to comment on
Browne's meandering thoughts about changelings, cohabitation with devils, and Satanic possession.

Ross concluded his criticisms of Part One of *Religio* by de-
nouncing Browne's doubts about the certainty of his salvation
because he realized his "unworthinesse." Besides, Browne had
written that "no infallible warrant" of salvation or, for that
matter, the existence of the city of Constantinople can be
given (I, 59). All of these remarks were abhorrent to Ross.
First, "to be fully perswaded, and not to sweare it, is a contradiction" (p. 65); then, there is much that must be accepted as true without empirical evidence; most important,
"doubting is not the fruit of humilitie, but of infidelitie."
Browne, indeed, was an infidel after the manner of the Church
of Rome, "which would rob us of the comforts wee reap in
our afflictions, and in death it selfe, from the assurance of our
salvation; For, if we doubt of our salvation, wee must doubt
also of our election, and of the certainty of all Gods promises."
The Sacraments and the words of Saint Paul (the last cited
in rebuttal to Browne's quoting of the Apostle) reaffirm the
closeness of our tie with Christ. Finally, Ross admitted that
some believers have doubts, but they are comforted "that
*Christ* prayeth for them, that their faith shall not faile";
Browne "to be still doubting, is a signe of a bad *Christian;* and

26. *On the Nature of Things,* trans. H. A. J. Munro, in *The
Stoic and Epicurean Philosophers,* ed. Whitney J. Oates, 166.

. . . of a bad man" (pp. 66–67). With that personal condemnation Ross ended his discussion of the first part of *Religio*; his magnanimity almost extended to doubting Christians, but certainly not to bad men.

## The Rejection of Introspection

The last group of Ross's criticisms may be best considered as rebuttals to Browne's personal allusions. All except the first refer to Part Two of *Religio*, in which Browne discussed charity, friendship, death, marriage, and other human experiences.

Browne expressed a certain disdain for death: "I finde not any thing therein able to daunt the courage of a man, much lesse a well resolved Christian . . . nor can I highly love any that is afraid of" death (I, 38). These remarks did not at all suit Ross; he cited David, Ezekiel, Christ, Seneca, and "the greatest of all philosophers" as among those who feared death. The last-mentioned he quoted directly although he neglected to state the context. Aristotle did indeed term death "the most terrible of all things," but he also said that man should not fear death in all situations. An honorable fear of death may be felt by the bravest men in battle where the danger of death is greatest (*Ethica Nicomachea*, 1115a30–3). There is no such tempering remark by Ross who says that even the good man fears death, for it "dissolves his fabrick" (p. 50). To this grim topic Ross brought no levity. Browne's equanimity and calm tone—death is a force to be considered and met with honor—is much closer to Seneca and Aristotle than Ross's evident terror. Even more important—Browne's mannered indifference parallels the Christian ethic that man should be so dissatisfied with this earthly life that he anticipates the next. Ross rejected this placation and quoted Scripture as authority for his fears.

Browne's confession (II, 5) that his love of friends exceeds his love of kin motivated a strong reaction from Ross, who expressed his belief that Browne was in danger of violating the Fifth Commandment. God has decreed "an order in our love," which must not be broken. So sure was Ross of this truth that he concluded, "But what needs the urging of this duty, which is grounded on the principles of Nature?" (pp.

70–71). He then misconstrued in the same manner as Digby a statement by Browne: "I have loved my Friend as I do vertue, and as I do my soule, my God." Both critics attacked Browne for alleged disrespect to God—surely a misreading of his parallelism! Ross countered that the love of God, the "universall good," transcends the "selfe-love" of friends, a "particular" good (p. 72).

A profession by Browne that his original sin had been cleansed by baptism and that he need not fear for the sins of his youth (II, 7)—that last probably meant ironically—provoked a stern rebuke that only the guilt and the curse of original sin are removed by baptism; the "root" of the sin remains like infectious *"leprosie . . . never . . . totally abolished,"* until death. Ross charged Browne with self-deception if he no longer feared for his sins (pp. 72–73). His humorless mind had missed the comfort Browne had whimsically drawn from the knowledge that he had "no sinnes that want a name" and that he was not of the nature to invent new sins. Such understatement was wasted on Ross, who was unwilling to study his capability for sin as did Browne.

Ross shared with many readers, including Digby, some moments of doubt over Browne's confession that he was thankful that he "escaped" the vice of pride (II, 8). Ross's response was strait-laced—far more so than Browne deserved—although Margaret Bottrall, who considers Ross's book "comparatively mild," compliments him for making a "good point" on this passage (pp. 40–41). After comparing Browne with the infamous Pharisee, Ross reminded him of the subtlety of pride and asked the question that nearly all readers consider: "And have you not pride, in thinking you have no pride?" (p. 74). Ross directed Browne to Saint Bernard's warning against bragging, the fourth of the twelve steps of pride: "But when increasing vanity begins to make the windbag swell, then the wind must be belched out through a larger opening, a wider passage, else it will burst . . . in the multitude of words you may recognize boastfulness."[27]

---

27. Bernard, Abbot of Clairvaux, *The Steps of Humility*, trans. George Bosworth Burch, 205–6. It is interesting to note that Bernard's definition of humility (125), is very close to Browne's (I, 59) with its emphasis on the self-knowledge of unworthiness.

Browne's disparagement of "the blind pursuit of knowledge" and his desire to rest in "a modest ignorance" (II, 8) revealed, for Ross, a lack of appreciation for the blessings that earthly knowledge will yield in heaven, an argument that Digby also presented. Ross pointed out that "by the knowledge of the *creature*, we come to know the *Creatour*; and by the effects, we know the supreme cause, whom to know in *Christ*, is life eternall." Knowledge brings us "neere to the *Angelicall* nature." God made nothing in vain, including man's "understanding, apprehension, judgement." Although some knowledge is "uncertaine," the Christian, through his accumulation of knowledge in "*Philosophy*, and other humane studies, did more hurt to *Gentilisme*, then all the opposition and strength of men could doe." To conclude that "ignorance is better than knowledge" is to conclude that "blindness is better than sight" (pp. 75–76). Once again, the irony of Browne's self-depreciation eluded Ross, who rendered instead a pious and evangelical call to Christian learning. Ross identified ignorance with religious confusion—to him an unbearable state.

Naturally, Browne's well-known renunciation of "the foolishest act a wise man commits in all his life" (II, 9) drew Ross's fire. Wisdom and God have conceived this method of procreation, so it is not folly; however, Ross admitted that the "circumstances" may be foolish at times, but not the act itself (p. 77). About the same time that Ross was registering his dislike, James Howell in a letter to Thomas Young, dated 28 April 1645, recorded his reaction to Browne's thoughts on marriage:

> But to come at last to your kind of *Wiving*, I acknowledge, that marriage is an honorable condition, nor dare I think otherwise without profaneness, for it is the Epithet the Holy Text gives it: Therefore it was a wild speech of the Philosopher to say, That if our conversation could be without women, Angels would com down and dwell amongst us; And a wilder speech it was of the Cynic, when passing by a Tree where a Maid had made herself away, wish'd, That Trees might bear such fruit. But to pass from these Motheaten Philosophers to a modern Phisician of our own, it was a most unmanly thing in him, while he displaies his own Religion, to wish that ther wer a way to propagat the world otherwise than by conjunction with women, (and Paracelsus undertakes to shew him the way), whereby he seems to repine (though I understand he was Wiv'd a little after) at the honourable degree of

*marriage, which I hold to be the prime Link of humane society, the chiefest happines of Mortals, and wherein heaven hath a special hand. (I, 373)*

Browne's fear, not of "the contagion of commerce without me," but of "the corruption . . . within me" (II, 10) led to nothing more than a reminder from Ross that Browne should, of course, fear both the inner and the outer corruption. After citing the proverbial pitch, which defiles, and the ubiquitous sun, which is not corrupted, Ross mentioned the restrictions placed upon the Israelites by God and Juvenal's advice in the Second Satire (lines 79–81) that "the scab of one sheep, or the mange of one pig, destroys an entire herd; just as one bunch of grapes takes on its sickly colour from the aspect of its neighbour" (pp. 23, 25). Ross either misread or was misled by an incorrect edition when he endorsed Browne's view that his "conversation must not be, like the Suns, with all men" (pp. 77–78). In Browne's magnanimous statement, the "not" is absent. All in all, Browne's emphasis on the psychology of inner corruption was wasted on Ross; introspective writers require introspective readers, ideally of kindred emotions or at least of pliable emotions.

## The Neglect of a "Maturer Judgement"

Ross concluded his pronouncement by addressing Browne directly: Browne had indicated his "aberrations . . . not out of an humour of contradiction or vain-glory, nor of any intention I have to bring you or your Booke into obloquie, that I have marked out its obliquities." Since Ross had repudiated Browne for his so-called impious loyalty to friends, it is worth while noting that Ross declared once again the motivation for his book to be "only to satisfie the desire of my friends (for whom we are partly borne) who have laid this charge on me; and to let green heads and inconsiderate young Gentlemen see, that there is some danger in reading your Book, . . . for, whilst they are taken with the *gilding* of your phrase, they may swallow unawares such *pills*, as may rather kill then cure them" (pp. 79–80). Some lesser errors by Browne had been omitted from Ross's critique, since he did not wish to appear "too Eaglesighted in other mens failings, whereas I have enough to doe with mine owne." Complimenting *Religio* for its "much worth and good language," Ross praised Browne for his "modesty" in admitting the relevance of "maturer Judgements" (I, 60) on what he had written. By this Ross meant himself. Ross protested his own lack of malice and concluded piously: "The God of truth direct all our hearts into the way of truth. *Amen*" (p. 80). A final blow indeed— Ross's prayer for Browne.

Seven years later Sir Thomas Urquhart, in his ΕΚΣΚΥΒ-ΛΛΑΥΡΟΝ *or, The Discovery of a Most Exquisite Jewel, . . . To frontal a Vindication of the Honour of Scotland,* offered these praises upon Ross's behalf (noteworthy today solely for their prolixity):

*Nevertheless being to speak a little of some of them [Scottish scholars], before I lanch forth to crois the seas, I must salute that most learned and worthy gentleman, and most endeared minion of the muses, Mr. Alexander Ross, who hath written manyer excellent books in Latin and English, what in prose, what in verse, than he hath lived years; and although I cannot remember all, yet to set down so many of them as on a sudden I can call to minde, will I not forget; to the end the Reader, by the perusal of the works of so universal a scholar, may reap some knowledge when he come to read*

*His Virgilius Evangelizans in thirteen several books (a peece truly, which when set forth with that decorement of plates it is to have in its next edition, will shew that he hath apparelled the Evangelists in more splendid garments, and royal robes, than (without prejudice be it spoken) his compatriots Buchanan and Jhonstoun, have, in their Paraphrastick translation of the Psalmes, done the King and Prophet David). His four books of the Judaick wars, intituled, De rebus Judaicis libri quatour, couched in most excellent hexameters; his book penned against a Jesuite, in neat Latine prose, called Rasuratonsoris; his Chymera Pythagorica contra Lansbergium; his Additions to Wollebius and Ursinus; his book called* The new planet no planet; *his Meditations upon predestination; his book intituled* the pictures of the conscience; *his Questions upon Genesis; his Religions Apotheosis; his Melissomachia; his Virgilius Triumphans; his four curious books of Epigrams in Latin Elegiacks; his Mel Heliconium; his Colloquia plautina; his Mystagogus-poeticus; his Medicus medicatus; his Philosophical touchstones; his Arcana Microcosmi; his observations upon Sir Walter Rawley; his Marrow of History, or Epitome of Sir Walter Rawleigh's works; his great Chronology in the English tongue (set forth in folio) deducing all the most memor-*

able things, that have occurred since the Macedonian war, till within some ten or twelve years to this time: and his many other learned Treatises, whose titles I either know not, or have forgot.

Besides all these volumes, books and tractates here recited, he composed above three hundred exquisite sermons, which were, by the merciless fury of Vulcan, destroyed all in one night, to the great grief of many preachers, to whom they would have been every whit as useful as Sir Edward Coke's reports are to the lawyers. But that which I as much deplore, and am as unfainedly sory for, is that the fire, which (on that fatal night) had seazed on the house and closet where those his Sermons were consumed, had totally reduced to ashes the very desks wherein were locked up several Metaphysical, Physical, Moral, and Dialectical Manuscripts; whose conflagration by Philosophers is as much to be bewailed, as by Theologically-affected spirits, was that of his most divine elucubrations.

This loss truly was irrecoverable, therefore by him at last digested, because he could not help it: but that some losses of another nature, before and after that time by him sustained, have as yet not been repaired, lyeth as a load upon this land, whereof I wish it were disburthened; seeing it is in behalf of him, who for his piety, theological endowments, philosophy, eloquence, and poesie, is so eminently qualified, that (according to the metempsychosis of Pythagoras) one would think that the souls of Socrates, Chrysostome, Aristotle, Ciceron, and Virgil, have been transformed into the substantial faculties of that entelechy, wherewith, by such a conflated transanimation, he is informed and sublimely inspired. He spends the substance of his own lamp, for the weal of others; should it not then be recruited with new oyle by those that have been enlightened by it? Many enjoy great benefices (and that deservedly enough) for the good they do to their coævals onely; how much more meritoriously should he then be dealt with, whose literate erogations reach to this and afterages? A lease for life of any parcel of land is of less value, then the hereditary purchase thereof: so he of whom posterior generations reap a benefit, ought more to be regarded, than they whose actions perish with themselves. Humane reason, and common sense it self instructeth us, that dotations, mortifications, and other honorary recompences, should be most subservient to the use of those, that afford literatory adminicularies of the longest continuance, for the improvement of our sense and reason.

Therefore could I wish (nor can I wish a thing more just) that this reverand, worthy, and learned gentleman Master Rosse, to whom this age is so much beholden, and for whom posterity will be little beholden to this age, if it prove unthankful to him, were (as he is a favorite of Minerva) courted by the opulent men of our time, as Danae was by Jupiter; or that they had as much of Me-

caena's soul, as he hath of Virgil's: for if so it were, or that this
Isle, of all Christendom, would but begin to taste of the happiness of so wise a course, vertue would so prosper, and learning
flourish, by his encouragements, and the endeavors of others in
imitation of him, that the Christians needed lie no longer under
the reproach of ignorance, which the oriental Nations fixe upon
them in termes of seeing but with one eye; but in the instance of
great Britain alone (to vindicate (in matter of knowledge) the
reputation of this our western world) make the Chinese, by very
force of reason (of whose authority above them they are not
ashamed) be glad to confess, that the Europeans, as well as themselves, look out with both their eyes, and have no blinkard minds.
Of which kind of brave men, renowned for perspicacy of sight in
the ready perceiving of intellectual objects, and that in gradu ex-
cellenti, is this Master Rosse: the more ample expressing of whose
deserved Elogies, that I remit unto another time, will I hope be
taken in better part, that I intend to praise him againe; because
Laus ought to be virtutis affecla; and he is always doing good.[28]

Despite this effusive praise, Thomas Keck could praise
Digby at Ross's expense. In his *Annotations* Keck wrote first
of *Religio* and then of its animadverters:

For the work it self, the present Age hath produced none that hath
had better Reception amongst the learned; it hath been received
and fostered by almost all, there having been but one that I know
of (to verifie that Books have their Fate from the capacity of the
Reader) that hath had the face to appear against it; that is Mr.
Alexander Rosse; but he is dead, and it is uncomely to skirmish
with his shadow. It shall be sufficient to remember to the Reader,
that the noble and most learned Knight, Sir Kenelm Digby, has
delivered his opinion of it in another sort, who though in some
things he differ from the Author's sense, yet hath he most candidly
and ingenuously allow'd it to be a very learned and excellent piece;
and I think no Scholar will say there can be approbation more
authentick. (Pp. 49–50)

It is pleasantly revealing that Keck, a consummate pedant in
his own right, praised the scholarly judgment of Digby while
dismissing that of Ross, a companion in pedantry.

Later, Dr. Johnson could accurately report that the *Medicus
Medicatus* was "universally neglected by the world" (Wilkin,

28. Urquhart, 171–76. Quoted by permission of The Huntington Library, San Marino, California. In quoting part of this eulogy
Wilkin adds dryly: "Alas for the person of poor Mister Ross,
which must, on this theory, have been rather thickly peopled with
souls" (I, lxii–lxiii, note).

I, xxv). And Foster Watson, who resurrected Ross in 1895, reported that, while "the *Religio Medici* is read and treasured; *Medicus Medicatus* is hardly known as a name" (p. 470).

Although W. K. Jordan grouped Ross under the "principles of moderation and latitude" and assessed Ross's *Pansebeia: Or, A View of all Religions in the World* (1653), unquestionably written on a controversial and dogmatic subject, as "marked by an objective temper of mind" (IV, 428), it is clear that Ross's attitude toward Browne lacked both objectivity and magnanimity. Ross preferred religious intolerance and philosophical semiconsistency. Even though he embroidered his argument with Aristotelian proofs, most of his conclusions rest solidly on preconceived notions no less metaphysical than those to which he objected. Many of Ross's rebukes are unfair because they ignore Browne's context—in some instances, contexts that state or imply ideas which Ross introduced as rebuttals. Although Browne derived many of his views from teleological and causative arguments, Ross persistently introduced just these arguments in his attempts at confutation. The more extended criticisms in Ross are elliptical, self-contradictory, irrelevant, and unimaginative in many instances. In no way did he submit his conclusions judiciously and fairly. By labeling Browne stupid and evil Ross brought no credit to his discussion. Rather, he presented himself as essentially a dull and ungracious commentator, unwilling either to rebuke or to respect Browne honestly. It is clear that the learned Mr. Ross missed Browne's point.

# V.

## THE CRITICISMS,
## ON BALANCE

Both of Browne's contemporary critics discounted his abilities to deal with matters of spiritual and philosophical depth. Digby, who demanded diligence, orderliness, and "pains" of his readers, doubted that the witty Dr. Browne, with his medical rather than philosophical education, could truly understand such subjects. Although pleased that Browne was not content to use simply the bald terms of the Scholastics, Digby disputed the vagueness of Platonic description and definition. For Ross, *Religio Medici* had been praised too often on the basis of what he considered surface readings. For Browne to ask to be read rhetorically and flexibly was, to Ross, cowardly and suspect. Ross set out to focus the full glare of reason on the text. That there might be a contradiction between his lack of objectivity, induced by his single-minded espousal of certain vested Christian truths, and his pledge of rationalism never occurred to Ross. Views that he regarded as Platonic and allegorical he rejected out-of-hand, just as they had been by Digby. And both commentators trod a slippery path when they essayed to explain the spiritual without plunging entirely into corporeal interpretations. Traditional Aristotelian and biblical authority did not usually fail Ross in this respect. Both sources of knowledge were at least plain and clear most of the time for him. Like Digby, Ross chose not to appreciate a metaphorical definition that interjected fancy into problems he thought must be treated with heavy exactitude. Neither cared to recognize that metaphor already inheres in Aristotle's arguments and definitions.

Having attacked Browne's Platonism, Ross attacked Digby's Aristotelianism in an appended thirty-page section called *Animadversions upon Sir Kenelme Digbie's Observations on "Religio Medici,"* in which he answered what he considered to be Digby's hasty and inaccurate "phrases." A glance at these comments will fill in Ross's views, particularly on certain points with which he did not deal in his reactions to

*Religio*; for example, he charged that Digby disliked Aristotle's definition of light as *actus perspicui* (I, 10; Digby, pp. 5–6) because he did not understand it. "The meaning is plaine," wrote Ross, "that light is the active qualitie of the aire or water, by which they are made perspicuous, or fit *mediums*, through which wee see visible objects; for in darknesse, though the aire be a bodie still, yet it is not the medium of our sight, but onely *potentially*; let the light come, then it is *perspicuous*, that is, through which wee may see the objects *actually*" (p. 85). He concluded, "Here are no naked termes obtruded in the Schooles upon easie minds, as Sir *Kenelme* thinketh" (p. 86). Thus, in a sentence or two Ross dismissed both problems: the inexactitude of traditional philosophical language and the quality–quantity debate. In the meantime Browne's preference for mystery instead of "rigid definition" had been lost sight of. Digby's main complaints against the Aristotelians in *Of Bodies* (Chapters VI and VII) are exemplified concretely by Ross's rebuttal.

While Digby expressed admiration and kinship for Browne's tolerance, particularly of Roman Catholics, Digby's asceticism and right reason narrowed the range of his own magnanimity. Whether the matter before him concerned the ancients or his fellow man, Digby's strictures of conduct and thought inhibited his tolerant instincts. No absolute conclusion can be reached about two men of such contradictory natures—Digby the gregarious extrovert, at least in the early years of his marriage, versus Browne the solitary investigator, surely as knowing as Digby, but not as widely known. Digby could be vaguely expansive on what he recognized as compassion in Browne; Ross, on the other hand, deliberately distorted Browne's forbearance by interjecting agreements between Browne and positions based on Catholic dogma that do not appear in Browne's reminiscences. The slightest signs of ecumenicalism were dangerous gullibility in Ross's eyes. Where questions of papal authority were even hinted at, Ross lost all sense of judicious understanding. His attacks on Browne's tolerance became a stalking-horse for his own bigotry. His use of guilt by association and the unsubstantiated allusion betray the partisanship of Ross's so-called rationalistic attack. Evidently, Ross loved a good fight so dearly he would start one himself, if need be, and then sustain it with a fervor vastly different from Browne's calm.

On the other hand, as we have seen, Digby proceeded, in his criticism of Browne, by substantiating the immortality of the soul by first examining the operations of the body through an investigation of their physical causes. He was troubled by attempts to explain the physical by means of the spiritual powers or qualities. Miraculous or hidden explanations he judged as unsound, since they render incomprehensible many questions that are susceptible to man's reason and understanding. Just as the spiritual is used mistakenly to explain the corporeal, so too the soul is wrongly explained through the corporeal and the occult. If the principles of the body can be understood, then it will be clear that the soul operates from different principles and from a different source. Digby assumed that a physician's intimate familiarity with the body would necessarily be a disadvantage when matters of the soul are examined. The soul is noncorporeal and self-moving. It can deal with negatives, contradictions, particularities, universals, and infinities. The soul and the mind are evidently inseparable.

Yet, when Digby came to consider the regenerated plant in *Religio*, he was forced to agree that the Idea endures so the form may live. A plant is formed through a union of the body's vital heat with air and moisture. As for the generation of animals, Digby rejected preformation and palingenesis while he supported epigenesis and pangenesis. Behind the creative process lies Divine Providence and the clockmaker-God, to become familiar later in Leibnitz's work. But no immediate agent, neither God nor nature, imprints "a determinate figure into a particular body." Digby could not, however, completely reject the idea of "a forming vertue or V*is formatrix* of an unknown power and operation," which he was content to define as "the complex, assemblement, or chayne of all the causes, that concurre to produce this effect." By these means, Digby answered the approach explained through qualities or faculties.

According to Digby, Browne's incapacity for understanding the soul extended to the nature of the resurrected body. Caught on the dilemma of accepting for religious reasons a unification of bodily particles with the soul that he regarded as "grosse," Digby turned to the perpetual atomic flux as an explanation for the unity of the matter with the form. Since the soul as form is absolute and unchangeable, its unity is individual and distinguishable. Thus, the reassumption of identity lies in the form and not in the matter, which lacks distinction.

Ross's conception of the immortal soul paralleled Digby's, but took an opposite tack. He first questioned Browne's ability to read the philosophical sources—which are themselves inconclusive on the question of mortalism—then offered his proposition for immortality. The soul is of a heavenly, not elementary, nature; it is simple, not compounded; it has neither matter nor form, and thus has no contraries; it is inseparable from life, and thus not accidental; it subsists of itself; it desires immortality naturally; and at death it resolves to nothing, being incorruptible. Ross's views apparently differed from Digby's primarily on the questions of matter versus form and on the ability of the soul to be compounded and contradictory. He agreed with Digby that, in the case of the regenerated plant, the form equals the soul of the plant and the vital heat equals the nutritive soul that Aristotle spoke of. But Ross felt it necessary to attack Browne's imaginative experiment by sarcastic quibbling over the natural plant versus the artificial plant and by lowering the analogy with art to a comparison with that which is ephemeral and insubstantial. By using these tactics, he separated his thinking from Browne's standards of art and from Digby's standards of religion. Digby was at least moved, to a degree, by the presence of the Divine Voice in Browne's system.

Ross devoted nearly a third (pp. 98–109) of his animadversions on Digby's *Observations* to answering Digby's views on I, 48 (Digby, pp. 28–31). Ross first stated that Digby was wrong to term the reuniting of each atom of the body "a grosse conception," because the "Almighty" can as well reunite the atoms "as he could at first create them"; Ross cited Tertullian as support (p. 99). With this curt dismissal Ross turned to Digby's lengthier explanation of the resurrection of the body and its identity in eternity. With respect to the broad question of the resurrection, Digby had, according to Ross, committed nine mistakes: (1) what Digby called resurrection is only the *"surrection"* of the body; (2) Christ transfigured or transformed "our vile bodies," but this would indicate "a *forming* of a new body . . . an *assumption* . . . or . . . a *Pythagoricall transanimation"*; (3) man was created so that both his body and soul could enjoy God; (4) "the essentiall forme of mans body" is not like other creatures susceptible to "corruption" so it remains the same; (5) "the same numericall body shall returne that fell, because the whole matter of it remaines"; (6) "though the union of the body to the soule in the resurrection be not *numerically* the same action that was in generation, yet the body shall be the same; because the *entity* and *unity* of the body is not hindered by the multiplication or iteration of accidents, such as union is"; (7) "our resurrection shall bee conformable to *Christs"* or Jonah's; (8) "if in artificiall things the introduction of a new forme makes not the matter to be identically different from what it was," then the same must be true of man's body, which never loses its essential form; and finally (9) "Gods justice and mans comfort" make it so (pp. 100–103).

Digby's second error, Ross declared, was to regard the form, not the matter, as giving "numericall individuation to the body." The opposite is nearly the case; after death the form— "the chiefe cause of *individuation"*—is gone; only the secondary cause—matter and accident—remains to distinguish one dead carcass from another (pp. 103–4).

His third error—that the matter has no actual being without form—was disproved, in Ross's thinking, by the fact that the matter is a substance, has entity, takes part in generation, and is the cause of motion. Although it has "that measure of actuall being" only after union with its form, Ross could not see how matter and form can ever be separate.

Digby's fourth error—that identity belongs to itself, not to its matter—may be answered by the argument that, while the "conjunction of the forme with matter makes *identity* . . . the particular parts of the matter have their particular *identities* and inclinations to such and such formes . . ." (p. 105).

His fifth mistake—that man's body is not the same as it was—Ross handled on the basis of the account of Ulysses' being recognized by his nurse upon his return home and by the admission that "if there be any deperdition [in the body], it is in respect of the fluid parts only, and that so slowly and insensibly" that there is little distinction between a man's body in old age or in childhood. Ross discounted "the common opinion" that there is continual "reparation of the matter by nutrition and auction." The "solid parts" and "the *primogeneall* or *radicall* humour" are the same until death, according to Ross (pp. 106–7).

Finally, Digby's sixth error lay in his choice of similes—the ship of new timber, the ever-flowing Thames, the glassful of water, and the soul of a newly dead man in another body—all of which are inaccurate analogies, according to Ross, since the ship's form would be "onely artificiall and accidentall"; the springs of the Thames, not the river itself, support its identity; the glass, but not water in it, would be the same; and it would be unjust for Dives' soul to enter Job's or Lazarus' body (pp. 107–9).

Nevertheless—returning to Digby's criticism of *Religio*—Ross thought that Digby must admit that the relationship of the soul to the body is a puzzling one. While rejecting traduction (I, 36; Digby, p. 16), he must admit a "dependance" of the soul on the body. To overcome this embarrassment Digby had reaffirmed emotionally the transcendence of the soul by arguing that even in its perfection it must achieve a level of judgment in relation to reason and to proper action, which reinforces the grandeur of what he called the well-ordered soul truly prepared for eternity. This statement of dependence evidently exasperated Ross almost beyond his patience, for he stated in his observations on Digby (pp. 92–93) that he had "already proved" otherwise. He complained that one may as well say "the Sun depends upon the earth, to *warme* and *illuminate* it." In examining further the body–soul unity Digby perceived along Cartesian lines an "I" that continued to exist although separated from the body. Agreeing with Ross that the soul can be accidental from the body, he concluded that it is an immortal substance not subject to change, local motion, the opposition of rarity and density, or "harme from contrariety." The progress of the soul will not be completed in this life, but in the next. He could accept sensory response to external stimuli even to the extent of nerve and brain responses, but he maintained that motion to the brain was carried on by spirits combining with "materiall participations of the bodies." Thus, the organic and the inorganic are reconciled on the level of the soul. The interactions of bodies have not jeopardized the spirituality of the soul.

For Ross, the question of traduction merited long discussion. He reaffirmed that the soul is immaterial, self-existent, immortal, noble, spiritual, nonseminal, and nontransmutable. Along with Digby, he maintained that the soul is superior to and separate from the body. He avoided preformation in his views and did not quite face up to the theory of epigenesis as did Digby. Ultimately, Ross tried to argue that intellect and reason are "infused" into the body, whereas the soul is "transfused." Whatever he meant by this, he concluded that the soul is inorganic and that the brain is indeed "the seat of reason" as well as of the senses and the fancy; the body is simply an "instrument."

Digby held so firmly to the unchangeability of the soul that even the idea that God would release a damned soul is execrable (I, 7; Digby, pp. 5–6). He believed that to do so would necessitate a radical change in the essence of the unsaved soul, while Ross argued moralistically that to do so would destroy the justice of God. Ross continued his criticism (pp. 84–85) with the statement that to change the essence of the soul from pain to happiness is possible, since "these are *accidents*, which may be present or absent, without the destruction of the subject in which they are." He would, however, limit the property of unchangeableness to God alone, with the "passive power or possibilitie of change" in "the things themselves, which are eternall." Digby's example of fire ceasing to be hot Ross countered with the biblical account of the three children in the Babylonian furnace as a case in point.

Ross had not commented directly in *Medicus Medicatus* on Browne's summary of the First Cause and Second Cause (I, 14), but he questioned Digby's view that the first matter does not have actual existence without the form (Digby, p. 8). Ross complained that Digby "must know, that the first matter is a substance, and hath a reall actuality, . . . called *Actus entitativus* . . . , without the forme, else it could not be the *principle*, or *cause* of things . . . when the forme comes, it receives *formall* actuality, without which it is but in possibilitie . . . " (p. 86). Related to this question is the matter of notions. Ross agreed with Digby that "notions have their being only in the mind," but he was unwilling to believe that matter and form are merely notions, as Digby said (pp. 8–9), because notions cannot be "the first principles and causes of all things. So likewise the objects of the two noblest Sciences, . . . *Physick* and *Metaphysick*, are onely *notions* and artificial termes, not reall things, which cannot be" (pp. 86–87). Also related to causation is the question of astrology and its possible impiety (I, 18; Digby, pp. 11–12), so Ross reminded Digby that "the Church and Fathers" settled the matter long since; belief in astrology "overthrowes the liberty of mans will" and "robs God of his honour" (pp. 87–88).

Ross used the immutability of the heavens as support for his argument for both the immortality of the soul and for the existence of "the Heaven of glory." The heavens are quantitative and material, but not subject to generation and corruption. Ross doubted that the world can be destroyed, but even if it can, that possibility does not threaten the eternity of the moral heavens, which are not only real but localized. Hell is hell as, it is supposed to be—real and localized as well. Just as hell is not mental or merely in the conscience, so too there will be a literal judgment day. To think otherwise is to overthrow morality and religion. Death is to be feared—not accepted calmly as Browne and sometimes Digby said.

As we have seen, both Digby and Ross turned to the principle of contradiction as a means for separating the spiritual from the material. According to Digby, God as Self-Entity cannot be Non-Entity, one of the terms of contradiction. God can work contradictions because He is omnipotent; however, annihilation cannot come from God for He is "selfe-existence" (Digby, p. 18). Ross, on the other hand, believed that God cannot work contradictions because certain actions are "repugnant to his wisedome, goodnesse, or power" (p. 41). In his animadversions Ross elaborated on the matter of annihilation, another point from *Religio* that he did not react to directly in *Medicus Medicatus*. He agreed that God cannot be "an efficient cause . . . yet we may safely say, that hee is the deficient cause. . . . There is then in the creature both a passive possibilitie of annihilation, and in God an active possibilitie to withdraw his assistance. . . ." Thus God is affirmed again as absolute cause (pp. 96–97).

Digby's thinking about angels centered on their knowledge which he assumed to be instant, timeless, and nonsuccessive. Ross was narrower in regard to this question and less clear. Neither tolerated Browne's association of light with angels; both regarded light as substantial and material rather than angelic or qualitative; Digby, in particular, argued for the corporeality of light. Ross, in his negative comments (pp. 89–92) discussed his reactions to Digby's views (Digby, pp. 14–15) on I, 33, particularly this question of the nature of light and of angels. Concerning angels, Ross presented four points of criticism of Digby's view that angels have instant and timeless knowledge: angels have grown in knowledge during the six thousand years since creation; they do not know our "free thoughts" (as Digby had said), for these are known only to God except for those made known "by outward signes, or by revelation"; they do not know the future, whether it be the day of judgment, "future contingencies," or "naturall effects," which come from divine causes and influences; finally, they do not know man's resolutions, which come only from his free will—again, subject only to God's knowledge. Concerning the substantiality of light, Ross was deterred for only one sentence by the fact that he had not seen Digby's fuller arguments on the subject. For if light were a body it would penetrate other bodies; it would have to move at impossible speeds from one end of the world to the other; and it would have to disappear and reappear each day with the sun, Ross reasoned.

There are two further areas of rebuttal in the criticisms, neither of which were discussed in *Medicus Medicatus*—first, the soul's relationship to the body (I, 37; Digby, pp. 16–18; and Ross, pp. 93–96) and then the nature of grace (I, 47; Digby, pp. 43–44; and Ross, pp. 109–11).

First, Ross doubted Digby's feeling that "terrene Soules" linger near their bodies in cemeteries, since he did not consider one soul more "terrene" than another, although one "may be more affected to earthly things then another." Besides, "that life, which united the soule to the body" is no more lost to the soul than the light is lost to the sun after it sinks below the horizon. For souls to take new bodies would involve a "*Pytha-goricall transanimation*," while for them to take their "cold and *inorganicall* bodies" would necessitate a return to the grave and a resurgence involving greater strength "then ever they had." More importantly, all "such apparitions are delusions of *Sathan* and *Monkish* tricks, to confirme superstition." As for the idea that souls go out of their bodies with affections to the objects they leave behind them, Ross disparaged the entire idea that the united soul could even have affections, which he defined as "motions of the heart, stirred up by the knowledge and apprehension of the object, good or bad; the one by *prosecution*, the other by *avoiding*." Since the affections work through the heart and the external senses, they have nothing to do with "the soule separated." The soul has only "the reasonable and inorganicall faculties of the *Intellect* and *Will*" after leaving the body. Finally, while Ross could not entirely deny that a murdered body might bleed at the approach of its murderer—which Digby conjectured and which Ross had read about in the case of an arm—he thought it unlikely: If the soul could induce bleeding, why would we need the physician to bleed us, or how can the congealed blood flow again without the vital spirits? Perhaps such a phenomenon can best be explained by "the prayers of these *soules* under the Altar, saying," like Browne (I, 46), "*Quousque, Domine?*"

With respect to the second area—that of grace—Ross was annoyed by Digby's belief that grace is "the whole complex of such reall motives . . . that incline a man to vertue, and piety; and are set on foote by Gods particular *Grace* and favour, to bring that worke to passe" (Digby's exact words, p. 44, rather than Ross's briefer, narrower, and vaguer version). He agreed that grace is not "any inherent or infused quality in us," because "grace in the matter of Justification is taken for the free acceptation, mercy and goodnesse of God in *Christ*. . . . This was given us before the world was made." If grace is taken "in a larger extent, then it signifieth every thing freely given . . . & so Nature it self." In stricter terms, Ross continued, grace is "those spirituall gifts of God, which more neerly concerne our salvation." He seems to say that, in this last sense—although he may have meant it in all three cases—grace is a quality. He perceived a contradiction in Digby's reasoning when he de-

nied that grace is a quality and yet would regard qualities such
as "gentlenesse and softenesse of . . . nature" as instruments of
grace. This view Ross deemed "a harsh and dangerous phrase."

Ross concluded his criticisms with praises of Digby couched
in the reminder that no man—Popes included—has a mo-
nopoly on truth (pp. 111–12).

In *Religio Medici* Sir Thomas Browne presented an implicit
view of himself as an inherently controversial thinker—controversial because he tolerated religious practices and dogmas
that were antipathetic to many of his contemporaries and because he professed a moral emphasis on charity and magnanimity that was to become increasingly dangerous in the combustible decade of the book's publication. The range of
Browne's vision extended beyond tolerance to a gentle skepticism reconciled by an imaginative balance between reason and
intuition.

An innate self-awareness in Browne's tracing of the microcosm in his personal life-fable, his interest in his dreams, his
pursuit of poetry through prose, a conscious striving for synthesis through an *oh altitudo* that perceived God's wisdom,
providence, and eternity, unify—at least tenuously—the arguments in *Religio*. Rather than being personal in his allusions,
Browne obviously related himself to and through certain nearly Faustian archetypes associated with the physician as atheist,
rationalist, and skeptic. Within this broad pattern, Browne
maintained self-love as an instrument for understanding and
charity. Not just *Know thyself*, but *Love thyself* emerges as a
persuasive method in Browne's argument. Defining his life as
a poem, a fable, and a dream, Browne mixed intimacies with
an Olympian perspective that macrocosmically studied its
own microcosm. Such a proportion is ironic simply by its self-
contained distance. Since he recognized his dreams as illusory,
evasive, and facetious in their religious revelation, he accepted
the need to search elsewhere for truth.

But this was no agonized search; instead, he sedately separated himself from those around him. No zealot, no self-
appointed reformer; rather, he determined to relate known
facts, make congruous the incongruous. The Christian faith
as he knew it was circumferent enough to contain him, and he

need not expel someone else to make himself room. Abhorring absolutism and contentiousness in themselves, he sympathized with rational investigation couched in terms of humble exploration. Since man's judgments and systems are temporal and fallible, Browne trusted his best inclinations toward faith and charity until death should reveal all.

Recognizing the historical cycles in religious speculations, Browne coordinated his *oh altitudo* with an all-embracing God-head who supersedes man's questions. A totally self-conscious faith overrides any incongruity of reason and imagination. Metaphor transcends definition, description eclipses prescription.

Probably the only absolute is God Himself—His causation, His revelatory force in nature, His divine numerology, His omnipotent craftsmanship, His providential companionship with mankind. The embodiment of God's presence may be found in the mysterious, the miraculous, the oracular, and the demonic. Man's existence in an amphibious state between matter and spirit reinforced for Browne the natural ambivalence of life and death. Man's essence—his soul—is inorganic and thus beyond the destructiveness of death. Along with life's other misfortunes, Browne was able to tolerate the fact of death. But resurrection will prevail, even to the extent of the regenerated plant, in which the immortality of the noncorporeal form and the indestructibility of the microcosmic Idea or seed will defeat the seemingly material basis of existence. A necessary harmony of man and God, of body and soul, of man and man will achieve final progression toward eternity.

Although Browne apologized in his brief preface for his *Religio* and rewrote and supplemented some passages in it, he left it a substantially controversial and—to some—an alarming work. His defense against the charge of atheism has the mark of an eagerly inquisitive mind, of a lover of "private truths" who could not help but prompt responses from many conservative readers. Two of these readers—as we have shown —responded pointedly and unfavorably in print. Browne's dislike for religious and intellectual quarrels could never counterbalance his hyperboles and paradoxes, which beg for retorts —both serious and facetious. While much of *Religio* is not controversial—especially today—it contains enough impor-

tant questions and answers to arouse a dogmatic reader or
one preoccupied with certain religious and scientific commit-
ments. Browne's equivocations and ambivalences are taken
today to be the words of a cautious rationalist or a compromis-
ing pietist, but to contemporaries like Digby or Ross such
hesitancies suggested cowardice and impiety.

For a reader of Sir Kenelm Digby's views, the question of
the soul's virtue was as significant as its immortality. The soul
perseveres over an inferior body that is affected by lowly
earthly desires while tied to an all-powerful God who acts
visibly and rationally through a chain of causation that is at
one time mechanistic and immaterial. For Digby, the intuitive and the Platonic were aëry and ephemeral, while the personal and the social were vulgar and temporal. Granting
Browne ingenuity and an even judgment, Digby doubted that
he was capable of truly understanding the immortality of the
soul. Both faith and demonstration affirmed the soul's immortality for Digby, but to approach the question accurately,
Digby thought, one must avoid explaining the physical by
means of miraculous or secret causes and the spiritual by
means of corporeal causes. So Browne as a physician was
guilty, by association, of the gross errors of materialism and
particularity. Worse, Digby accused the medical mind of
overlooking universal causes, thus rendering itself incapable
of perceiving the true nature of the soul and its immortality.
To lack the mind to perceive the soul may be to lack also the
soul itself, he feared. The soul can be strengthened and educated in this life through spiritual judgments that rise above
the particular, the sensual, and the merely human. He observed this capability in himself but not in Browne.

In seeking an explanation for the mechanical responses of
the nervous system, Digby assumed an immortal substance
independent of the body and its properties. In terms of the
purely physical—plants and animals—Digby looked for physical explanations that do not contradict possible nonphysical
ones. The absoluteness of causation aids in all explanations
anyway, even those touching on fortune, astrology, palmistry,
and even demonology.

Digby's Aristotelian-based concept of the Deity predicated
a positive, active force in the universe, capable of performing

every rational action necessary for existence. Distrustful of metaphors and quibbles other than his own, Digby demonstrated a progressive continuum in nature and beyond, as substantial and quantitative as he could posit while still maintaining the spiritual qualities. He found Browne too negative, too obscure, and too indiscriminate in his thinking and expression. For one matter, Browne failed to distinguish the word from the thing, and the quality from the quantity. The same general quarrel carried back to Digby's views on the particular versus the universal. In determining the truly universal from the accidental it is necessary to avoid subtlety. Perception and understanding are unified by a careful and accurate use of analogy. Ultimate understanding comes after death, but it is clearly foreshadowed by the anti-contradictory and immutable character of God's actions through nature. The progressive character of mankind culminates in a union with the unchanging spiritual world. The sympathetic yearning of the soul for spiritual existence solely, and then for a reunion with a body cleansed of its carnality epitomized for Digby the nature of the resurrection. By such an action the spirit reaffirms and consolidates its superiority over the body as well as the transcendence of the form over the matter. Final identity in eternity is spiritual, not material. By such an orderly procedure, true understanding can be achieved without recourse to mysterious or poetic explanations. Most significantly, Digby declared that no leap from the material to the spiritual, such as he found in Browne, is necessary. No divine voice or universal spirit need be invoked.

Digby's God is intimately related to the nature of virtue and grace. Virtue is sustained for its own sake—not for a reward— and culminates through grace or God's favor represented in the beatific vision. The soul's desire to achieve this state is so strong that it grows to hate the body's earthly life. The correspondence found here between human and divine excellence reduces to vulgar insignificance any motivation based on a system of reward and punishment, in Digby's view. Virtue as a temper of mind is also closely related to right reason. The presence of grace can make itself known to such a receptive mind, although sometimes misfortune may be needed to signal this presence. The power of grace reaffirms the chain of causation so carefully ordered by God. Even charity must be defined in terms of man to God, rather than man to man. All worldly endeavors are necessary and rational preparations for the next life. Ultimately, all matters of love and charity are synthesized by the power of divine love. Thus, for Digby, this chain of devotion represented a tangible and reliable explanation for all relevant questions raised by Browne.

While the extravagances of Browne's mind and art may amuse and excite most readers, Digby's extravagances simply irritate and annoy. Whereas Browne intrigued the reader with mysteries unexplained and oxymorons unforeseen, Digby indulged in underdeveloped rebuttals and immaterial explanations. Digby, as a controversialist, was not to be satisfied with factual arguments. While Browne's inconsistencies seem personally based and the results of private contemplation, Digby's contradictions strike the reader as arbitrary and ill-humored. Actually, the two men could have been compatible in their thinking, if Digby were not so inflexible in his moralisms. Apparently, he was so preoccupied by his version of existence that he could not respect the ingenuity of Browne's views. A tendency to disagree for the sake of disagreement does not enhance the quality of Digby's retort.

Contrarily, Alexander Ross promised to peruse Browne's "matter, not words," with a rational, not rhetorical, eye. Instead, his rationalism is often mere subjectivity and preconception. Far oftener than Digby, Ross simply misrepresented Browne's meaning. As for Browne's tolerance for Roman Catholicism, Ross in his anti-Catholicism and antipapism merely adopted guilt by association as an argumentative maneuver with occasional cries of heresy to heighten the effect. For Ross the middle way was the dangerous and ridiculous path in a time of crisis calling for absolute commitment, not compromise. Clearly, Ross was not inclined to avoid controversy and conflict.

The pedant in Ross seldom resisted the temptation to lecture Browne on what sources he should consult to reconstruct his understanding of such complex matters as the soul's immortality. Ross's eclectic Aristotelianism served his purposes well; he could attack what he regarded as myth and metaphor in Platonism while asserting the rationalism of Aristotle in his own behalf. An uncertain blend of a philosophic soul with a moralistic system of reward and punishment, based on heaven and hell as final reality, satisfied all doubts for Ross. Browne's too-expansive reliance on God's mercy was a spiritual blight, in Ross's sterner vision. There's no escape for the cowardly sinner, Ross warned. All such equivocation reinforced, for Ross, Browne's dangerous ambivalences and uncertainties. Such misconceptions usually met with sarcasm, so when Browne's imagination soared to its heights, whether it be concerning the body–soul or the regenerated plant, Ross grounded it with literalism and flat matter-of-factness.

In Ross's work, arguments against obscure metaphors and quantitative definitions are lumped together with propositions based on the absolute validity of circularity and constancy in the universe and in God's method. Dogmatic claims based on literalistic readings of Aristotle are presented to counterattack and dismiss Browne's views. Errors that touched on salvation and damnation provoked Ross to righteous anger.

Similar literalism characterized Ross's use of Scripture. He regarded Browne's reading as "mysticall." There were few ambiguities for Ross, so he labeled Browne's views as impious, heretical, and at the very least "ridiculous." Fully confident of his authority, Ross laughed at what he considered Browne's vacillations.

On the matter of God's omnipotence and wisdom Ross simply summarized Thomistic and Augustinian positions as contrasts to inaccuracies and limitations he perceived in Browne's thinking. He regarded Browne's views on fortune and astrology as profane and Satanic, for they diminished a benevolent God. Man's very nature emanates from God and to doubt this providential care is atheistic. Mankind must then respond morally; doubt of any kind is un-Christian and infidel.

Levity, mannered indifference, irony, equanimity, candor, whimsy, understatement, objectivity, self-declared ignorance, magnanimity, and introspection—the major qualities that characterize *Religio Medici*—were utterly wasted on Ross, who must attack the book as a warning to those "green hands and inconsiderate young Gentlemen" who "are taken with the *gilding* of your phrase."

So Digby seems sympathetic to Browne when compared with the mean-tempered Ross whose fixed Aristotelianism and Scottish Presbyterianism prevented an equable reading of either author. However, the extremity of Ross's sometimes foolish objections actually make his *Medicus Medicatus* more enjoyable reading than Digby's *Observations,* but the work is a curiosity rather than valid argument. Ross rebuked Browne's arguments more by misrepresentation or by irrelevancy than by any germane facts. Much of the time he deluged Browne's point with a catalogue of Aristotelian assumptions or scriptural principles without directly relating either to what Browne had said. For those readers of Ross's cast of mind such attacks have severe effect, but to most readers the imaginative idealism of Browne withstands such blanketing. When Ross and Browne substantially agreed on some moral and religious matters, only the extremity and rigidity of Ross's arguments separated them. But after Ross had elaborated one of his points, the gap between the two writers widened. It is fascinating to watch Ross separate himself from the moderation of Browne's views. All in all, Ross brought a most unsatisfactory—but provocative—perspective from which to judge a mind and talent like Browne's.

Usually Digby and Ross did not attack the broad lines of Browne's tolerance, skepticism, faith, or personal confession; instead, they attached their rebukes to specific contentions, many times of a minor or subordinate significance, and thus weakened their cases by ignoring the broader lines of Browne's argument. Only Ross's frontal attack on Browne's tolerance or Digby's confusing rebuttal to Browne's doctrine of moral charity raised major and substantial debates. Usually Ross and Digby only carped at minutiae in Browne, whether it be an occasional hyperbole or witticism, or a metaphorical sally or conceit. Instead of attacking Browne's *oh altitudo* itself, both critics objected only to the individual paradoxes his imagination and speculativeness allowed them to see. Thus, many of the more formidable debates degenerated to a mere contrast of Browne's vision with their own. A modern reader is often surprised by what Browne perceived—either his idea itself or the language through which he expressed it—while in reading Digby or Ross the reader's enjoyment is often dulled by redundant objections. That ultimately Browne was neither radical nor revolutionary in his thinking renders Digby's and Ross's objections all the more perverse. In some ways both critics outreached Browne in their modernity, but neither neared his imaginative levels.

Browne's genius lay in the ingenious and the provocative. Any reader who too quickly rejects the insights of *Religio Medici* need only turn to his contemporaries' criticisms to see superfluities and prejudices sufficient to underscore the intellectual pleasures that can be gained from this product of Browne's mind. Even though Browne was ultimately conservative—looking back to scholasticism and Neoplatonism rather than forward to rationalism and science in the later seventeenth and early eighteenth century senses—his ideas were presented with such a high quality of expression and vigor that they carry a weight and authority much greater than might be expected. Browne's attackers increased this authority by making his ideas appear more controversial and uncompromising than they truly were. But even without the defamers and the historical hindsight, many readers still find *Religio* a most invigorating book. As an escape from the mundane and the temporal, *Religio* can scarcely be rivaled. Perhaps we can object as strongly to Digby and Ross's attempts to pull Browne back from his elevated and idiosyncratic viewpoint as to any counterattack that they launched against him.

Once the reader recognizes that a mental progression, not a logical one, unfolds in *Religio*, then he releases himself to the sweeping rhythms of the very copiousness of that mind: the personal touches, the Janus-like quality, the pursuit of religious mysteries and beauties, the sweep of its faith, the degree to which it seeks out correspondences between man and God, the divinity and the artistry it perceives in nature, the tempered skepticism of its rationalism, its superstitiousness, its grandiloquence, its paradox, its humanitarianism—these are the valued intellectual and mental qualities in *Religio Medici*. They are durable enough to reward any reader who, like Browne, wrestles with the philosophical, scientific, and moral problems posited by the sudden expansions of all horizons in the reader's place and time. *Religio Medici* remains in its controversialness one of the most viable bridges the "ingenuous Reader" has between himself and the seventeenth-century mind.

# BIBLIOGRAPHY

Adam, Charles. "Descartes: Ses Correspondants Anglais," *Revue de Littérature Comparée*, 17 (1937), 437–60.

Allen, Don Cameron. *The Legend of Noah*. Illinois Stud. in Lang. and Lit., Vol. 33, Nos. 3–4. Urbana: University of Illinois Press, 1949.

Allers, Rudolf. "Microcosmus: From Anaximandros to Paracelsus," *Traditio*, 2 (1944), 319–407.

Aquinas, St. Thomas. *Summa Theologica*, trans. Fathers of the English Dominican Province. 3 vols. New York: Benziger Bros., 1947–1948.

Aristotle. *The Works . . . Translated Into English Under the Editorship of W. D. Ross*. 12 vols. Oxford: The Clarendon Press, 1910–1952.

Aubrey, John. *Aubrey's Brief Lives*, ed. Oliver Lawson Dick. London: Secker and Warburg, 1950.

———. *Brief Lives . . .* , ed. Andrew Clark. 2 vols. Oxford: The Clarendon Press, 1898.

———. *Miscellanies*. London: 1696.

———. *The Natural History of Wiltshire*, ed. John Britton. London: J. B. Nichols and Son, 1847.

———. *Remaines of Gentilisme and Judaisme*, ed. James Britten. London: W. Satchell, Peyton, 1881.

Augustine, Saint. *The City of God*, trans. Marcus Dods. New York: Modern Library, 1950.

Bacon, Roger. *The Opus Majus . . .* , trans. Robert Belle Burke. 2 vols. Philadelphia: University of Pennsylvania Press, 1928.

Baker, Herschel. *The Wars of Truth*. Cambridge: Harvard University Press, 1952.

Bamborough, J. B. *The Little World of Man*. London: Longmans, Green, 1952.

Bennett, Joan. *Sir Thomas Browne*. Cambridge: Cambridge University Press, 1962.

Bernard, Abbot of Clairvaux. *The Steps of Humility*, trans. George Bosworth Burch. Cambridge: Harvard University Press, 1940.

Bethell, S. L. *The Cultural Revolution of the Seventeenth Century*. New York: Roy, 1951.

Bevan, Edwyn. "Hellenistic Judaism," *The Legacy of Israel*, eds. Edwyn Bevan and Charles Singer. Oxford: The Clarendon Press, 1927.

Blackmur, R. P. *The Double Agent*. 1935; rpt. Gloucester, Mass.: Peter Smith, 1962.

Bligh, E. W. *Sir Kenelm Digby and His Venetia*. London: S. Low, Marston, 1932.

Blount, Charles. *The Miscellaneous Works*. . . . London: 1695.

Bocalini, Trajano. *I ragguagli Di Parnasso, or, Advertisements from Parnassus: in two centuries. With the Politick Touchstone*, trans. Henry Earl of Monmouth. 3d ed., corr. London: 1674.

Bottrall, Margaret. *Every Man a Phoenix*. London: Murray, 1958.

Bowle, John. *Hobbes and His Critics*. London: J. Cape, 1951.

Bradley, Robert I., S. J. "Blacklo and the Counter-Reformation: an Inquiry into the Strange Death of Catholic England," *From the Renaissance to the Counter-Reformation: Essays in Honor of Garrett Mattingly*, ed. C. H. Carter. New York: Random House, 1965.

Bredvold, Louis I. *The Intellectual Milieu of John Dryden*. 1934; rpt. Ann Arbor: University of Michigan Press, 1956.

Brehier, Emile. *The Seventeenth Century*, trans. Wade Baskin. *The History of Philosophy*, Vol. 4. Chicago: University of Chicago Press, 1966.

Briggs, K. M. *Pale Hecate's Team: an Examination of the Beliefs on Witchcraft and Magic among Shakespeare's Contemporaries and His Immediate Successors*. London: Routledge and Kegan Paul, 1962.

Brome, Alexander. *Songs and Other Poems*. London: 1661.

Browne, John. *Adenochoiradelogia. . . .* London: 1684.

[Browne, Sir Thomas, and Sir Kenelm Digby]. *Browne's "Religio Medici" and Digby's "Observations."* Tudor and Stuart Library. Oxford: The Clarendon Press, 1909.

Browne, Sir Thomas. *Religio Medici*. London: 1642.

———. *Religio Medici*. London: 1643.

———. *Religio Medici*, ed. Jean-Jacques Denonain. Cambridge: Cambridge University Press, 1953.

———. *Religio Medici*, ed. Jean-Jacques Denonian. Cambridge: Cambridge University Press, 1955.

———. *Religio Medici and Other Works*, ed. L. C. Martin. Oxford: The Clarendon Press, 1964.

———. *Sir Thomas Browne's Works including his Life and Correspondence*, ed. Simon Wilkin. 4 vols. London: William Pickering, 1835.

Burtt, Edwin Arthur. *The Metaphysical Foundations of Modern Physical Science*. 2d ed. rev. Garden City, N. Y.: Doubleday, 1954.

Bush, Douglas. *English Literature in the Earlier Seventeenth Century*. 2d ed. rev. *The Oxford History of English Literature*, Vol. V. Oxford: The Clarendon Press, 1962.

Calvin, John. *Institutes of the Christian Religion*, trans. John Allen. 7th ed. 2 vols. Philadelphia: Presbyterian Board of Christian Education, 1936.

Cardano, Gerolamo. *The Book of Games of Chance: "Liber De Ludo Aleae,"* trans. Sydney Henry Gould. New York: Holt, Rinehart, and Winston, 1961.

Cassirer, Ernst. *The Platonic Renaissance in England*, trans. James P. Pettegrove. Austin: University of Texas Press, 1953.

Cawley, Robert Ralston, and George Yost. *Studies in Sir Thomas Browne*. Eugene: University of Oregon Books, 1965.

Chalmers, Gordon Keith. "Sir Thomas Browne: True Scientist,"
   *Osiris*, 2 (1936), 28–79.
Cicero. *De Natura Deorum, Academica*, trans. H. Rackham. Loeb
   Classical Library. Cambridge: Harvard University Press,
   1933.
Clarendon, Edward Hyde, Earl of. *The History of the Rebellion
   and Civil Wars in England*, ed. Bulkeley Bandinel. 8 vols.
   Oxford: 1826.
———. *The Life*. 2 vols. Oxford: The University Press, 1857.
Cohn, Norman. *The Pursuit of the Millennium*. Fairlawn, N. J.:
   Essential Books, 1957.
Coleman, Christopher Bush. *Constantine the Great and Chris-
   tianity: Three Phases: the Historical, the Legendary, and the
   Spurious*. New York: Columbia University Press, 1914.
*Coleridge on the Seventeenth Century*, ed. Roberta Florence
   Brinkley. Durham: Duke University Press, 1955.
Colie, Rosalie L. "Sir Thomas Browne's 'Entertainement' in
   XVIIth Century Holland," *Neophilologus*, 36 (1952),
   162–71.
Collop, John. *Poesis Rediviva or, Poesie Reviv'd*. London: 1656.
*Conway Letters; the Correspondence of Anne, Viscountess Con-
   way, Henry More, and their Friends, 1642–1684*, ed. Marjorie
   Hope Nicolson. New Haven: Yale University Press, 1930.
Conford, F. M. *The Unwritten Philosophy and Other Essays*, ed.
   W. K. C. Guthrie. Cambridge: Cambridge University Press,
   1950.
Curry, Walter Clyde. *Shakespeare's Philosophical Patterns*. Baton
   Rouge: Louisiana State University Press, 1937.
Dampier, William Cecil. *A History of Science and Its Relations
   with Philosophy and Religion*. 4th ed. rev. Cambridge:
   Cambridge University Press, 1949.
Danielou, Jean. *Origen*, trans. Walter Mitchell. New York: Sheed
   and Ward, 1955.
Davies, R. Trevor. *Four Centuries of Witch-Beliefs: with Special
   Reference to the Great Rebellion*. London: Methuen, 1947.
Debus, Allen G. "Sir Thomas Browne and the Study of Colour
   Indicators," *Ambix*, 10 (February, 1962), 29–36.
Denonain, Jean-Jacques. *La Personnalité de Sir Thomas Browne:
   Essai d'application de la caracterologie à la critique et
   l'histoire littéraires*. Publications de la faculté des lettres et
   sciences humaines d'alger, XXXIII. Paris: Presses Univer-
   sitaires de France, 1959.
Digby, H. M. *Sir Kenelm Digby and George Digby, Earl of Bristol*.
   London: Digby, Long, 1912.
Digby, Sir Kenelm. *A Discourse concerning the Vegetation of
   Plants*. London: 1661.
———. *Observation on the 22. Stanza in the 9th Canto of the
   2nd Book of Spencers Faery Queen. Full of excellent Notions
   concerning the Frame of Man, and his rational Soule*. Lon-
   don: 1644.
———. *Private Memoirs*. . . . London: Saunders and Otley, 1827.
———. *Two Treatises: in the one of which, The Nature of Bodies;*

in the other, the Nature of Mans Soul, Is Looked Into: In Way of Discovery of the Immortality of Reasonable Soules. Paris: 1644.

Dijksterhuis, E. J. *Archimedes*. Acta Historica Scientiarum Naturalium et Medicinalium, Vol. 12. Copenhagen: E. Munksgaard, 1956.

Dowden, Edward. *Puritan and Anglican*. London: K. Paul, Trench, Trubner, 1901.

Drummond, William. *The Works*. . . . Edinburgh: J. Watson, 1711.

Dunn, William P. *Sir Thomas Browne*. 2d ed. rev. Minneapolis: University of Minnesota Press, 1950.

Edelstein, Ludwig. "The Golden Chain of Homer," *Studies in Intellectual History*. Baltimore: The Johns Hopkins Press, 1953.

Empedocles. *The Fragments* . . . , trans. William Ellery Leonard. Chicago: The Open Court Publishing Co., 1908.

Endicott, N. J. "Some Aspects of Self-Revelation and Self-Portraiture in *Religio Medici*," *Essays in English Literature from the Renaissance to the Victorian Age Presented to A. S. P. Woodhouse 1964*, eds. Millar MacLure and F. W. Watt. Toronto: University of Toronto Press, 1964.

Epictetus. *Moral Discourses*, trans. Elizabeth Carter, ed. W. H. D. Rouse. London: E. P. Dutton, 1933.

Evelyn, John. *Diary and Correspondence* . . . , ed. William Bray. 4 vols. London: G. Bell and Sons, 1887.

————. *The Diary* . . . , ed. E. S. DeBeer. 6 vols. Oxford: The Clarendon Press, 1955.

————. *Fumifugium*. London: 1661.

————. *The Miscellaneous Writings* . . . , ed. William Upcott. London: H. Colburn, 1825.

[Ficino, Marsilio]. *Marsilio Ficino's Commentary on Plato's "Symposium,"* trans. Sears Reynold Jayne. The University of Missouri Studies, Vol. 19. Columbia: The University of Missouri Press, 1944.

Finch, Jeremiah S. *Sir Thomas Browne*. 1950; rpt. New York: Collier Books, 1961.

Finney, Gretchen L. "Music: a Book of Knowledge in Renaissance England," *SRen*, 6 (1959), 36–63.

Fulton, John. *Sir Kenelm Digby*. New York: P. and Katharine Oliver, 1937.

Fussell, G. E. "Crop Nutrition in the Late Stuart Age (1660–1714)," *Annals of Science*, 14 (1958, pub. 1960), 173–84.

Gabrieli, Vittorio. *Sir Kenelm Digby: Un Inglese Italianato Nell'eta Della Controriforma*. Roma: Edizioni di Storia e letteratura, 1957.

Galen. *On Anatomical Procedures: "De Anatomicis Adminstrationibus,"* trans. Charles Singer. Pub. of the Wellcome Historical Medical Museum, N. S., No. 7. London: Oxford University Press, 1956.

Gillow, Joseph. *A Literary and Biographical History, or Bibliographical Dictionary of the English Catholics. From the*

*Breach with Rome, in 1534, to the Present Time.* 5 vols. London: Burns and Oates, 1885–1903.

Glanvill, Joseph. *A Praefatory Answer to Mr. Henry Stubbe. . . .* London: 1671.

Gosse, Edmund. *Sir Thomas Browne.* English Men of Letters. New York: The Macmillan Co., 1905.

Grant, Robert M. *Miracle and Natural Law in Graeco-Roman and Early Christian Thought.* Amsterdam: North Holland Pub. Co., 1952.

Green, Peter. *Sir Thomas Browne.* Bibliog. Ser. of Supplements to "British Book News" on Writers and Their Work, No. 108. London: Longmans, Green, 1959.

Grenell, Robert Gordon. "Sir Kenelm Digby, Embryologist," *Bull. Hist. Med.,* 10 (1941), 48–52.

Grotius, Hugo. *The Rights of War and Peace,* ed. A. C. Campbell. Washington: M. W. Dunne, 1901.

Hakewill, George. *Apologie or Declaration of the Power and Providence of God.* London: 1627.

Hammond, Henry. *A Practicall Catechisme.* London: 1646.

Harnack, Adolf von. *History of Dogma,* trans. Neil Buchanan. 7 vols. New York: Russell and Russell, 1958.

Harris, Victor. *All Coherence Gone.* Chicago: University of Chicago Press, 1949.

Harrison, Charles Trawick. "The Ancient Atomists and English Literature of the Seventeenth Century," *Harvard Stud. in Classical Philology,* 45 (1934), 1–79.

Harvey, Gideon. *The Conclave of Physicians, detecting their intrigues, frauds, and plots, against their patients. . . .* London: 1683.

Hazlitt, William. *Lectures on the Literature of the Age of Elizabeth, and Characters of Shakespear's Plays.* London: Bell and Daldy, 1884.

Henderson, Ernest F., trans. and ed. *Select Historical Documents of the Middle Ages.* London: Bell and Sons, 1892.

Hilberry, Conrad. "Medical Poems from John Collop's *Poesis Rediviva* (1656)," *Jour. Hist. Med. and Allied Sciences,* 11 (1956), 384–411.

Hinman, Robert B. *Abraham Cowley's World of Order.* Cambridge: Harvard University Press, 1960.

Historical Manuscripts Commission. *Report of the Manuscripts of the Late Allan George Finch, Esq. of Burley-on-the-Hill, Rutland.* Ser. 71, 4 vols. London: H. M. Stationery Office, 1913–1965.

Hobbes, Thomas. *Of Liberty and Necessity,* ed. Baron Cay V. Brockdorff. Kiel: Schmidt and Klaunig, 1938.

Horace. *Satires, Epistles, and Ars Poetica,* trans. H. Rushton Fairclough. Loeb Classical Library. Cambridge: Harvard University Press, 1936.

Howell, Almonte C. "Sir Thomas Browne and Seventeenth-Century Scientific Thought," *SP,* 22 (1925), 61–80.

Howell, James. *The Familiar Letters,* ed. Joseph Jacobs. 2 vols. London: D. Nutt, 1892.

Hughes, Merritt Y. "The Themes of Pre-existence and Infancy in
    *The Retreate,*" *Renaissance Studies in Honor of Hardin
    Craig,* eds. Baldwin Maxwell, W. D. Briggs, Francis R.
    Johnson, and E. N. S. Thompson. Stanford: Stanford Uni-
    versity Press, 1941.

Huntley, Frank Livingstone. *Sir Thomas Browne.* Ann Arbor:
    University of Michigan Press, 1962.

———. "Sir Thomas Browne and His Oxford Tutor; or Academic
    Guilt by Association," *The History of Ideas News Letter,* 2
    (1956), 50–53.

———. "Sir Thomas Browne, M.D., William Harvey, and the
    Metaphor of the Circle," *Bull. Hist. Med.,* 25 (1951),
    236–47.

Jenkins, Harold. *Edward Benlowes (1602–1676): Biography of a
    Minor Poet.* Cambridge: Harvard University Press, 1952.

Johnson, Francis R. *Astronomical Thought in Renaissance Eng-
    land: A Study of Scientific Writings from 1500 to 1645.*
    Huntington Library Pub. Baltimore: Johns Hopkins Press,
    1937.

Jones, Richard Foster. *Ancients and Moderns: A Study of the
    Background of the "Battle of the Books."* Washington Univ.
    Stud., N.S., Lang. and Lit. No. 6. St. Louis: Washington
    University, 1936.

———. *The Seventeenth Century.* Stanford: Stanford University
    Press, 1951.

Jordan, W. K. *The Development of Religious Toleration in Eng-
    land from the Accession of James I to the Convention of the
    Long Parliament (1603–1640).* 4 vols. London: G. Allen and
    Unwin, Ltd., 1932–1940.

Jortin, John. *Tracts, Philological, Critical, and Miscellanies.* 2
    vols. London: 1790.

Josephus. *Jewish Antiquities,* trans. H. St. J. Thackeray. 8 vols.
    Loeb Classical Library. London: W. Heinemann, 1926–
    1939.

*Julian the Emperor, containing Gregory Nazianzan's Two In-
    vectives and Libanius's Monody,* trans. Charles William
    King. Bohn's Classical Library. London: 1888.

*Juvenal and Persius,* trans. G. G. Ramsay. Loeb Classical Library.
    London: W. Heinemann, 1928.

[Keck, Thomas]. "Annotations Upon *Religio Medici,*" in Sir
    Thomas Browne, *Works.* London: 1686.

Kemsley, Douglas S. "Religious Influences in the Rise of Mod-
    ern Science: a Review and Criticism, Particularly of the
    'Protestant-Puritan Ethic' Theory," *Annals of Science,* 24
    (September, 1968), 199–226.

Keynes, Sir Geoffrey. *The Life of William Harvey.* Oxford: The
    Clarendon Press, 1966.

King, Daniel. *The Vale-Royall of England, or The County Pala-
    tine of Chester Illustrated.* London: 1656.

Kocher, Paul H. *Science and Religion in Elizabethan England.*
    Huntington Library Pub. San Marino: Huntington Library,
    1953.

Kristeller, Paul Oskar, ed. *Catalogus Translationum et Commentariorum: Mediaeval and Renaissance Latin Translations and Commentaries*. Washington: Catholic University of America Press, 1960.

Lamprecht, Sterling P. "The Role of Descartes in Seventeenth Century England," *Studies in the History of Ideas*, 3 (1935), 181–240.

Laud, William. *The Works*, eds. William Scott and James Bliss. 7 vols. Oxford: John Henry Parker, 1846–1860.

Leroy, Olivier. *Le Chevalier Thomas Browne (1605–1682): Medecin, Styliste and Metaphysicien*. Paris: Librairie J. Gamber, 1931.

Letts, Malcolm. "Sir Thomas Browne and His Books," *N&Q*, 11th ser., 10 (1914), 321–23, 342–44, 361–62.

Lilly, William. *History of His Life and Times*. London: J. Roberts, 1715.

[Longueville, Thomas]. *The Life of Sir Kenelm Digby by One of his Descendants*. London: Longmans, Green, 1896.

Lovejoy, Arthur O. *The Great Chain of Being*. 1957; rpt. New York: Harper, 1960.

Lowell, James Russell. *Literary Essays*. 4 vols. Boston: Houghton Mifflin, 1890.

Matthiessen, F. O. *American Renaissance*. London: Oxford University Press, 1941.

McKeon, Richard, ed. and trans. *Selections from Medieval Philosophers*. 2 vols. New York: Charles Scribner's Sons, 1930.

McLachlan, H. John. *Socinianism in Seventeenth-Century England*. London: Oxford University Press, 1951.

Mead, G. R. S. *Thrice-Greatest Hermes*. 3 vols. London: John M. Watkins, 1949.

Merryweather, John. *Directions for the Latine Tongue*. London: 1681.

Merton, Egon Stephen. "The Botany of Sir Thomas Browne," *Isis*, 47 (1956), 161–71.

——. "Old and New Physiology in Sir Thomas Browne: Digestion and Some Other Functions," *Isis*, 57 (1966), 249–59.

——. *Science and Imagination in Sir Thomas Browne*. New York: King's Crown Press, 1949.

——. "Sir Thomas Browne as Zoologist," *Osiris*, 9 (1950), 413–34.

——. "Sir Thomas Browne's Interpretation of Dreams," *PQ*, 28 (1949), 497–503.

Merton, Robert K. "Science, Technology and Society in Seventeenth Century England," *Osiris*, 4, part 2 (1938), 360–632.

Millerd [Smertenko], Clara Elizabeth. *On the Interpretation of Empedocles*. Chicago: University of Chicago Press, 1908.

Millington, E. C. "Theories of Cohesion in the Seventeenth Century," *Annals of Science*, 5 (1945), 253–69.

Mintz, Samuel I. *The Hunting of the Leviathan*. Cambridge: Cambridge University Press, 1962.

More, Henry. *An Explanation of the Grand Mystery of Godliness*. London: 1660.

More, Paul Elmer. *Shelburne Essays, Sixth Series, Studies of Religious Dualism.* New York: G. P. Putnam's Sons, 1909.

Morley, Christopher. *Sir Kenelm Reads in Bed.* New York: P. C. Duschnes, 1937.

Nathanson, Leonard. *The Strategy of Truth: A Study of Sir Thomas Browne.* Chicago: University of Chicago Press, 1967.

Needham, Joseph. *A History of Embryology.* 2d ed. rev. New York: Abelard-Schuman, 1959.

———. *Time: the Refreshing River.* New York: Macmillan, 1943.

Nicoll, Allardyce. "Sir Kenelm Digby, Poet, Philosopher, and Pirate of the Restoration," *The Johns Hopkins Alumni Magazine,* 21 (1933), 330–50.

Nicolson, Marjorie Hope. *The Breaking of the Circle.* Evanston: Northwestern University Press, 1950.

———. "The Early Stages of Cartesianism in England," SP, 26 (1929), 356–74.

Oates, Whitney J., ed. *The Stoic and Epicurean Philosophers.* New York: Random House, 1940.

Oppenheimer, Jane M. "John Hunter, Sir Thomas Browne and The Experimental Method," *Bull. Hist. Med.,* 21 (1947), 17–32.

Ore, Oystein. *Cardano: The Gambling Scholar.* Princeton: Princeton University Press, 1953.

Origen. *Contra Celsum,* trans. Henry Chadwick. Cambridge: Cambridge University Press, 1953.

*The Oxinden and Peyton Letters, 1642–1670,* ed. Dorothy Gardiner. New York: Macmillan, 1937.

Pagel, Walter. *Paracelsus.* Basel: S. Karger, 1958.

———. "Religious Motives in the Medical Biology of the XVIIth Century," *Bull. Instit. Hist. Med.,* 3 (1935), 97–128, 213–31, 265–312.

———. "The Religious and Philosophical Aspects of van Helmont's Science and Medicine," Suppl. No. 2, *Bull. Hist. Med.* Baltimore: 1944.

———. *William Harvey's Biological Ideas.* New York: Hafner, 1967.

Paracelsus. *The Hermetic and Alchemical Writings,* ed. Arthur Edward Waite. 2 vols. London: J. Elliott, 1894.

Patrides, C. A. "Renaissance and Modern Thought on the Last Things: A Study of Changing Concepts," *Harvard Theo. Rev.,* 51 (1958), 169–85.

Peacham, Henry. *The Compleat Gentleman.* 2d ed. London: 1634.

Petersson, R. T. *Sir Kenelm Digby.* Cambridge: Harvard University Press, 1956.

Plato. *The Collected Dialogues,* eds. Edith Hamilton and Huntington Cairns. Bollingen Series 71. New York: Pantheon Books, 1961.

Plotinus. *The Enneads,* trans. Stephen McKenna. 3d ed. rev., B. S. Page. London: Faber and Faber Ltd., 1962.

Powell, Anthony. *John Aubrey and His Friends*. Rev. ed. New York: Barnes and Noble, 1964.

Price, Derek J., ed. *An Old Palmistry*. Cambridge, England: W. Heffer, 1953.

Rabelais, Francis. *The Works*. . . . , trans. Sir Thomas Urquhart and [Peter] Motteux, 2 vols. Rev. ed. London: 1863.

Raven, Charles E. *Natural Religion and Christian Theology*. Cambridge: Cambridge University Press, 1953.

———. *Synthetic Philosophy in the Seventeenth Century*. Oxford: B. Blackwell, 1945.

Raven, J. E. *Pythagoreans and Eleatics*. Cambridge: Cambridge University Press, 1948.

Remusat, Charles de. *Histoire de la philosophie en Angleterre depuis Bacon jusqu'à Locke*. 2 vols. Paris: Didier, 1875.

Rosenberg, Edgar. *From Shylock to Svengali*. Stanford: Stanford University Press, 1960.

Rosenfield, Leonora Cohen. "Un Chapitre de L'Histoire de L'Animal-Machine (1645–1749)," *Revue de Littérature Comparée*, 17 (1937), 461–87.

Ross, Alexander. *Leviathan Drawn Out With a Hook*. London: 1653.

———. *Medicus Medicatus: or the Physicians Religion Cured, by a Lenitive or Gentle Potion: with some Animadversions upon Sir Kenelme Digbie's Observations on Religio Medici*. London: 1648.

———. *Pansebeia: Or, a View of all Religions in the World*. London: 1653.

Rust, George. *A Letter of Resolution Concerning Origen and the Chief of His Opinions*, ed. Marjorie Hope Nicolson. The Facsimile Text Society. New York: Columbia University Press, 1933.

Ryan, John K. "The Reputation of St. Thomas Aquinas Among English Protestant Thinkers of the Seventeenth Century," *The New Scholasticism*, 22 (1948), 126–208.

Sayle, Charles. *Sir Thomas Browne: An Essay*. Cambridge, England: 1915.

Schneck, Jerome M. "Sir Thomas Browne, *Religio Medici* and the History of Psychiatry," *Amer. Jour. Psychiatry*, 114 (1958), 657–60.

Seaton, Ethel. *Literary Relations of England and Scandinavia in the Seventeenth Century*. Oxford: The Clarendon Press, 1935.

Selden, John. *Table Talk*, ed. Sir Frederick Pollock. London: Quaritch, 1927.

Sencourt, Robert. *Outflying Philosophy*. Hildesheim: 1924.

Seneca, Lucius Annaeus. *Ad Lucilium Epistulae Morales*, trans. Richard M. Gummere. 3 vols. Loeb Classical Library. Cambridge: Harvard University Press, 1961–1962.

———. *Seneca's Tragedies*, trans. Frank Justus Miller. 2 vols. Loeb Classical Library. London: W. Heinemann, 1927, 1929.

———. "De Vita Beata," in *Moral Essays*, trans. John W. Basore.

3 vols. Loeb Classical Library. Cambridge: Harvard University Press, 1928–1935.

Seznec, Jean. *The Survival of the Pagan Gods,* trans. Barbara F. Sessions. 1952; rpt. New York: Harper and Row, 1961.

Shotwell, James T., and Louise Ropes Loomis. *The See of Peter.* Records of Civilization: Sources and Studies. New York: Columbia University Press, 1927.

Stephen, Leslie. *Hours in a Library.* 3 vols. New York: G. P. Putnam's Sons, 1892–1899.

Strachey, Lytton. *Books and Characters.* New York: Harcourt, Brace, 1922.

Stubbe, Henry. *The Plus Ultra Reduced to a Non Plus.* London: 1670.

Taylor, Jeremy. *The Whole Works . . . ,* ed. Reginald Haber, rev. ed. Charles Page Eden. 10 vols. London: Longman, Brown, Green, and Longmans, 1855.

Tertullian. "On the Soul," trans. Edwin A. Quain, and "Apology," trans. Sister Emily Joseph Daly, in *Apologetical Works.* The Fathers of the Church, Vol. 10. New York: Fathers of the Church, Inc., 1950.

Thompson, D'Arcy Wentworth. *On Form and Growth,* ed. John Tyler Bonner. Abr. ed. Cambridge: Cambridge University Press, 1961.

Thompson, Elbert N. S. "Mysticism in Seventeenth-Century Literature," *SP,* 18 (1921), 170–231.

Thorndike, Lynn. *A History of Magic and Experimental Science.* Vols. VII–VIII: *The Seventeenth Century.* 8 vols. New York: Columbia University Press, 1923–1958.

Tulloch, John. *Rational Theology and Christian Philosophy in England in the Seventeenth Century.* 2 vols. London: 1872.

Tuveson, Ernest Lee. *Millennium and Utopia.* Berkeley: University of California Press, 1949.

Tyler, Dorothy. "A Review of the Interpretation of Sir Thomas Browne's Part in a Witch Trial in 1664," *Anglia,* 54 (1930), 178–95.

Underhill, Evelyn. *Mysticism.* 12th ed. 1910; rpt. Cleveland: World Pub. Co., 1955.

Urquhart, Sir Thomas. ΕΚΣΚΥΒΑΛΑΤΡΟΝ *or, The Discovery of a Most Exquisite Jewell. . . . To frontal a Vindication of the Honor of Scotland. . . .* London: 1652.

Walzer, Richard. *Galen on Jews and Christians.* Oxford Classical and Philosophical Monographs. London: Oxford University Press, 1949.

Watson, Foster. "Alexander Ross: Pedant Schoolmaster of the Age of Cromwell," *Gentleman's Magazine,* 279 (1895), 459–74.

Webster, Charles. "The Recognition of Plant Sensitivity by English Botanists in the Seventeenth Century," *Isis,* 57 (Spring, 1966), 5–23.

West, Robert M. *Milton and the Angels.* Athens: University of Georgia Press, 1955.

Westfall, Richard S. *Science and Religion in Seventeenth-Century England.* Yale Historical Publications, Miscellany 67. New Haven: Yale University Press, 1958.

Whichcote, Benjamin. *Moral and Religious Aphorisms,* ed. Samuel Salter. London: 1753.

White, Hayden V. "The Gregorian Ideal and Saint Bernard of Clairvaux," *JHI,* 21 (1960), 321–48.

White, Thomas. *De Mundo, Dialogi Tres.* Paris: 1642.

———. *Of the Middle State of Souls.* London: 1659.

———. *Peripateticall Institutions.* London: 1656.

Wiley, Margaret L. *The Subtle Knot.* London: Unwin Brothers, Ltd., 1952.

Willey, Basil. *The Seventeenth Century Background.* Garden City, N. Y.: Doubleday, 1955.

Williams, Arnold. *The Common Expositer.* Chapel Hill: University of North Carolina Press, 1948.

Williamson, George. *Seventeenth Century Contexts.* Chicago: University of Chicago Press, 1961.

Wilson, F. P. *Seventeenth Century Prose.* Berkeley: University of California Press, 1960.

Wood, Anthony à. *Athenae Oxonienses,* ed. Philip Bliss, 4 vols. London: 1813–1820.

Worthington, Dr. John. *The Diary and Correspondence,* eds. James Crossley and R. C. Christie. 2 vols. Manchester: The Chetham Society, 1847–1886.

Wycliffe, John. *Three Treatises,* ed. James Henthorn Todd. Dublin: 1851.

Yolton, John W. "Locke and the Seventeenth-Century Logic of Ideas," *JHI,* 16 (1955), 431–52.

Ziegler, Dewey Kiper. *In Divided and Distinguished Worlds.* Cambridge: Harvard University Printing Office, 1943.

# INDEX

A. B., 61
Abraham, 22
Accidental properties, 69, 103, 173, 175, 182
Accommodation, theory of, 153
Achilles, 15
Actuality, 135, 137–39, 170, 175–76
Adam, 20, 44, 48, 100, 106, 146
Æsculanus, 157
African and Asian churches, 21, 130
Aging, 99–100
Albertus Magnus, 44
Allegorical, 107–8, 135
Allen, Thomas, 58, 83
Anastasius, 128, 130
Anatomy, 35, 43, 146
Angels: nature of, 35, 146; as guardians, 41–42; knowledge of, 81, 177; and light, 87–88; habitation of, 90, 92–93, 146
Anglicanism, 18, 25, 64
*Apocrypha, The,* 125
Apollo, 33, 97
Apuleius, Lucius, 138–39
Aquinas, Thomas: on guardian angels, 42; on Providence, 81; theory of knowledge, 88, 95, 136, 155–56; on miracles, 154; on evil, 156; mentioned, 9, 41, 52, 184
Archimedes, 117
Argentarius, 157
Arianism, 128, 130
Aristotle: on sleep, 15; the mean, 18; entelechy, 29; eternity, 32; heavens, 32,

132, 147; soul, 32, 43, 71–72, 131–33, 135–39; triad, 32–33; causation, 35–36, 96; nature and art, 35–36, 142; on virtue, 49; on the heart, 71; on creativity, 75; on chiromancy and palmistry, 83–85; contraries, 84, 132; time, 85; light, 87–90, 170; unity of the world, 91; theory of knowledge, 94–95; logical figure, 117; plant generation, 141–43; on honorable death, 161; on philosophical language, 143–44; on defining nature, 143, 145; on the "right" side, 145; mentioned, 6, 8–9, 21, 42, 59, 97, 105, 136, 148, 166, 168–69, 172, 181, 183–85
Astrology, 15–16, 37, 51, 82–83, 176, 181
Atheism, 10, 14, 16, 37–38, 48, 158–60, 179–80, 184
Athena, 33
Atomism, 105–6, 158, 172
Aubrey, John, 50, 57–58, 60n8
Augustine, Saint: eternity, 31; on cohabitation with the devil, 41; light and angels, 90, 136; millennium, 98; grief, 116; evil, 156–57; mentioned, 42, 184
Aurinus, 157n22
*Automatum,* 73
Averroes, 95

## B

Bacon, Francis, 3, 19, 39, 77
Bacon, Roger, 64–65

## About the Author

James N. Wise is Associate Professor of English at the University of Missouri—Rolla. Previously, he served on the faculties of Kentucky Southern College, Western Kentucky University, University of Florida, and Georgetown College. Professor Wise received the B.S. (1957) and M.A. (1958) degrees from West Virginia University and the Ph.D. (1964) from the University of Florida.

To gather material for this book, Professor Wise used the resources of the Henry E. Huntington Library and Art Gallery, San Marino, California, on a grant from the University of Missouri. His articles have appeared in a number of scholarly publications, including *The Arlington Quarterly, Costerus Essays in Philology and English Literature,* and *The Kentucky Folklore Record.*